To Dan -
Best always and
please enjoy the book -
Cheryl Pula 2/17/11

DAN
KEEP READIN.
Bob

Dan - Best wishes
and thanks for
buying. Enjoy! 2/17/11
Dennis K-----

"WITH COURAGE AND HONOR"

ONEIDA COUNTY'S ROLE IN THE CIVIL WAR

EDITED BY

JAMES S. PULA & CHERYL A. PULA

ETHNIC HERITAGE STUDIES CENTER
UTICA COLLEGE

PUBLISHED BY THE

EUGENE PAUL NASSAR ETHNIC HERITAGE STUDIES CENTER

AT

UTICA COLLEGE

ISBN 0-9660363-7-9
Ethnic Heritage Studies Center
Utica College
1600 Burrstone Road
Utica, N.Y. 13502

FOR
KAITLIN PULA

The first Civil War monument in Oneida County was
erected in Glenside Cemetery in New York Mills.
(James S. Pula)

TABLE OF CONTENTS

Introduction

The Civil War was one of the most traumatic events in American history. Almost every family had at least one person directly affected by the war. A higher percentage of Americans were in uniform between 1861 and 1865 than at any time in the nation's history. More Americans were killed in one day at the Battle of Antietam than in the entire eight years of the American Revolution. More Union soldiers died during the Battle of Gettysburg than there were Americans killed in the first two weeks of the Normandy invasion during World War II. An estimated 628,222 people lost their lives during the Civil War, as many as were killed in the American Revolution, the War of 1812, the Mexican War, the Spanish-American War, all of the Indian Wars, World War I, World War II, the Korean Conflict, and Vietnam combined. And this did not include those who lost arms, legs, eyesight, or were otherwise maimed for life.

For those who survived, and their descendants, the Civil War changed the fundamental social, economic and political fabric of the nation, affects that can still be felt today. Socially, the war increased the participation of women in the economy by opening the doors to professions such as medicine and education that had previously been largely reserved for men, and it increased the growing impetus for women's civil and political rights. Passage of homestead legislation and the Morrill Land Grant Act, which would not have been possible with the South in the Union, stimulated the westward movement, made inexpensive land available for farmers, led to a variety of internal improvements, and created the precedent for federal aid to education through the establishment of "Land Grant" colleges in each state. And the Civil War settled the divisive issue of slavery.

Economically, the war led to a dramatic increase in federal spending and the national debt. It has been estimated that the war cost the federal government alone two million dollars per day, or a total of $6.19 billion by 1866. When the interest on loans, veterans' pensions, widows' pensions and other post-war costs directly associated with the war are added, by 1911 the cost had nearly doubled to $11.5 billion. This led to a dramatic rise in the national debt. To pay off the accumulating financial burdens, Congress authorized the printing of paper money, or "greenbacks," for the first time and began unprecedented borrowing through the sale of government bonds with their attending interest payments. These were accompanied by tax increases, along with the implementation of entirely new taxes. One of the "temporary" taxes instituted to pay off the Civil War debt was the federal personal income tax, a good reason for Americans to remember the Civil War every April 15.

Politically, the war led to a major realignment of influence in America. In the 32 years leading up to the secession of South Carolina in 1860, six Democrats and only two Whigs held the office of president. All were either from the South, or were moderate Northerners who favored compromise with the South. The Civil War brought an abrupt change. In the 72 years beginning with the election of Abraham Lincoln and ending with the selection of Franklin D. Roosevelt in 1932, there were eleven Republican presidents and only two Democrats. The only Southern Democrat during this entire period was Woodrow Wilson who, though born in Virginia, spent most of his adult life in New Jersey and was known more as a "progressive" than were traditional Democratic conservatives of the day. Control of Congress shifted from Southern Democratic agriculturalists, to Northern Republican merchants and industrialists. This signaled a major shift in how people viewed the federal government and how the government viewed its own role in society. The long controversy between the strict constructionist "States' Rights" view of the Constitution favored by the South and the loose constructionist view based on "implied powers" favored by the North ended with a definitive Northern victory with the resulting dramatic increase in the reach and authority of the federal government.

Three amendments were added to the Constitution as a direct result of the Civil War and resulting Northern Republican control of the Congress. The Thirteenth prohibited slavery, the Fourteenth defined citizenship and representation, and the Fifteenth made it illegal to discriminate in voting rights based on "race, color, or previous condition of servitude." The war brought the admission of West Virginia as a new state, carved from a portion of what had been Virginia. It also led to the first absentee ballots in American history to allow soldiers in the Union army to vote. Equally important, the war began to change fundamentally the manner in which Americans viewed their government. Prior to the war people most often spoke of "these" United States and used the plural verb "are," emphasizing that the country was an alliance of various states. Following the war people increasingly referred to "the" United States and used the singular verb "is." *The* United States was no longer thought of as a grouping of semi-independent states, but a *single* nation.

In the long road leading to the beginning of the war that would change the nation so dramatically, and indeed actually create *a* nation, the most emotional issue dividing the country into two parts was clearly the question of slavery. Among the regions of the nation that became early forerunners in the anti-slavery movement, and developed a more radical strain of abolitionist agitation, were New England and Central New York. Of the latter, the clear leader was Oneida County. From the development of the "Underground Railroad" to the preaching of Charles Grandison Finney that motivated people to become active in social reform movements, from the funding and practical motivation provided by Gerrit Smith to the Oneida Institute which was the first school in the nation to enroll black and white students on an equal basis, Oneida County was an early leader in the anti-slavery crusade. As Gerald Sorin asserted, "The New York abolitionist leaders were radical. They held ideas which were radical in substance—specifically, immediate emancipation and political and economic equality for blacks. ... they experienced a total commitment to abolitionism."[1] Historian Edward Magdol was more specific, concluding in *The Antislavery Rank and File* that "Abolitionism in Utica and its environs was sparked by some of the nation's most important advocates of immediatism."[2] Immediatism meant *Abolitionism*: the uncompromising demand for *immediate* emancipation of *all* slaves *without any compensation* to their owners. Among the most outspoken were the people of Oneida County, as the reader will learn from chapters one and two of this work.

In 1860, Oneida County's population of 101,626 included 672 blacks, with 43 percent of the residents born in foreign lands, notably England, Ireland, Germany, Scotland, and Wales. If the children of the immigrants are included, fully 67 percent of the county's inhabitants were first or second generation Americans. Utica was the largest city, boasting 22,524 residents, with Rome second at 10,720. Once the secession movement exploded into open warfare, the people of Oneida County backed their rhetoric by contributing their blood to the causes of preserving the Union and eliminating slavery. According to Frederick Phisterer, 2,772,408 Northerners served in the Union army during the course of the war. Of these, 448,850, or 16.2 percent, were New Yorkers. Although it is difficult to be precise since men often enrolled in regiments outside the bounds of their geographic home, it is believed that some 10,000 men who served in the Union army hailed from Oneida County.[3]

Men from the county served by ones and twos, and handfuls in thirty-three infantry regiments (3rd, 17th, 19th, 21st, 24th, 34th, 37th, 40th, 47th, 53rd, 57th, 61st, 68th, 75th, 76th, 78th, 80th, 81st, 93rd, 101st, 102nd, 103rd, 106th, 115th, 128th, 141st, 161st, 164th, 179th, 189th, 192nd, 193rd,194th), twelve cavalry regiments (2nd, 3rd, 7th, 8th, 11th, 13th, 15th, 20th, 22nd, 24th, 1st Mounted Rifles, Oneida Independent Company), sixteen artillery batteries (Battery A, 1st; Batteries G, L, and M, 2nd; Battery C, 3d; 4th, 5th, 7th, 9th, 10th, 11th, 12th, 13th, 14th, 16th, 24th Independent Batteries), and two engineer regiments (15th and 50th).[4] Most, however, served in five infantry regiments (14th, 26th, 97th, 117th and 146th) that were known locally as the First through Fifth Oneida Regiments and an artillery battery (Battery A, 1st New York Light Artillery, known as the "Empire Battery"). All of these were raised predominantly in the county. They form the basis for six of this book's chapters. Along with a concluding chapter on the postwar activities of the veterans, they illuminate the county's military contribution to the Northern war effort. Since Oneida County was also home to several military and naval officers and politicians prominent during the conflict, an appendix presents brief biographical portraits of notable individuals not otherwise covered in the preceding chapters.

The various authors and editors wish to express their gratitude to Donald Wisnoski who generously shared his extensive Civil War *carte de visité* collection as illustrations for this book; the staff and volunteers of the Oneida County Historical Society who provided access to materials and illustrations; and the staffs of the National Archives and Records Administration, the Library of Congress, and the U.S. Army Military History Institute, all of whom provided access to their archival and photographic collections.

---

[1]Gerald Sorin, *The New York Abolitionists* (Westport: Greenwood Press, 1971), 3.

[2]Edward Magdol, *The Antislavery Rank and File* (New York: Greenwood Press, 1986), 43.

[3]Frederick Phisterer, *Statistical Record of the Armies of the United States* (Edison, NJ: Castle Books, 2002; reprint of 1883 original), 10.

[4]Hobart L. Morris, Jr., "A Tabular Compilation of Some Data About Oneida County Civil War Servicemen," unpublished manuscript, Utica College of Syracuse University, May 1959, in the Oneida County Historical Society.

CHAPTER 1

"BORN IN SLAVERY"

THE UNDERGROUND RAILROAD IN ONEIDA COUNTY

by

Jan DeAmicis

Long before the clouds of war raced across the nation, citizens of Oneida County were actively involved in one of the growing issues of the day, opposition to the ownership of one human being by another. To a great extent, these early efforts were centered on local religious groups, notably congregations of Quakers, Methodists, Presbyterians, and Baptists. By 1850, there were four Quaker meeting houses in Oneida County, along with 43 Methodist, 29 Baptist, and 23 Presbyterian churches.[1] In many of these, committees existed to aid escaped slaves seeking their freedom. These groups were part of a widespread network throughout the northeast that was especially active in New York. According to Wilbur Siebert, who wrote the first history of the Underground Railroad, the Rev. Charles B. Ray, a member of the Vigilance Committee of New York City and editor of *The Colored American* explained that "He knew of a regular route stretching from Washington, by way of Baltimore and Philadelphia, to New York, thence following the Hudson to Albany and Troy, whence a branch ran westward to Utica, Syracuse and Oswego, with an extension from Syracuse to Niagara Falls.[2]

Oneida County's history includes some features of the Underground Railroad that many believe to be typical, such as secret hiding places, slave-catchers, violent resistance, and station-masters. Here there are also other less-understood features of the Underground Railroad: community-centered defiance, the settlement of fugitives among white residents in relative safety, clusters of freedom-seekers living openly near each other, and the abolitionist activities of the Welsh. Long before the Civil War ended the debate on slavery, the people of Oneida County made it clear that no law protecting slavery would be enforced here. The county's Underground Railroad "stations" linked this region to the nation's network of resistance.

THE UNDERGROUND RAILROAD IN AMERICA

While the history of the Underground Railroad in the United States is still being uncovered, some of its features are well known. An informal network of "stations" began to emerge around 1800. It was not a formally organized system with a national "headquarters." Instead it took different forms in different places and usually involved people of face-to-face acquaintance. Sometimes there were well-organized local systems of stationmasters and supporters, usually rooted in county, state, and sometimes national abolitionist networks. Free blacks were as deeply involved as whites. There was no national center, no formal structure, and no roster of station-masters. In some places it operated in total secrecy because of popular resistance to abolitionism, a desire for a share of the bounty, and legal reprisals. It was illegal to assist a fugitive, and local governments were bound by law to assist in the recapture of freedom-seekers. But in other places, the underground railroad was publicly flaunted in open defiance of the law.[3]

Henrietta Buckmaster's account is typical of many stories that relate how, around 1830, the Underground Railroad acquired its name.

> A fugitive named Tice Davids crossed the (Ohio) River at Ripley (Ohio). He was escaping from his Kentucky master, who followed so closely on his heels that Tice Davids had no alternative when he reached the river but to swim. His master spent a little time searching for a skiff, but he never lost sight of his slave, bobbing about in the water. He kept him in sight all the way across the river and soon his skiff was closing the distance between them. He saw Tice Davids wade into shore, and then—he never saw him again. He gave the only explanation possible for a sane man, "He must have gone on an underground road."[4]

The significance and character of the Underground Railroad is still a matter of historical debate. It was extremely difficult for slaves in the Deep South to escape, so most successful freedom-seekers came from the border slave-holding states of Delaware, Maryland, Tennessee, Kentucky, and Virginia. Slavery in such places as Alabama, Mississippi, and South Carolina was not seriously challenged by escapes to the North. Lacking maps or real information, no fugitive knew for sure where to go or whom to trust, so they usually sought out local African-Americans for help rather than white "stationmasters." There was relative security in reaching a free state such as New York, but fugitives could not be totally safe until they reached Canada. Many lived and worked openly along the Canadian border in places such as Oswego, New York, ready to flee if slave-hunters threatened. The number of successful escapes did not threaten slavery. Estimates are that about 1,000 enslaved Americans escaped each year from 1830 until the Civil War, not a large number since there were more than 4,000,000 slaves by 1861. Of course, we will never know how many efforts to escape were unsuccessful. However, the very existence of a northern-wide Underground

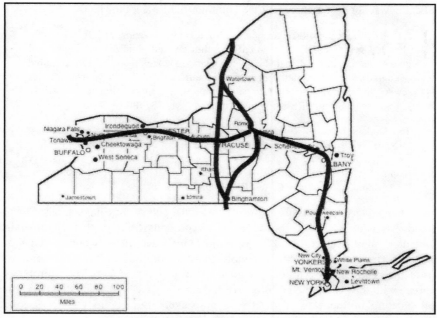

Major Underground Railroad routes through New York.

Railroad, rather than the actual number of escapes, convinced many Southerners that there was no room for compromise with the abolitionists.

SLAVERY AND ANTI-SLAVERY IN ONEIDA COUNTY

Oneida County's important role in the abolition movement and Underground Railroad might seem unlikely in light of the region's slaveholding history. Some Revolutionary War veterans who settled the area after the war brought their slaves with them. Some of the most prominent citizens in the county were also slave-holders, men such as Alexander Coventry, William Floyd, and Benjamin Walker. Newspapers regularly advertised the sale of slaves:

> For Sale, A young Black woman. She is healthy and active, and is accustomed to all kinds of house work. For further particulars inquire of R. W. MADDOCK, Whitestown, October 21, 1805.[5]

> For Sale, a Negro Wench, a slave for life, aged 20 years—honest and faithful. For terms apply at this office or go to the subscriber in Vernon. Rufus Pettibone, Vernon, March 25, 1816.[6]

Local newspapers also informed the community of escaping slaves:

> Ran away from the subscriber on the 23rd, a lad by the name of JOHN LEWIS, alias JOHN SYMOND, 15 years of age, thin favored, light coloured eyes, had on a butternut coloured coat, swans down striped jacket, nankeen light coloured overalls and an old felt hat. Whoever will return said lad shall have two shillings reward and all necessary charges paid. All persons are forbid trusting or harboring him at their peril. Roseel Lewis, Deerfield, May 5, 1806.[7]

> Ten Dollars Reward: Runaway from the subscriber on Friday evening last, DINAH COOK, a black slave, very large and fleshy, and has lost one of her fore teeth. Ten dollars reward and all reasonable charges will be paid for her delivery to me, or for securing her in any jail in the county. All persons are forbid harboring her on penalty of law. C. W. HIEST, Utica. May 4, 1815.[8]

Such advertisements suggest that some local people may have assisted local freedom-seekers, a precursor of the Underground Railroad that emerged in Oneida County in the 1830s. However, most Oneidans probably considered abolitionists stridently self-righteous, unpleasantly disruptive, and likely to compromise the region's reputation as a good place to do business. Many probably agreed with the "gentlemen of property and standing"[9] who disrupted the inaugural meeting of the New York State Anti-Slavery Society in Utica's Second Presbyterian Church on Bleecker Street in 1835. Oneida County was not an obvious place for abolitionism to take root.

But Oneida County not only participated in, but indeed became a leader of the nation's anti-slavery crusade. Several abolitionist newspapers were published in the county. Men and women, black and white alike, organized abolitionist societies across the county, including New York State's first Anti-Slavery Society itself. Oneidans participated in political campaigns in support of abolitionism. Thousands of Oneidans signed at least 1,200 pages of petitions protesting slavery, which they sent to the United States Congress. This moral crusade can be partly attributed to the fervor roused by the Rev. Charles Finney's religious revivalism which began in the 1820s, earning upstate New York the nickname of "The Burnt-Over District." While Finney did not advocate for abolitionism, he helped prepare many New Yorkers to act on their moral convictions. Social-religious experiments emerged across upstate New York, such as the Oneida Community and the Mormons. Among these moral communities was the Oneida Institute in Whitestown, Oneida County.

THE ONEIDA INSTITUTE, 1827-1844

Oneida County's abolition movement and Underground Railroad activity can be said to begin when Beriah Green assumed leadership of the Oneida Institute in 1833. The Oneida Institute thereafter became a beacon of progressive educa-

Bill of sale for the slave girl Patience.
(Clinton Historical Society)

tion and led the struggle in the county for immediate emancipation. The Institute enrolled black and white male students on an equal basis, the first college in America to do so. Some of them became prominent in the abolition movement, such as Jemaine Loguen, Alexander Crummel, and Henry Highland Garnet. Here debates were held and an abolitionist newspaper, *The Friend of Man*, was published.[10] Speakers from Oneida Institute fanned out across the county carrying the abolitionist message. And it was here that, in July 1833, 35 students banded together to form New York State's first anti-slavery society dedicated to immediatist principles, meaning slavery should be abolished immediately rather than

The Oneida Institute
(Oneida County Historical Society)

Beriah Green
(Oneida County Historical Society)

gradually over a long period of time. The Oneida Institute quickly became a station on the Underground Railroad: "He (Beriah Green) welcomed fugitive slaves to his home and to the campus, where students hid them in their dormitory rooms. Fugitives from 'the peculiar institution' (as slavery was often called) enjoyed the safety of the 'Old Hive,' Green's home in Whitesboro."[11]

By the Fall of 1835, there were seventeen town societies in Oneida County including Hamilton College, Oneida Castle, Vienna, Camden, Marshall, and New York Mills, which included a Ladies' Society and both a Utica Juvenile Males and Juvenile Females Society. Before long, most towns supported at least one anti-slavery society. Although the first meeting of the New York State Anti-Slavery Society was dispersed by a mob,[12] the Society convened in Utica the following year and several years after that without public protest. Fanning out across the county, abolitionists distributed tracts, wrote and sang songs, debated in public meetings, formed abolitionist churches, held rallies, and circulated scores of petitions protesting slavery. One year after the first meeting of the New York State Anti-Slavery Society in Utica, local citizens struck a powerful blow on behalf of the movement, and thus made visible the region's emerging Underground Railroad.

THE UTICA RESCUE, 1836

Federal law required local magistrates to authorize the arrest of any African-American who was claimed as an escaped slave by any agent of the owner. This meant that all black people who could not immediately prove that they were legally free were at risk of arrest and enslavement solely on the word of a slave-hunter. Slave-hunters traveled throughout the North, including upstate New York.[13] So when Spencer Kellogg stood outside his leather goods shop on Genesee Street on Thursday morning, December 29, 1836, and noticed two black men riding in a carriage in the custody of two constables, he had reason to be suspicious. When the party stopped at the office of Judge Chester Hayden on 96-98 Genesee Street (the building still survives), Kellogg asked about their offense. The reply was, "stealing potatoes." Following them into Hayden's office, he found two white Virginians. He asked if the black men had been arrested as fugitive slaves, and was told yes. Judge Hayden seemed eager to resolve the matter as quickly and quietly as he could. The two captives, Harry Bird and George, had been living in Utica for four months and denied that they were fugitives. Kellogg sent for Alvan Stewart, an abolitionist lawyer, who quickly arrived. Stewart argued that there was no proof that these really were fugitives and that they should therefore be granted a trial like any free citizen. Hayden agreed and settled the black men and the Virginians in an adjacent room until later that evening. Men and boys milled about the office all day, and some even visited with the captives. Then, shortly before the judge was to return, a struggle erupted. Jermaine Loguen described what happened.

The masthead from *The Friend of Man*, an early abolitionist newspaper published in Utica by William Goodell. *(Cornell University)*

But the brave colored men of Utica, armed with clubs, broke into the prison, and after a battle which made sore heads among the captors and bullies, rescued the slaves, and detained the claimants and bullies in the same prison, until the former were out of reach. So sudden and bold was this deed that the enemy was dumfounded, and the black heroes were never known to them.[14]

The headlines of William Goodell's abolitionist newspaper *The Friend of Man* indignantly proclaimed: "Kidnapping in Utica! The Slave Coast in Oneida County. Piracy and Law in the State of New York!!! The scenes of Senegal, upon the banks of the Mohawk!!!!"[15]

Such rescues also occurred in other places, one of the most notable being the Jerry Rescue fifteen years later in Syracuse. They put slave-hunters on notice that it would be very difficult indeed to claim a fugitive, even with the authority of the law on their side. Freedom-seekers sometimes felt encouraged to remain in a "safe" area as Oneida County, even keeping their names and admitting to Census takers their slave-state birthplaces. Others moved as close to the Canadian border as they could, notably Oswego, where they lived openly but could easily reach Canada on short notice.[16] One route led from Utica north toward Boonville, through the Welsh communities in Remsen and Steuben.

THE WELSH COMMUNITY

Abolitionism flourished throughout the county and wherever it was most active, there too was the Underground Railroad. Nowhere did it so solidly reflect a community's will as among the Welsh inhabitants of Remsen and Steuben, under the leadership of Dr. Robert Everett. Born of a Scottish-English father and a Welsh mother in 1797 in Wales, he was called to the ministry at Bethesda Welsh Congregational Church in Utica in 1823. "He was an abolitionist from the time he arrived in Utica; the Everetts' wagon driver was either a slave or a former slave and had told them much about slavery."[17] Everett attended the famous inaugural meeting of the New York State Anti-Slavery Society and became one of the region's most ardent abolitionists. He published two anti-slavery periodicals in Welsh. He also published a Welsh language edition of Harriet Beecher Stowe's *Uncle Tom's Cabin* (*Caban f'ewythr Twm*) in Remsen. Everett helped organize "The Welsh Anti-Slavery Society of Steuben, Remsen, Trenton, and Vicinities" at

Capel Ucha on January 27, 1842. At least one anti-slavery petition was sent to Congress by the "Welsh Residents of Remsen and Steuben."[18]

Everett served at the Second Presbyterian Church in Utica but, wanting to work with Welsh-speaking Congregationalists, he took on the ministry at Capel Ucha in Steuben, an area thickly inhabited by Welsh immigrants, with a capacity of about 500 people. Capel Ucha, first built of logs in 1804, was a Methodist stone church during the days of the Underground Railroad.[19] It is likely that fugitives spoke here.

> Those walls had sheltered the church home of our parents, and the grandparents of many of us, there our own childish hearts had learned to love the house of God, there had been heard the impassioned eloquence of so many of our old Welsh ministers in this country, and from Wales, thrilling addresses from the immortal Finney, in behalf of temperance, of Alvan Stewart, Beriah Green, and others of anti-slavery note, and even the plaintive story of the fleeing bondsman, who, when he had told his tale, was secretly hurried to the next station on the underground railroad, on his forced flight to liberty in the Queen's dominions.[20]

Everett's entire family was heavily involved in abolitionism. His two sons attended the Oneida Institute. One of them, John Robert, helped John Brown's antislavery faction in Kansas. He moved his family to a farm in Osawatomie, Kansas during the days of the free soil movement. His other son, Robert Everett, Jr., helped his father print the *Cenhadwr*, an abolitionist periodical, and lectured on abolitionism and temperance. Both names appear on several anti-slavery petitions of 1837 from Whitestown. His daughter Elizabeth attended Rev. H. G. Kellogg's Ladies Seminary in Clinton, which was run by abolitionists and admitted African-Americans.

There is clear evidence of active support for abolitionism and the Underground Railroad among the Welsh inhabitants of the rural towns of Remsen and Steuben. By the 1840s Oneida County had become well known for its abolitionist sentiments.[21] Heartened by the strength of white support, some fugitives decided to remain in the area. The Village of Paris offers an example of how freedom-seekers settled openly among a white community.

THE PARIS FUGITIVE COMMUNITY

John Thomas, a fugitive from Maryland, arrived with another fugitive in Utica in 1844 by way of Philadelphia, New York, and Albany. He made his way to the home of William Johnson, 16 Post Street, Utica. Johnson was active in the Negro Conventions, and was appointed Vice President of a "Convention of colored persons" at the African M. E. church in Rome on May 10, 1853, that passed ten resolutions opposing the Liberia colonization plan. Post Street at that time

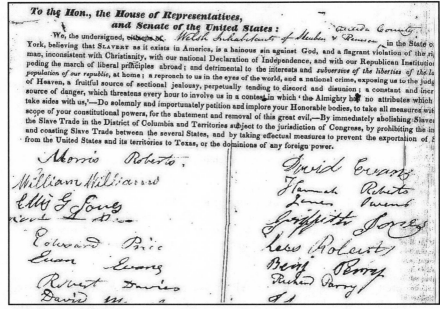

Anti-Slavery petition from the Welsh citizens of Oneida County to the U.S. Congress.
(National Archives)

was a predominantly black residential area, and as such would have been a logical destination of any fugitive in the area. Johnson sent the two freedom-seekers to Wesley Bailey, editor of *The Liberty Press*, at his home at 63 Genesee Street, Utica. Bailey directed Thomas to the Village of Paris, about twenty miles away, where he was harbored by Jesse Thompson, a prominent white abolitionist.

Thomas was befriended by John and David Roberts, freedom-seekers from the Baltimore area with whom he eventually purchased a house from Jesse Thompson.[22] Thomas was employed variously by J. M. Simmons, Val Pierce, and Henry Crane, all of whom signed anti-slavery petitions in 1836, 1837, 1838, and 1845.[23]

We find evidence of the Paris Fugitive Community in the United States Census. The U.S. Census provides one method for identifying freedom-seekers. African-Americans who claimed a slave-holding state as their place of birth were probably fugitives.[24] After Congress banned the importation of slaves in 1808, the value of domestic slaves rose steeply, making it unlikely that bondsmen would be freed. John and Mary Roberts, and John and Sarah Thomas are listed in both the 1850 and 1860 United States Censuses, and all identify the slave-holding state of Maryland as their birthplaces. It is remarkable that they continued to live openly among this white community even after the Fugitive Slave Law of

1850, which strengthened the power of slave-hunters and stiffened the penalties for harboring fugitives. This could only happen if freedom-seekers felt confident of the protection of their white neighbors. There were many abolitionists in the Town of Paris, if the sheer number of anti-slavery petitions (17) and signatures (including those of the people who helped John Thomas) are an indication. In fact, the citizens of Paris sent more anti-slavery petitions to Congress than any other community in the county except Utica (27).

In the Village of Paris in Hillcrest Cemetery lie the graves of seven freedom-seekers. On the middle grave marker an inscription reads: "IN MEMORY OF JOHN ROBERTS, MARY HIS WIFE AND FIVE FRIENDS. BORN WHILE SLAVES, FOUND HOME AND FREEDOM AT PARIS BETWEEN 1846 & 1881." Fugitives settled elsewhere in Oneida County as well, and sometimes they lived close enough to be considered small communities.

FUGITIVE COMMUNITIES IN ONEIDA COUNTY

Freedom-seekers were never entirely free from the danger of recapture in upstate New York. But events such as the Utica Rescue and the Jerry Rescue in Syracuse meant that recapture would be very difficult. It is likely some fugitives remained in the area rather than continuing on to Canada, as indicated by the Paris Fugitive Community. In the United States Census, wherever we find black Oneidans claiming a slave state, Canada (the assumption being that they had escaped and then crossed back into the country), or "unknown" as their place of birth, it is an indication that they sensed no danger in revealing themselves. Their ability to live openly depended on the cooperation of white sympathizers as well as the companionship of fellow freedom-seekers. After passage of the Fugitive Slave Law in 1850, many escapees fled to the relative security of the Canadian border. Across the North the proportion of Census-identified fugitives and their dependents dramatically fell. However, there was only a slight decrease of probable freedom-seekers in Oneida County, where 8.5% (n = 58) in 1850 and 7.7% (n = 48) in 1860 of all African-Americans were plausibly slavery-born. It appears there were clusters of freedom-seekers throughout the county. The list below includes only those fugitives who lived close to other freedom-seekers, and it does not include their dependents who claimed Northern birth.

FUGITIVE COMMUNITIES IN ONEIDA COUNTY

1850

Kirkland: 13 people, mostly from Tennessee and Maryland;
Florence: 11 people, mostly from Washington DC, including James Lax, 115
    years old, from Africa;
Rome: 10 people, mostly from Delaware;

Utica: 12 people, mostly from Virginia, including Elizabeth Ludden, born on the "Ocean."

1860

Kirkland: 3 people from Maryland;

Florence: 4 people, including Joseph Young, 77 years old, born in the West Indies;

Rome: 20 people, mostly from Washington DC and Maryland, including James Danson, 49 years old, from the West Indies;

Utica: 7 people, mostly from Maryland.[25]

Many people, black and white, provided support for those freedom-seekers who decided to settle, but most probably moved on after a brief stay at one or more of the many stations across the county.

ONEIDA COUNTY'S UNDERGROUND RAILROAD "STATIONS"

Some of the county's Underground Railroad was organized around local networks: Utica, Paris, Remsen and Steuben, and the Oneida Institute. There were many other individual "station-masters" throughout the county whose connections to these networks is unknown. Some probably worked with only a few trusted people. Their common connection everywhere, of course, was their active roles in the abolition movement. Some of the most prominent of these people are identified here.

James DeLong, a "morocco dresser," owned a tannery on Water Street, Utica, and his house on 101 John Street was a station. DeLong attended Utica's New York State Anti-Slavery Convention in 1835, fleeing before the mob to Peterboro. He served as chair of the executive committee of the organization.

The DeLongs quit the (Methodist) church and became abolitionists, opening a station of the underground railroad in their house on John street. The back door of the house was left unlocked for fugitive slaves from the South on their way to Canada traveled only by night and hid by day. How they found their way to places of refuge was a mystery. When the DeLongs arose in the morning it was not unusual for them to find one or two Negroes asleep on the kitchen floor. These people were fed and during the day were kept secluded in the garret. When darkness fell their son Martin was detailed as guide to start the fugitives on their way north. They crossed the river bridge at the foot of Genesee Street and went through to Deerfield Corners. Having showed the fugitives the way north, Martin returned to the city.... One who recalls the sight states that twenty-one refugees turned up in Utica, at one time, and inquired the way to Mr. DeLong's house. There they found him ready, as always, with food and warmth, and plans for further advance. The next day was a Sunday and with his strong reverence for religion, Mr. DeLong marched the whole company off to the (Bleecker Street) Methodist church which he attended. No general ever felt prouder of his troops, says the narrator, than Mr. DeLong walking in the midst of this band of degraded and poverty stricken but suffering fellow-beings.[26]

Joshua Howe, of Utica, was an African-American station-master whose cabin was on the "gore," an unsurveyed wedge-shaped stretch of land in what is now part of Roscoe Conkling Park, probably near the Utica Zoo. His cabin offered a secluded retreat for fugitives. The U.S. Census records his presence from 1810 to 1840 in New Hartford (the "gore," now part of Utica) with a household of up to six people. When he died, Howe was buried in the old cemetery No. 4 in the eastern part of New Hartford. In 1915 Thomas R. Proctor placed a monument consisting of a large boulder to mark the spot and to commemorate "his services to the runaway from the South, during the years before the Civil War."[27] Unfortunately the boulder has not been located, but Joshua Howe certainly lived here.

Elihu Gifford II lived in a large house in the town of Florence, on the Williamstown Road, now Route 13. He was born in New Bedford, Massachusetts in 1797, probably after his seafaring father had departed on his fatal whaling voyage. He moved to Peterboro, home of Gerrit Smith, where he and his wife grew up. In 1834 he bought 187 acres of land from Gerrit Smith on Florence Hill, and in 1835 they moved to the main road where he became a station-master. Freedom-seekers were usually relayed from his place to Canastota, where they were forwarded on the canal to Oswego.[28] It is likely that he used a hidden room to conceal escapees and a specially designed grain wagon to transport them to the next station.

> Under the cellar floor of his house, Elihu had a room dug 8' x 8' x 6'. Perhaps as many as 10 adults could hide out in there. A trip to the grist mill in Williamstown (being farther up the valley towards Canada) would become necessary. The grain would be arranged on the wagon in such a way that a false bottom provided concealment for desperate runaways. From here they could go to Oswego. In later years, "Aunt Gene," a granddaughter of Elihu II born in 1854, would speak of the secrecy whenever there were any people in the cellar. She does remember how a little boy fell ill and was left behind as his parents resumed their flight towards freedom. (Perhaps his death seemed imminent and their need to move quickly superceded staying any longer.) In any case, he became a favorite with the family but later died of a childhood disease.[29]

William Seymour Laney, Jr. was born in the town of Lee in 1808, the son of William and Rachel Laney. He attended Whitestown Seminary (previously the Oneida Institute) and later served as an officer in the Army until 1837. In 1832 he purchased land in Lee, now used as the Kiwanis Camp on Kiwanis Road. After his Army service he built a post and plank, cape-cod style house on this property. The residence soon became known as one of the local stations of the Underground Railroad. Laney was a member of the Taberg Presbyterian church. When the church softened its views on slavery in 1845, many of the abolitionist members, including Laney, left the membership. Laney was a member of the Freed Men's Aid Society, an organization formed to help the freed slaves. He is buried in Lee Valley cemetery.[30]

Dr. Arba Blair of Rome was a delegate at the inaugural meeting of the New York State Anti-Slavery Society in 1835 and served on its executive committee. Marcus. L. Kenyon was proprietor and operator of a stage line from Rome to Boonville. His house was on Dominick and George, Rome. The two apparently cooperated in their Underground Railroad activities.

> One Saturday evening while busy in my store, a colored man, trembling with fear, came in. His appearance showed me at once what he was. As it was a cold day, he was directed to take a seat by the stove, and was furnished with something to eat. He told me had had been three days in the swamp, and had nothing to eat. His master was in pursuit of him, and he barely escaped being taken. He was taken to Dr. Blair's, who had a room where he kept them in safety. On Monday morning he was given in charge of that noble-hearted man, Kenyon, who owned the daily line of stages to Oswego. Kenyon was ever true to the trust thus given him to see them safely given up to the Freedman's Depot at Oswego. And the drivers of his stages dare not violate the trust he put in them to thus deliver them. Kenyon was a Democrat, but did not with his party believe in the justice of the infamous law.[31]

William Blaikie owned a pharmacy on Genesee Street, Utica.

> A dramatic episode of Mr. Blaikie's life had to do with the part he took preceding the Civil War in behalf of the slaves of the South. A dedicated Abolitionist, he voted that party ticket when it not only was unpopular to do so but sometimes dangerous, so strong was the feeling hereabouts against the minority working for the emancipation of the slaves. Threats were made against Mr. Blaikie's family and at times they were compelled to leave their residence on this account. Mr. Blaikie frequently sheltered runaway slaves and his home in the outskirts of the city (now the residence of his remaining daughter, Miss H. G. Blaikie, 2203 Genesee) became widely known as station of the 'underground railway.' Many an escaping slave heading for Canada slept in the Blaikie home or the barn and on several occasions the pharmacist found concealment for the fugitives in a building belonging to a well-known Utica Southern sympathizer— but needless to say, without the latter's knowledge or consent.[32]

CONCLUSION

The sites, people, and events identified here can be documented with confidence, but more information is required to establish details of their participation.

There are many suspected and other as-yet unidentified activists on the Underground Railroad to be uncovered. Evidence suggests that fugitives were sheltered in Boonville, Bridgewater, Clayville, Sauquoit, and Clinton. Freedom-seekers certainly must have found their way to the black communities along Post Street near the center of Utica, and in "Hayti" on Utica's eastern edge along Broad Street. There was possibly a second Utica Rescue that must also be documented. Fortunately, there are still many resources to explore in the unfolding story of the Underground Railroad.

The people of Oneida County were part of a dramatic chapter in the nation's history. Black and white men and women[33] not only voiced opposition to slavery, but stood behind their words, sometimes at their peril.[34] In both the rural and urban areas of the county, individuals and communities sheltered fugitives, and apparently encouraged some of them to settle amongst them. By challenging slavery in every way they could, they made an important contribution to the struggle by helping to move the country towards its fateful Civil War. Southerners realized that northern abolitionists would never accept slavery. While relatively few slaves escaped to freedom, their daring success and the abolitionists' open defiance proved that increasingly people in places like Oneida County, New York, would not only flaunt the laws protecting slavery, but would not rest until slavery had been eliminated.

---

[1]William J. Swittala, *Underground Railroad in New York and New Jersey* (Mechanicsburg, PA: Stackpole Books, 2006), 110.

[2]Wilbur Siebert, *The Underground Railroad from Slavery to Freedom* (1898). See also Henrietta Buckmaster, *Let My People Go* (New York: Harper & Brothers, 1941); John Walsh, *Vignettes of Old Utica* (Utica, NY: Utica Public Library, 1982); and Horatio Strother, *The Underground Railroad in Connecticut* (Middletown, CT: Wesleyan University Press, 1962).

[3]There are different accounts of how organized the system actually was. Larry Gara challenges the romanticized accounts of the underground railroad: the numbers have been exaggerated; the degree of organization has been overstated; the importance of sympathetic whites has been exaggerated; most fugitive slaves escaped for a few days only before returning; most of the risks of escape had been taken long before fugitives encountered sympathetic whites. "Far from being secret, it was copiously and persistently publicized and there is little valid evidence for the existence of a wide-spread underground conspiracy. The legend not only distorts the nature of the activity but exaggerates its impact on national events." Larry Gara, *The Liberty Line: The Legend of the Underground Railroad* (Lexington: University of Kentucky Press, 1961), 192-93

Henrietta Buckmaster, however, describes the underground railroad as a fairly coherent system of regular routes and very public supporters. "In the East, well-run 'tracks' lay from Washington to Rochester with branches or stops at New York, where a militant Vigilance Committee under the leadership of the colored clergyman, Charles Ray, was meeting the dangers of so exposed and important a city, and sending their 'clients' by boat to New England or up the Hudson River valley to Albany, where Stephen Myers, the colored publisher of The Elevator, an Abolition Sheet, was chief stationmaster. From there they went to Syracuse where J. W. Loguen, himself a fugitive, had been put in sole charge of all activities, and so on to Rochester where Frederick Douglass had established a terminal that looked across the lake to freedom. Through Pennsylvania, east, west and north the lines stretched through Philadelphia, Harrisburg, Pittsburgh, or east to Trenton and so on through New York state, to Albany, Schenectady, Utica; or up from Wilkes-Barre through the station kept by Gerrit Smith at Peterboro. All passed through the little towns, the isolated farms that were the strong links in the line. Up the western coast of New York other 'tracks' lay, through Westfield, Fredonia, Buffalo, Niagara and across the bridge, a short quick palpitating distance, taken many times on the run...." Buckmaster, *Let My People Go*, 200-01

[4]Buckmaster, *Let My People Go*, 59.

[5]*Utica Patriot*, December 2, 1805, 4. See Jan DeAmicis, "For Sale: A Young Black Woman," *Afro-Americans in New York Life and History*, Vol. 27, No. 2 (2003), 69-134.

[6]*Utica Patriot*, April 23, 1816, 4.

[7]*Utica Patriot*, May 13, 1806, 4

[8]*The Utica Club*, June 12, 1815, 4.

[9]Leonard Richards, *"Gentlemen of Property and Standing": Anti-Abolition Mobs in Jacksonian America* (New York: Oxford University Press, 1970). Richards uses this term to describe the mob because many rioters were prominent members of local society.

[10]*The Friend of Man* was one of several abolitionist newspapers that were published locally as Utica was the center of printing for the abolitionist movement, behind Boston and New York, according to Hugh Humphreys, "Let My People Go: Abolitionists in Upstate New York" (2000) in the Oneida County Historical Society.

[11]Milton Sernett, *Abolition's Axe: Beriah Green, Oneida Institute, and the Black Freedom Struggle* (Syracuse: Syracuse University Press, 1986), xv. An 1836 anti-slavery petition protesting the slave trade in Washington, DC, from the citizens of Whitestown includes the signature of Beriah Green and his African-American student Alexander Crummell, who became prominent in the abolitionist movement.

[12]See Richards, *"Gentlemen of Property and Standing."* Most of the delegates afterwards met at Geritt Smith's estate in nearby Peterboro, Madison County.

[13]See Solomon Northrup, *Twelve Years a Slave* (Baton Rouge: Louisiana State University Press, 1968; reprint of 1853 edition); also Roy Gallinger, *Oxcarts Along the Chenango* (Sherburne, NY; Heritage Press, 1965).

[14]Jermaine Loguen, *The Rev. J. W. Loguen, As a Slave and as a Freeman* (New York: Negro Universities Press, 1968, reprint of 1859 edition), 352.

[15]*The Friend of Man*, January 5, 1837, 1.

[16]See Judith Wellman, "This Side of the Border: Fugitives from Slavery in Three Central New York Communities," *New York History*, October, 1998.

[17]Millard Roberts, *Narrative History of Remsen, New York* (Syracuse, NY: Lyman Brothers, 1914), 127.

[18]Lorena Reynolds, "Early Welsh Settlers in Remsen and Steuben," unpublished manuscript dated 1968 found in Oneida County Historical Society collection, 19; see also Edna Robb, *Honey Out of the Rock* (Middleburg, VA: Middleburg Press, 1960); and Howard Thomas, "The Welsh Came to Remsen," *New York History,* Vol. XXX, January,

1949.

[19]"This served for 83 years and would have done services for many more years had it not been for a spring under the northwest corner of the foundation which with the alternate freezing and thawing slowly but surely undermined the corner and wrecked the structure. So it was removed and a wood structure was built in 1903 and served until it was closed and auctioned off in 1948 to be used for lumber. This was at first a Union Church, its members being from Calvinistic Methodist and Congregational churches in Wales. In 1804 the church was due to be incorporated and friendly discussion followed and that same year the Congregationals were advised by their sister church in Utica to form a church of their own. Thus a Congregational Church was organized in 1804. The Methodist members were happy to remain with the church until in 1824 they built a Calvinistic Whitfield Methodist Church just east of Remsen, called Pen-Y-Caerau. These two churches were the Mother Churches of each faith and were responsible for other churches being built nearby because of distances members would have to walk to attend week-day services as well as Sunday services." Margaret Davis, 25-26. A monument in Capel Ucha Cemetery marks its location, but no structure survives.

[20]Mary Everett, no date. Read at the dedication of the New Chapel, June 23, 1904. Mary Everett, *An Historical Sketch of the First Welsh Congregational Church of Remsen, N. Y.* (Remsen: Capel Ucha), 13. Mary H. Everett was the daughter of Dr. and Mrs. Robert Everett. He served as pastor of Capel Ucha from April 29, 1838 until his death on February 29, 1875.

[21]The only other report of slave-hunters challenging community resolve after the Utica Rescue appears to have ended in a second Utica Rescue. See "Son of Fugitive Slave Tells of Negro Race's Love for Gerrit Smith," *Utica Observer Dispatch*, May 29, 1936.

[22]John Roberts was also a recipient of Gerrit Smith's land distribution and received 30 acres in Franklin County, New York.

[23]Martha Smith, "A Runaway Slave at Paris Hill," *Waterville Times,* May 29, 1996.

[24]See Judy Wellman, "This Side of the Border: Fugitives from Slavery in Three Central New York Communities," *New York History,* October, 1998.

[25]United States Census of the Population, 1850, 1860.

[26]*Utica Herald*, obituary, April 16, 1883.

[27]*Utica Daily Press*, January 4, 1908, 5.

[28]Roy Snyder, *Camden Chronology II* (Rome, NY.: Pub. by author, 1991), 35.

[29]Patricia R. James, "The Gifford Family," *Genealogical Journal of Oneida County, New York* (Boise, ID: Second annual issue, 1998), 44. James cites reminiscences of John D. Gifford, the great-grandson of Elihu Gifford.

[30]Maryellen S. Urtz, "Cemeteries in the Town of Lee, Oneida County, New York," *Lee Tidings* (Town of Lee, NY: Lee Town Board, 1982), Vol. 7.

[31]Col. A. Seymour, *The Rome Citizen*, February 23, 1872.

[32]*Utica Observer-Dispatch,* October 25, 1953.

[33]Perhaps half of the 1,200 signees of antislavery petitions from Oneida County were women.

[34]Beriah Green and Alvan Stewart in particular faced unfriendly opponents. "Effigies of Beriah Green and Alvan Stewart were carried through the streets while two hundred people followed behind blowing horns and ringing bells. A platform was erected in the public square in front of the hotel in which Stewart lived, and a barrel of tar was lit. While

the effigies burned, the mob danced around the burning tar barrel. No attempt was made by city authorities to break up this demonstration. The Common Council tried to have Beriah Green indicted for treason, but the measure failed to pass for lack of one vote." Alice H. Henderson, "History of the New York State Anti-Slavery Society" (Ann Arbor, MI: Ph.D. Dissertation, University of Michigan, 1973), 14.

CHAPTER 2

"THE SECOND GREAT AWAKENING"
ABOLITIONISM IN ONEIDA COUNTY

by

James S. Pula

October 21, 1835, dawned cool and overcast. By afternoon a crowd estimated at upward of 600 people began assembling at the Second Presbyterian Church on the corner of Charlotte and Bleecker Streets in Utica to listen to speakers from Central New York's growing anti-slavery movement. As the orators ascended the rostrum, noise began to intrude on the proceedings from a crowd gathering in the streets outside. Quickly the noise rose to levels that disrupted the meeting, then leaders from the outside group burst through the church doors into the aisles between the benches. Shouts, curses, and threats disrupted the proceedings. Most of the anti-slavery group escaped with only ruffled feelings and clothing, but some were physically attacked suffering personal injuries.[1]

What caused this riot in otherwise peaceful Utica? The story begins in 1792 with the birth of Charles Grandisson Finney in Warren, Connecticut. When he was but two years old, Finney's family moved to Oneida County, New York, where he grew to maturity amid the fields and forests of what was then a largely rural frontier. Educated in local schools, he married a woman from Whitesboro before pursuing a career in the law. A self-professed skeptic, he was employed as a legal clerk in Adams, New York, when he first attended a religious service led by the Rev. George Washington Gale. "As I read my bible and attended the prayer meetings," Finney recalled in his autobiography, "heard Mr. Gale preach, conversed with him, with the elders of the church and with others from time to time, I became very restless. A little consideration convinced me that I was by no means in a state of mind to go to heaven if I should I die."[2] Attracted by Gale's zeal for the religious revivals then beginning to spread throughout Central New York, Finney became a willing convert. When Gale moved to a small farm in Western, Finney followed. There the former law clerk absorbed Gale's philosophy of uniting traditional academics with manual labor in the preparation of clergy for the Presbyterian ministry.

Soon Finney, sponsored by the Female Missionary Society of Utica, began

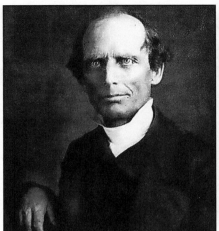

Charles Grandisson Finney
(Oneida County Historical Society)

George Washington Gale
(Oneida County Historical Society)

preaching on his own in small, local village churches. Yet, in his ministry Finney parted with the strict traditional Calvinist view preached by Gale, the belief that a person could do nothing to gain salvation since only God could ordain salvation. Rather, Finney believed that man had free will, and with it the ability to influence his own salvation. No longer was the individual powerless to effect his salvation. This new view brought with it a closer relationship between the individual and God because Finney's preaching taught that by doing good, by actively participating in reform movements for the betterment of society, an individual could contribute to his or her own salvation. One could, in effect, earn a place in heaven. "Unless the will is free, man has no freedom," wrote Finney, "and if he has no freedom, he is not a moral agent."[3] Laced with liberal democratic ideals and anti-aristocratic overtones that fit well with the popular Jacksonian ideas of the day, Finney's ardent preaching struck a responsive chord in an era of religious and social revival. Converts embraced this emphasis on individualism and self-determination, often gaining renewed confidence in themselves and their abilities to exist in and shape the world around them.[4]

An ardent believer in his new religious view of social responsibility, Finney proved to be an excellent speaker, his warm and compelling mannerisms and mesmerizing oratory attracting converts wherever he spoke. The effect of his well-organized, thoughtful and logical presentations was magnified by his physical presence and compelling delivery. "He was tall and spare," wrote Richard L. Manzelmann, "a handsome and commanding figure in appearance. He had a voice that could reach, penetrate and stir, and a tongue that could shape words and images easily. He was master of the appropriate gesture; in fact his whole body expressed his preaching. It was especially his eyes, often remarked on, that could pierce the individual and compel the masses. He had the uncommon ability to control and sustain the attention of his congregations for hours on end. He had, in short, what we call 'charisma.'"[5] "I have heard many celebrated pulpit orators in various parts of the world," commented one observer. "Taken all in all, I never heard the superior of Charles G. Finney."[6]

Finney arrived in New York Mills in 1826 at the invitation of his brother-in-law, George Andrews, who was then a superintendent in the textile mills. The clergyman described what transpired next in his autobiography:

> I was invited to go and preach at that place, and went up one evening and preached in the village school-house, which was large and was crowded with hearers. The word I could see took powerful effect among the people, especially among the young people who were at work in the factory.
>
> The next morning after breakfast I went into the factory to look through it. As I went through I observed there was a good deal of agitation among those who were busy at their looms, mules, and other implements of work. On passing through one of the apartments, where a great number of young women were attending to their weaving, I observed a couple of them eyeing me, and speaking very earnestly to each other, and I could see that they were a good deal agitated, although they both laughed. I went slowly toward them. They saw me coming and were evidently much excited. One of them was trying to mend a broken thread, and I observed that her hands trembled so that she could not mend it. I approached slowly, looking at the machinery on each side as I passed, but observed that this girl grew more and more agitated, and could not proceed with her work. When I came within eight or ten feet of her I looked solemnly at her. She observed it, and was quite overcome and sunk down, and burst into tears. The impression caught almost like powder, and in a few moments nearly all in the room were in tears. This feeling spread through the factory. Mr. W[alcott], the owner of the establishment, was present, and seeing the state of things, he said to the superintendent, "Stop the mill, and let the people attend to religion, for it is more important that our souls should be saved than that our factory should be run." The gate was immediately shut down, and the factory stopped. But where should we assemble? The superintendent suggested that the mule room was large, and the mules being run up, we could assemble there. We did so, and a more powerful meeting I scarcely ever attended. It went on with great power. The building was large and had many people in it from the garret to the cellar. The revival went through the mill with astonishing power, and in the course of a few days nearly all in the mill were hopefully converted.[7]

Finney was favorably impressed with Walcott, describing him as "a gentleman of high standing and of good morals." Walcott must have been even more impressed with the clergyman because Finney's preaching appears to have converted him unequivocally to the cause of religious activism, a conversion that would result in long-term financial support for local churches and the future activities of Finney, Gale and other religious reformers of the day.[8]

Following his successful preaching in New York Mills, and a revival he conducted in Rome, Finney received an invitation to engage in "a season of preaching" in Utica. There his oratory reached new levels of impassioned appeal, casting him as a leader in the religious transformation overtaking western New York. From Utica, as his reputation grew, he traveled to Auburn, Rochester, Lockport and points in between, contributing greatly to the movement that brought to central and western New York the sobriquet "The Burned-Over District" in recognition of the fires of religious revival that consumed its towns and villages in the late 1820s and early 1830s.[9] "If Northampton, Massachusetts, was the birthplace of the First Great Awakening with Jonathan Edwards in the 18th century," wrote historian Richard L. Manzelmann, "Oneida County was the birthplace of what has been called the Second Great Awakening with the Rev. Charles Grandisson Finney. If the First Great Awakening influenced the founding of the nation, the Second Great Awakening helped to determine the great reform movements of the nineteenth century and influenced dramatically the great debate on slavery that ended in the Civil War. 1826 in Oneida County was a portentous moment for the history of the United States."[10]

Finney's preaching, through its emphasis on social activism, united the fire of religious revival with the cause of abolitionism in a powerful new moral imperative that would not be denied. Adding further to the effects of Finney's ministry was the founding by Rev. George Washington Gale of the Oneida Institute of Science and Industry in Whitesboro as a training ground for Finney's converts. Basing his ideas on the precedent of Swiss educator Phillip Emmanuel von Fellenberg's efforts to combine classical education with manual labor in Europe, Gale established the Oneida Institute on the theory that young men were better fitted for society through the combination of classical and practical education. In time, this philosophical underpinning would become the organizing philosophy for several of the nation's socially-oriented private educational institutions including Oberlin College and Lane Theological Seminary in Ohio and Knox College in Illinois.[11]

From its earliest inception, the Oneida Institute was also closely associated with the growing abolitionist crusade. Among its first class in 1827 was Theodore Dwight Weld, destined to be one of the most active and influential of Finney's converts on the national level. A student at Hamilton College in 1826, he came under Finney's influence when his aunt took him to one of the preacher's revival meetings in Utica. In time, Weld would go on to a distinguished career that included authoring *Slavery as It Is*, generally considered to be the most famous of all abolitionist pamphlets, helping to organize the first national anti-slavery petition campaign, and being credited by contemporaries and historians alike with "singlehandedly abolitionizing northeastern Ohio."[12]

One of Weld's first converts when he began his own preaching career was Beriah Green. Born in Preston, Connecticut, in 1795, Green was brought up in a strictly religious family environment in which children were expected to contribute manual labor from an early age. After graduating first in his class from Middlebury College in 1819, he began a preaching career noted for its reliance on simple deductive logic rather than the more elaborate allusions to the classics as was then the norm. In 1833 he succeeded Gale as president of the Oneida Institute, bringing with him a renewed sense of abolitionist purpose. At the Institute, Green encouraged the enrollment of black and white students on an equal basis, making it the first institution in America to boast a completely integrated student body. He founded the first abolitionist society in New York State at the Institute, which also became an active stop on the Underground Railroad. Deeply committed to the proposition that Christians had a moral duty to act against sin, he argued in *Things for Northern Men to Do*, a discourse published in 1836: "[A]ct as if you felt that you were bound with those in bonds, as if their cause was all your own, as if every blow that cuts their flesh, lacerated yours. [Then] you can plead their cause with the earnestness, and zeal, and decision, which self-defense demands."[13]

But Green did not limit his activities to the Institute. He also played a leading part in organizing anti-slavery activity throughout the Utica area and took an active part in the heated debates between the advocates of colonization and abolitionism. When, for example, in 1833 the Rev. Joshua Danforth characterized colonization as a "Christian and practical endeavor," Green responded, arguing instead the virtues of abolitionism. The shouting match of mutual denunciation that followed ended with an enraged crowd marching through the streets of Utica calling for the abolitionists to be arrested as traitors and burning in effigy both Green and attorney Alvan Stewart, an outspoken supporter. In the aftermath, the Utica Common Council failed by only a single vote to indict Green on a charge of treason.[14]

As the nascent abolitionist spirit in Oneida County grew, propagated through the Oneida Institute where the first immediatist anti-slavery society in New York State was formed in 1832, several local churches and a variety of itinerant speakers, conflicts with anti-abolitionist groups multiplied. On the lecture circuit, abolitionist speakers like Theodore Weld were met as often with curses as converts, many of them being "pelted with eggs and struck on the head with stones" by angry anti-abolitionist crowds.[15] In 1832, the Utica Common Council approved a resolution referring to the abolitionists as "misguided philanthropists" whose actions were "little short of treason." The resolution recommended that "the slavery question not be discussed since slavery is constitutional and since discussion would only provoke sectional rifts that would otherwise disappear."[16] Yet, this did not mean that Uticans, or others in Oneida County, were necessarily in favor of slavery. Rather, the prevailing sentiment favored the gradualist approach to the elimination of slavery as espoused by the American Colonization Society. At a meeting of the Society held in the Presbyterian Church in Utica in 1834 a resolution was adopted proclaiming the colonizationist strategy "the instrument under providence best calculated to alleviate the induction of the free Negro and secure the emancipation of the slave."[17]

Friction between the various groups came to a head in 1835 with the announcement that the abolitionist group planned to convene an anti-slavery convention in Utica. Weeks before the gathering was to take place a public meeting held at the courthouse in Utica denounced those calling for the meeting as "incendiaries," while on September 17 the Oneida County grand jury proclaimed that anyone organizing antislavery societies "'for the purpose of printing pictures and inflammatory publications' were guilty of sedition and ought to be punished. Moreover, said the grand jury, it was the 'duty of all our citizens' who were 'friendly to the Constitution' and the 'future quiet and happiness of this people' to destroy these publications *'whenever and wherever* found.'"[18]

Nor was the proposed convention only a local issue. The Albany *Argus* joined both the Utica *Whig* and the Utica *Observer* in calling for the cancellation of the proposed convention, while New York City's *Courier and Enquirer*, demanded the convention be "put down" by state law or "the law of Judge Lynch."[19] In far-away Richmond, Virginia, the here-to-fore moderate *Enquirer* testified to the national import of the proposed convention when it stated ominously that

> Utica has to choose between two courses — Will she enjoy the honour of repelling the disunionists and fanatics from her gates? or will she be degraded by the presence of another Hartford Convention? Every eye of the south is fixed upon the meeting of the Convention within her borders. Every tongue is busy in discussing the probability and the consequences of the meeting. We call upon the citizens of New-York to arrest these madmen in their career — who know not themselves what mischiefs they are inflicting upon the country, and especially upon the coloured population, whose interests they are professing to serve. We call, above all, upon the good citizens of Utica, to keep this moral pestilence from their door. We call upon their respectable mayor, who was the chairman of the late anti-abolition meeting, to rouse up, and with the aid of all the patriots of Utica, to arrest this mischievous meeting. Stop the madmen's hands, that would apply the firebrands to the union itself.[20]

Opposition to the convention crossed otherwise rigid political lines. On October 15 the Oneida County Democratic convention passed the following motion:

> Resolved, That the citizens of Utica owe it to themselves, to the state, and to the union, that the contemplated Convention of incendiary individuals is not permitted to assemble within its corporate bounds; that their churches, their court, academy, and school-rooms, be closed against these wicked or deluded men, who, whatever may be their pretensions, are riveting the fetters of the bondsman, and enkindling the flames of civil strife.[21]

Not to be outdone, the *Oneida Whig* announced that the citizens of Utica would "never permit it to be carried into force,"[22] while an anonymous author writing under the pseudonym "Defensor" asserted that

> The agitators are those who are endeavoring, by deception and fraud, to subvert the constitution, and change the settled policy of this country. These fanatics, by means of their incendiary meetings and publications, have long been labouring to inflame the public mind against the abolitionists, by misrepresenting their sentiments and designs. They have industriously circulated throughout the southern states publications of the most inflammatory and incendiary character, calculated to produce an insurrection among the slave-holders, and a dissolution of the union. With such assiduous and untiring zeal have their disorganizing schemes been pursued, that they have agitated the country to its utmost bounds with excitement and alarm, which threaten to sunder the most endearing relations and most sacred ties.[23]

Tensions rose further when the Utica Common Council voted 7 to 4 to allow the assemblage to take place in the county court house. Opponents of the proposed meeting filed a petition requesting that the Council "not submit to the indignation of an abolition assemblage being held in a public building of the city ... developed to be used for salutary public objects and not as a receptacle for the deluded fanatics or restless incendiaries."[24]

On October 17, just days before the proposed abolitionist meeting was to convene, a meeting of the Utica Common Council with Mayor Joseph Kirkland presiding witnessed heated discussion as the opponents of the abolitionist meeting voiced forceful arguments for withdrawing permission for the gathering. "Sir, for what purpose has a State Convention been called?" asked congressman Samuel Beardsley rhetorically:

> To promote the objects they have in view. Sir, what are these objects? Mainly to bring about the immediate abolition of slavery at the south. They seem like downright idiots. No man, in his sober senses, can doubt that every movement of this kind, instead of elevating the condition of the slaves, renders their condition more degraded, debased, and oppressive than before. It has heretofore been, and the constant tendency is, to reduce the slave still lower, and make him more a slave than he was before. It is clear that this is the tendency of the efforts of the abolitionist. ... And why are these abolitionists intent on holding a convention in this city to promote their designs? It is intended to insult us. It is intended to degrade the character of the city in the esteem of the world. And especially to us, who live here, to treat us with the utmost contempt. Insult us to our faces where they cannot muster a corporal's guard. They, sir, in contempt of the open, public, and express sentiment of this community, come here to hold a disgraceful and scandalous assembly, to rush in and insult us to our faces with an assemblage of this kind. The laws of propriety forbid that they should come here. We are to be picked out as the head-quarters of Abolitionism in the state of New

York. As have this, I would almost as soon see it [the city] swept from the face of the earth, or sunk as low as Sodom and Gomorrah. Nothing is due to these men if they come here.[25]

"If they [the abolitionists] should persist in holding their convention in this city, they are responsible for all the consequences that should follow," opined Beardsley in a thinly veiled insinuation of future disturbance. Augustine G. Dauby, editor of the *Observer*, was less circumspect: "For one, Mr. President, I will be here, I will prevent their coming here, peacefully if I can, *forcibly if I must*."[26]

Finally, Beardsley offered the following resolutions:

> Resolved, that this meeting unmoved by passion or prejudice, but influenced only by a just regard for itself and for what is due to the quiet and repose of the whole community, *will not submit to the indignity of an abolition assemblage being held in a public building in this city*, reared as this was by the contributions of its citizens, and designed to be used for salutary public objects, and not as a receptacle for deluded fanatics and reckless incendiaries.

> Resolved, That it is the incumbent duty of every citizen to make use of all lawful and proper measures to arrest the disgrace which would settle upon this city by the public assemblage of the Convention appointed to be held on the 21st instant....[27]

Denied the use of public facilities by a new vote of the Common Council, abolitionist organizers moved the meeting venue to the Second Presbyterian Church on the corner of Charlotte and Bleecker Streets. With this, the stage was set for confrontation.

Some 600 people assembled in the Presbyterian Church on October 21, 1835. They represented a cross-section of society from near and far. Merchants and tradesmen were well represented, along with clergy including the Rev. Oliver Wetmore and the Rev. Lewis H. Loss from New York Mills. A high proportion were immigrants, with Welsh Baptists and Presbyterians being especially prominent in both the temperance and anti-slavery movements.[28] As the speakers began their denunciations of slavery inside the building, outside a raucous crowd gathered in the streets. Among the leaders were prominent civic figures including bankers, merchants, attorneys and elected officials. John C. Devereux, one of the wealthiest people in the city, was there, as were attorney and former mayor Horatio Seymour, bank president A. B. Johnson, attorneys William Tracey and J. Watson Williams, and Justice of the Peace John B. Pease. Many feared the negative impact the abolitionist convention might have on commerce with other cities and states, while others worried that left unchecked the abolitionists would drive a divisive and unnecessary wedge between North and South.[29]

When yelling and hallooing from the street did not prevent the abolitionists from commencing their business, some of the more aggressive protesters burst through the doors to the church into the middle of the assemblage. Crowding down the center aisle, screaming insults and threats, the mob thoroughly disrupt-ed the proceedings. When an aged minister rose to protest the invasion, Rutger B. Miller, a future United States Congressman, threatened to cane the cleric with his own stick. The shouting, commotion and physical threats combined to make it impossible to continue the meeting. Then, when the assembly finally adjourned, its members were subjected to a barrage of sticks, rocks, eggs and other missiles as they retreated through the threatening mob outside the church. Later that night, while most of the mob retired to the local saloons, a portion moved to Oneida, some seventeen miles away, where they attacked the office of the pro-abolition-ist *Oneida Standard and Democrat,* destroying type, cases and other printing equipment.[30]

In the gallery observing the abbreviated convention was Gerrit Smith. Born in Utica on March 6, 1797, he was the son of Peter Smith, a partner in the fur trade with John Jacob Astor and cousin of Robert Livingston who administered the oath of office to President George Washington. Through deft investments in land in the Alleghenies, the Mohawk Valley and the Adirondacks, Peter accumu-lated a fortune, a small portion of which he used to remove his family to a new home west of Utica in 1806 that he named for himself—Peterboro. Upon his death, he left his son Gerrit over one million acres in Virginia, Pennsylvania and New York worth approximately $400,000. With an annual income of more than $60,000 from these investments—well over a million dollars in today's funds—Smith was one of the richest men in America.[31]

Yet, Smith did not rest on his inheritance. Graduating with honors from Hamilton College in 1818 where he gave the valedictory address, he quickly launched himself into an active life of business, politics, social reform and phi-lanthropy. A cousin of the noted women's rights advocate Elizabeth Cady Stanton, he became a business partner of her father, Daniel Cady. In 1822 Smith married Ann Carroll Fitzhugh from Livingston County, the daughter of a promi-nent Maryland family related to Robert E. Lee and Fitzhugh Lee of Virginia, both of whom would later become prominent generals in the Confederate army.[32]

Although his father had once owned slaves, Smith became an early support-er of the American Colonization Society that sought to free slaves and return them to Africa. As early as 1827, Smith considered founding a school in Peterboro to train Black missionaries for work in Africa under the auspices of the Colonization Society. In 1834 he attempted to establish a manual labor school in Peterboro, but it lasted only one year. Although Beriah Green and others attempt-ed to interest Smith in the upcoming anti-slavery meeting in Utica, he shied away from the immediatist approach of the leaders planning the convention. "I feel a confidence, which my heart refuses to let go," Green wrote to Smith, "that you will, sometime or other, give us your heart and your hand." Nevertheless, Smith confided to his diary: "I think I cannot join the Antislavery Society as long as the

War is kept up between it and the American Colonization Society—a war, however, for which the American Colonization Society is as much to blame as the other Society."[33]

Regardless of his adherence to the more conservative Colonization Society, Smith was curious about the Utica meeting. En route to Schenectady with his wife, Smith spent the evening in Utica and decided to walk over to the meeting to see what was happening. He was among the spectators as the meeting opened, only to be brought to an abrupt end by the disruptive mob. Appalled by the lack of respect for the right of free speech, when it became apparent that the meeting would have to disband Smith rose from his seat to invite the participants to reassemble at his home in Peterboro the following day to continue their discussions.[34]

More than half of the 600 who met in Utica reconvened at Peterboro on October 22 where they heard Smith offer the following resolution.

> Resolved, That the right of free discussion, given to us by God, and asserted and guarded by the laws of our country, is a right so vital to man's freedom, and dignity, and usefulness, that we can never be guilty of its surrender, without consenting to exchange that freedom for slavery, and that dignity and usefulness for debasement and worthlessness.[35]

Beriah Green's confidence had been rewarded. Deploring the reaction to the anti-slavery meeting, while at the same time experiencing a growing frustration with the failure of the Colonization Society to actively pursue an anti-slavery agenda, Smith soon resigned from the Colonization Society to throw his considerable zeal and fortune behind the abolitionist cause. Slavery is "robbery," he wrote, "and the worst species of it — for it plunders its victim, not of goods and money, but of his body, his mind, his soul." It was a major turning point toward radicalizing Central New York to anti-slavery activism.[36]

Although the aggressiveness of the mob in Utica reflected a widespread lack of support for the abolitionists in 1835, a dramatic change unfolded during the two years following the aborted meeting. In addition to Smith's conversion to their cause, the abolitionists benefited from other events that began to very quickly shift the balance of popular opinion in their favor.

Theodore Weld, whose ardent rhetoric had already converted most of the faculty and students of the Oneida Institute to the cause of abolitionism in the spring of 1834, delivered an extraordinarily popular series of sixteen lectures in the Utica area that attracted overflow crowds of hundreds to the cause of human liberation. "Weld's fervent style and the acuity of his argument were eminently persuasive," concluded historian Edward Magdol, "as the mass response to him indicated." It was estimated that his emotional appeals added some 600 new members to the Utica Anti-Slavery Society alone, led to the formation of a young people's anti-slavery society in New York Mills that enrolled 100 people, and sewed

Theodore Dwight Weld in old age
(Oneida County Historical Society)

William Goodell
(Oneida County Historical Society)

the seeds of abolitionism throughout the county's towns and villages.[37]

While Weld spoke to enthusiastic audiences that strained the capacities of the venues, affluent attorney Alvan Stewart railed against the evils of slavery to other meetings and clergy from area Methodist and Presbyterian Churches preached the evils of human bondage in their sermons. Their efforts were furthered by William Goodell. Born in Chenango County in 1792, Goodell began his reform career in the temperance movement where he edited the periodical *Investigator*, which later merged with the *National Philanthropist* to become the respected *Genius of Temperance*. Soon, however, his interests changed to the anti-slavery movement where he became editor of the *Emancipator*. In 1836 Goodell moved to Utica where he began publishing *The Friend of Man* in support of the New York Anti-Slavery Society. Printed at the Oneida Institute, the newspaper provided a vehicle for the dissemination of abolitionist thought not only to the immediate Central New York region, but to a much larger national audience.[38]

Evidence of the dramatic success of the abolitionists in energizing the anti-slavery movement in Oneida County swiftly appeared. In 1836, only a year after the mob violence at the first anti-slavery meeting in Utica, a second convention convened in complete peace to ratify the constitution of the New York Anti-Slavery Society. A measure of the significance of the county in the statewide anti-slavery movement can be seen in the results of the elections to office in the new organization. Six Uticans were selected for the executive committee, while Uticans were also tapped for the leadership positions of vice president, corresponding secretary, recording secretary, and treasurer.[39] By the end of the decade, the Utica area was the unrivaled "upstate hub of social reform, religious revival, temperance, and the anti-Masonic and Workingmen's party movements," concluded historian Edward Magdol. "None of the others equaled the electric effect of Utica's waves of revivalism, as the city grew from frontier village into bustling canal town and finally into the metropolis of a regional factory-town network."[40]

While solidifying its role as the leader of New York State's abolitionist movement, Oneida County continued to make its influence felt in the national debates. As the dispute over slavery intensified, Theodore Weld led a movement, along with John G. Whittier and Henry B. Stanton, to collect signatures on petitions opposing the continued existence of slavery in the District of Columbia. In 1836 some 1,200 names were secured on anti-slavery petitions from the Utica area, while a similar drive in 1837 resulted in pleas to the United States House of Representatives from Steuben, Remsen, New York Mills, Utica, Rome, and almost every location of any size in Oneida County, opposing the extension of slavery into the western territories.[41] Compared with the hostility to the abolitionist cause in October 1835, the change in popular sentiment in Oneida County over the following two years was striking and unprecedented.

The beginning of the petition drives clearly established Oneida County as a voice on the national scene, yet the influence of the county's growing abolitionist sentiment on the national dialogue increased significantly through many simultaneous avenues. Chief among these were the graduates of the Oneida Institute who spread the abolitionist philosophy throughout the North. Following his successful petition drive, Weld continued his work of spreading abolitionism into the Midwest. Widely respected as a popular abolitionist lecturer, Weld was instrumental in founding the Lane Theological Seminary in Cincinnati on the principles of manual labor and evangelism. In fact, 24 of the 40 students enrolled in the first class at Lane were people who followed Weld west from the Oneida Institute. When the seminary's trustees objected to the strident abolitionism preached by Weld and his flock, the entire Oneida Institute group left for the more welcoming environment of Oberlin College.[42]

Following his marriage to the prominent abolitionist Angela Grimké in 1838, Weld authored the influential *Slavery As It Is*, the virtual bible of the early immediatist movement, then worked in the office of the American Anti-Slavery Society during early 1840s. There, he labored tirelessly to inspire congressmen and senators in the fight against slavery, providing many with information and arguments to be used against the supporters of the "peculiar institution." Among the prominent public figures Weld is credited with strongly influencing on behalf of abolitionism were Joshua Giddings, Owen Lovejoy, Thaddeus Stevens, and Benjamin Wade.[43]

Other students educated at Oneida Institute included some of the most prominent Black leaders of the early nineteenth century. Augustus Washington, a supporter of the colonization movement, served as an agent for the *Colored American*, taught in Brooklyn's African Public School No. 1, then moved to

Alexander Crummell
(Oneida County Historical Society)

Jermain W. Loguen
(Oneida County Historical Society)

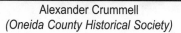

Liberia where he became a legislator and judge.[44] Another leading proponent of the colonization movement was Alexander Crummell. Born to free parents in Brooklyn in 1819, he enrolled in the Institute in 1835, graduating in the fall of 1838 from what he described as "3 years of perfect equality with upwards to 100 white students, of different denominations." When racial discrimination prevented him from gaining admittance to an Episcopal seminary, he persisted, engaging private tutors until he gained consecration as a deacon in 1842 and priest in 1844. Traveling to England four years later, Crummell earned his baccalaureate degree from Queen's College, Cambridge, in 1853. The man the *Washington Bee* called "the most educated Negro in America," spent two decades as a missionary in Liberia before returning to the United States to serve for a quarter-century as rector of St. Luke's Episcopal Church in Washington, D.C. He died in 1898.[45]

Jermain W. Loguen was born into slavery in Tennessee, but escaped to Canada around 1834. Eventually moving to Rochester, New York, he enrolled in the Oneida Institute in 1839. While there, he began the first school for Black children in Utica, then moved to Syracuse where he founded a second school before being ordained in the African Methodist Episcopal Zion Church. Although he preached in several upstate communities, his major contribution was to the abolitionist cause where he became known as the "General Superintendent of the Underground Railroad" in Syracuse. An effective speaker, his themes increasingly revolved around his belief that those enslaved should "strike a blow for themselves, and not wait for the hairsplitting of politicians and speakers." Following the Civil War Loguen was active in providing for the welfare of ex-slaves. He passed away in Syracuse in 1872.[46]

No doubt the most famous of the Institute's Black alumni was Henry Highland Garnet. A Maryland slave for the first nine years of his life, Garnet's parents escaped north with him where he received an elementary education at the African Free School in New York City. In 1831 he entered the High School for Colored Youth, receiving a classical education including the study of Greek and Latin. From there, Garnet registered at the Oneida Institute, serving at the Liberty Street Presbyterian Church in Troy after his graduation in 1839. Known for his superior public debating skills, he became an active and influential member of the American and Foreign Anti-Slavery Society where he fought tire-

Henry Highland Garnet
(Oneida County Historical Society)

lessly for the right of Blacks to vote in New York State. His work led to the establishment of African state conventions. Soon, however, he came to the belief that slavery would never be ended except by the efforts of the slaves themselves. In a speech delivered at the Convention of Free People of Color in Buffalo in 1843, he admonished those still enslaved that "voluntary submission" constituted a sin.

> To such degradation it is sinful in the extreme for you to make voluntary submission.... The diabolical injustice by which your liberties are cloven down, neither God nor angels, or just men, command you to suffer for a single moment. Therefore it is your solemn and imperative duty to use every means, both moral, intellectual, and physical, that promises success. ... You had far better all die — *die immediately,* than live slaves, and entail your wretchedness upon your posterity. If you would be free in this generation, here is your only hope. However much you and all of us may desire it, there is not much hope of redemption without the shedding of blood. If you must bleed, let it all come at once — rather *die freemen than live to be slaves....* In the name of the merciful God, and by all that life is worth, let it no longer be a debatable question, whether it is better to choose *liberty or death.*[47]

An early rival of Frederick Douglass for leadership of the African abolitionist movement, Garnet's increasing radicalism, along with Douglass's establishment of the newspaper *The North Star* as an outlet for his work, led to Garnet's eclipse by Douglass as the primary Black spokesperson. After journeys to England, Scotland and the West Indies, Garnet was eventually appointed U.S. Minister Resident to Liberia. After returning to America to serve as pastor of the

Shiloh Presbyterian Church in New York City, he was again named to the minis-
terial post in Liberia in 1881, dying there while on duty the following year.[48]

The number and quality of the abolitionists going out from Oneida County
had a profound effect on the growth and development of the national anti-slavery
movement. A popular pathway along the "Underground Railroad," Gerrit Smith
offered to pay slave owners for the freedom of those held in their bondage, while
also giving liberally of his fortune to assist runaways including some who had
escaped from the famous Virginia political leader John Mason, later a
Confederate minister to Europe. When Frederick Douglass moved to Rochester
to found his antislavery newspaper, Smith proved "a strong and vital supporter."
In 1839, he donated 21,000 acres of land to support the abolitionist training institution at Oberlin College. Six years later he set aside 120,000 acres in northern
New York's Adirondack Mountains to be sold at low cost as homesteads to free
Blacks. The land was to be divided into parcels large enough to qualify the owners to vote under New York State law, eventually resulting in the settlement of
1,985 families.[49]

Smith was also active as a leading figure on the national scene. As Lawrence
J. Friedman pointed out, many historians date the radicalization of noted abolitionist leader William Lloyd Garrison from the time in 1837 when he "embraced
the perfectionist ideas of John Humphrey Noyes," the founder of the Oneida
Community, a utopian society located in western Oneida County. By 1840 a
schism took place in the American Anti-Slavery Society between the Garrisonian
radicals centered in Boston and the more conservative and moderate anti-slavery
elements led by the Tappans in New York City. Smith urged reconciliation for the
good of the movement. Although he was not successful in forging an accommo-
dation between the two groups, he did remain on good terms with both, acting as
a stabilizing force to prevent internecine conflict.[50]

Smith's attempts to preserve unity among the anti-slavery factions did not,
however, preclude the Tappans from ridiculing another approach to the slavery
problem increasingly adopted by Smith and his Oneida County followers. From
the cauldron of the religious revivals that swept the Burned-Over District, Smith
drew the lesson that it was much easier to realize change in small towns where
family, neighbors and friends could exert influence on one another. Such group
pressure was difficult to achieve in the more anonymous atmosphere of larger
cities. "A dollar spent at Utica," declared Alvan Stewart, "is worth three spent at
New York [City]."[51] It was this focus on "localism" that propelled men like
Theodore Weld to fan out across the North to develop local organizations capable of carrying on the anti-slavery fight among their own friends and neighbors.

Smith also believed in "cultural voluntarism," the theory that in conditions
of cultural and political freedom, people would naturally be inclined to behave in
a moral manner. In places where the freedom of some was restricted, he deduced,
no one was truly free. Therefore, it was the responsibility of the government to

Gerrit Smith (standing, center, with tie)and Frederick Douglass
(seated, center, at table) appeared at this abolitionist rally in
Peterboro in around 1849. *(Madison County Historical Society)*

provide the free environment in which the natural propensity to follow God's laws could take place. Supported by Alvan Stewart's legal training and opinions, Smith argued that slavery was illegal under the provisions of the Constitution; thus, if the Federal government would only enforce the Constitution the slavery question would be solved. As historian Friedman explained it, "By simply exercising the supreme law of the land, he came to insist, the Federal government could secure to every American citizen the freedom to fulfill his moral obligations."[52]

These two beliefs, "localism" and "cultural voluntarism," were expounded by Oneida County activists throughout the North by means of the anti-slavery lecture circuit and the products of Oneida County's publishing industry, the third largest in the nation behind only New York City and Boston. Articles appearing in abolitionist newspapers published in Central New York were distributed nationally, while also finding their way into publications in other cities in an era where the press routinely re-published material from other publications. These periodicals were supplemented with printed lectures, occasional treatises on abolitionist theory, and the publication of monographs by noted social, religious and political leaders. In *The Democracy of Christianity*, William Goodell expounded the case for cultural voluntarism, while his *Views on American Constitutional Law, in Its Bearing upon American Slavery* became the classic statement of the abolitionist argument that the Constitution prohibited slavery. The claim, he wrote, that the Constitution "can secure general liberty and at the same time guarantee local slavery, or even compromise or permit its existence, is to affirm the greatest of moral absurdities, to deny self-evident truths, to falsify human history." Goodell's other work, *Slavery and Anti-Slavery*, provided a useful synthesis of anti-slavery thought. "The sole job of the abolitionists was to 'publish the truth,'" Smith had said. Through these activities, Friedman concluded, Smith and his followers were able to merge "the cultural voluntarism of their evangelistic Burned-Over District into Northern and national political life."[53]

While Oneida County's abolitionists influenced the national dialogue toward their brand of radicalism, the political debate on the slavery question was also informed by activities in Central New York. In 1839 an anti-slavery convention in Warsaw, New York, attempted unsuccessfully to nominate a candidate for president. In a letter to the *Emancipator* in January 1840, Alvan Stewart argued: "An independent abolition political party is the only hope for the redemption of the slave!" Slavery was a political issue, supporters of the idea claimed; consequently, it could be eliminated through control of the ballot box. The idea gained instant popularity among Oneida County's radicals, with Smith and Goodell taking the leadership in developing the new faction, which Smith suggested be called the "Liberty Party." The new party held its first national convention in Albany in 1840, nominating James G. Birney, Smith's brother-in-law, for the presidency.[54]

Consumed by their fervent abolitionism, inflamed by the excitement of the campaign, the novice national politicos produced catchy lyrics they repeated at rallies throughout Upstate New York. One, sung to the tune of "America," lamented the fate of a nation soiled by the blight of slavery:

> "My country, 'tis of thee,
> Dark land of slavery,
> For thee I weep;
> Land where the slave has sighed,
> And where he toiled and died
> To serve a tyrant's pride—
> For thee I weep."

Another, ironically sung to the tune that would later become associated with the Confederacy as "The Bonnie Blue Flag," encouraged people to enlist in the abolitionist cause. The chorus went as follows:

> "Come join the Abolitionists,
> Ye young men, bold and strong,
> And with a warm and cheerful zeal
> Come help the cause along."

Yet another, the "Ode to Birney," extolled the virtues of the candidate.

> "We hail thee, Birney, just and true,
> The calm and fearless, staunch and tried,
> The bravest of the valiant few,
> Our country's hope, our country's pride!
> In freedom's battle take the van;
> We hail thee as an honest man."[55]

Musical creativity notwithstanding, Liberty Party leaders were greatly disappointed when they attracted less than one percent of the national vote.[56] Nevertheless, despite the poor showing, Smith, Goodell and their followers made plans to broaden their base of support. Throughout the next two years a procession of speakers, including William Lloyd Garrison, Lucretia Mott and other prominent national anti-slavery leaders, toured Central New York to energize supporters. "In this section a Liberty party convention is an abolition convention, and an Abolition convention a Liberty party convention," Smith wrote to Salmon P. Chase, a prominent Senator and future Secretary of the Treasury and Supreme Court justice. The ballot box, Goodell trumpeted in the *Friend of Man,* was "an element of reformation which God has put into the hands of abolitionists." Their efforts were rewarded by only 7,000 votes in the statewide off-year elections in 1842, but the total was a significant improvement over the 1840 tally. More importantly, their speeches and arguments were disseminated throughout the North, influencing other candidates and local elections.[57]

Undeterred by the poor showing in its initial campaigns, the Liberty Party convened its second national convention in Buffalo in 1843 with 148 delegates from twelve states in attendance. Strongly endorsed by Garnet, Loguen and other products of the Oneida Institute, the Buffalo meeting was the first national political convention in American history to include Blacks among its leadership positions.[58] Although resting its political hopes on a single issue, the convention issued the longest platform statement of the century. To oppose the Democrat James K. Polk and the Whig Henry Clay, the Liberty Party once again chose James G. Birney. Once again they did poorly in the national race, winning only three percent of the vote in New York State and 2.3 percent nationally. But the 16,000 votes they attracted in New York, taken almost entirely from those who would otherwise have voted for Clay, were enough to swing the state to Polk. Ironically, the increasing vote total of the abolitionists secured the presidency for Polk whom the Liberty Party distrusted because of his pledge to annex Texas, an area ripe for the expansion of slavery.[59]

Polk's election victory, followed by the annexation of Texas, resulted in the outbreak of the Mexican War, an event Smith decried as "folly and wickedness."[60] With the American victory, the Treaty of Guadalupe Hidalgo brought the territory of the Mexican Cession — today's California, Nevada, Arizona and New Mexico — under United States ownership, providing additional territory that promised to become a battleground between North and South over the potential expansion of slavery. Political maneuverings and increasing rhetoric amplified the tension between the sections throughout the remainder of the 1840s. In New York, William Goddell spoke in 1847 at a Liberty League meeting supporting both abolitionism and free trade. Goodell believed strongly that the Constitution could not "secure general liberty ... and at the same time guaranty local slavery." He argued, echoing the now familiar arguments, that God's law provided that people were free to act morally. "Neither the slave nor the laborer facing protective tariffs possessed full 'self-ownership' and consequently neither could fully guide his behavior in conformity with God's moral imperatives."[61]

Despite the emotional oratory and appeals to religion, in 1848 most Liberty Party followers switched their allegiance to the new Free Soil Party formed in Buffalo by anti-Slavery Whigs, anti-slavery Democrats, and former Liberty Party supporters. Smith, Goodell and a smaller circle of radicals refused to support the Free Soilers who they felt were not sufficiently extreme to achieve their ends. In this presidential election year, feelings ran high in Oneida County as both the New York State Liberty Party meeting and the convention of New York anti-slavery Democrats met in Utica. The Liberty Party meeting was rife with the usual speechifying, while the tone for the anti-slavery Democrats, or "Barnburners," as they were called, was struck by Martin Grover's bold assertion that he would rather live in a monarchy than a nation controlled by 300,000 slave-holders. "If the schemes of the South succeed, farewell to liberty," he warned. With diminishing ranks, the Liberty Party nominated Gerrit Smith as its presidential candidate to oppose Democrat Lewis Cass, Whig Zachary Taylor, and Free Soiler Martin van Buren. Once again, support for the Liberty Party was negligible.[62]

The controversy over the Mexican Cession was finally settled, at least temporarily, by the Compromise of 1850. Abolitionists viewed this as a sell-out to Southern slaveholders because of its provision for Fugitive Slave Laws requiring that Northerners actively assist Southerners in reclaiming runaway slaves. Its passage ignited another storm of protest across Central New York, bringing politicians from around the nation to debate the issues in the cities and towns of Oneida County. William Hemstreet was fifteen years old when Senator Henry Clay visited New York Mills. Later in life he recalled being "one of an improvised brass band that, riding in an old omnibus, greeted the noble statesman and conducted him to 'Uncle Ben' Walcott's for luncheon. A pleasant social session, at which refreshments were served, concluded the event."[63] Pleasant though that occasion might have been, the reaction of Oneida County was once again a clarion to act. Speeches roused the people to action, petitions flowed, with Roscoe Conkling capturing the mood of the populace when he asserted that "American slavery is spoken of as an unmixed and unmitigated social, political and moral evil. I believe it is one of the blackest and bloodiest pictures in the book of modern times. Surely there can be fewer great monstrosities than the proposition that one race has the right to enslave another."[64]

Amid the turmoil, the 1852 national election pitted the Democratic candidate Franklin Pierce against Whig Winfield Scott and Free Soiler John P. Hale, with the Compromise of 1850 and the spread of slavery into the territories as pivotal issues in the ensuing debates. In the same year, Gerrit Smith led a mob that forcibly freed a fugitive slave from a Syracuse jail, ratcheting Central New York's response to the Fugitive Slave Laws significantly upward from oratory to illegal action. That fall, he was elected to the House of Representatives on the Liberty Party ticket, causing Horace Greeley to opine in his New York *Tribune* that "We are heartily glad that Gerrit Smith is going to Washington. He is an honest, brave, kind-hearted Christian philanthropist, whose religion is not put aside with his Sunday cloak, but lasts him clear through the week." Once in office, Smith immediately made himself abhorrent to Southerners by delivering several strong abolitionist speeches.[65]

As tensions continued to mount, the Kansas-Nebraska Act of 1854, providing for "popular sovereignty" in the territories, emerged as another compromise repugnant to abolitionist principles. A particular object of derision was Stephen A. Douglas, the Illinois Democrat who assumed the lead of Northern politicians seeking a peaceful solution to the questions surrounding the admission of Kansas to the Union. The *Utica Herald* labeled Douglas a "demagogue," a "scavenger," a "second Benedict Arnold," and an "enemy of Liberty."[66] In Whitesboro, a citizen's committee placed the following announcement in the newspaper:

> The traitor Douglas will be ordered down at 8 this evening and burned in a tar barrel at the stake. By order of the Guard of Liberty. Whitesboro, June 15, 1854.
>
> P.S. A band is expected to play the rogues march and other appropriate airs on this occasion, for the Prince of Doughfaces and enemy of Liberty.[67]

At the appointed time, a large crowd gathered, as described the following day in the pages of the *Utica Morning Herald:*

> Amid the hurrahing, the Court House, Academy, Furnace, Baptist, and Presbyterian bells commenced tolling. Someone with a pitchfork picked up the effigy and put it on the bier. Behind it was a sign saying "Douglas, Successor to Arnold. The Traitor's Doom." They walked up and down Main Street for a while, while the band played a "mournful dirge." ...such unearthly groans were given as *told* in unison with the tolling of the bells, that the North is not wholly

given up to Slavery. There is still a nucleus around which the friends of Liberty will rally and achieve a freedom from Doughfaces and Slavocratic rule worthy of the blood of our Revolutionary sires. Then, they went to the schoolhouse lot, erected a stake, and put *him* on it. In a few moments, the flames reached the object and it WITHERED as we trust the real Douglas now withers under the SCORCHING indignation of the enraged and intelligent friends of freedom everywhere.[68]

Nor were symbolic gestures Central New York's only response. Utica alone sent a petition with 755 names to Congress protesting the Kansas-Nebraska Act, the second largest number from any geographic area in New York State. Rome sent over 400 names, with petitions from New Hartford, Whitestown, New York Mills, Remsen, Prospect, and a host of other county towns and villages reflecting once again the fervent abolitionist sentiments of the area, beliefs that contributed substantially to the fratricidal conflagration about to envelop the land. Dozens of other petitions arrived in Washington from other towns and villages. In Congress, Representative Gerrit Smith spoke eloquently against the Kansas-Nebraska Bill, allying himself closely with Salmon P. Chase of Ohio and Charles Sumner of Massachusetts, personal friends who led the opposition to the bill in the Senate. He also pledged $1,000 per year to the National Kansas Committee.[69]

As the crisis over Kansas intensified, Senator Sumner took the floor of the Senate in May 1856, to denounce the advocates of slavery, and those who would strike bargains with them, in his famous "Crime Against Kansas" speech. Among the former he singled out Senator Andrew P. Butler of South Carolina; among the latter, Senator Stephen A. Douglas of Illinois, the champion of popular sovereignty. Outraged by Sumner's verbal attack on Butler, Preston Brooks, a member of the House of Representatives from South Carolina, and nephew of Butler, strode into the Senate chamber the following day intent upon defending his uncle's honor. Approaching Sumner, Brooks began pummeling Sumner with his walking cane, inflicting serious injuries to the senator's head and torso. Throughout the South, Brooks was hailed as a hero who stood up for Southern honor. In the North, editorials portrayed Brooks as a barbarian whose violence had debased the halls of the Senate. Oneida County's reaction to the incident was described by the *Utica Herald*:

> Slavery, which respects nothing, annihilates by a blow the Senatorial privilege, and fells the statesman to the earth. Slavery, which is a monarch absolute in the counsels of the "first Republic on earth," stalks into the Senate Hall and strikes with ruffian hand the Senator who questions its divinity — Slavery which is converting to its use the untrodden worlds of the West, and driving freedom, at bayonet's point to the wall, cracks its whip in Pennsylvania Avenue, carries its shackles into the Hall of Legislation, and fetters the limbs and tongues of the representatives of twenty-seven millions of people! Slavery, which puts morality to the blush, and laughs justice to scorn, rides in its crimson car over the necks, not of three million blacks, but of eighteen millions of whites.[70]

Furious at the growing assertiveness of the pro-slavery faction, Gerrit Smith journeyed to Chicago to incite opposition to the Fugitive Slave Laws. There, he openly called for the arming of antislavery settlers in Kansas, a precursor to the outbreak of open civil war in that territory shortly thereafter. That December the instigator of the violence in Kansas, John Brown, visited Smith at his home in Peterboro to relate to him the abolitionist's experiences in Kansas. Brown found his host "furious" at what he perceived to be the federal government's support for the pro-slavery faction.[71] Shortly after Brown's visit, Smith wrote to him:

> Captain John Brown, — You did not need to show me letters ... to let me know who you are. I have known you many years, and have highly esteemed you as long as I have known you. I know your unshrinkable bravery, your self-sacrificing benevolence, your devotion to the cause of freedom, and have long known them. May heaven preserve your life and health, and prosper your noble purposes![72]

Now allied with the most radical of abolitionists, Smith's influence would be felt more than ever in the growing rift between North and South.

Against the backdrop of violence in Kansas, the election campaign of 1856 promised to be even more important than the preceding national ballots. The Democrats nominated James Buchanan, while the Republicans, a combination of the various anti-slavery elements from other parties including former Free Soil and Whig supporters running a national presidential candidate for the first time, chose John C. Frémont as their standard-bearer. Called upon to support the Republican anti-slavery platform, Smith donated $500 to Frémont's campaign, but could not bring himself to leave the increasingly irrelevant Liberty Party. "The Republican party refuses to oppose slavery where it is, and opposes it only where it is not," complained Smith in attempts to urge Republican leaders to adopt a more decided abolitionist stance, while William Goodell echoed this message in his own editorials. Many leading Black abolitionists concurred with Smith and Goodell, including the Oneida Institute's Jermain W. Loguen and Amos Beman.[73]

The election of Buchanan on a platform of sectional compromise did not entirely relieve the mounting tensions. Instead, with the ferocity of open conflict in Kansas still fresh in the national consciousness, the Supreme Court weighed into the slavery crisis with its famed Dred Scott Decision, ruling that slaves were legally property protected under the Fifth Amendment to the Constitution. What the court's opinion implied was that slaves could be taken anywhere, including New York, regardless of local law because slaves were property and the right to own property was guaranteed in the Constitution. Anti-slavery Northerners were outraged. "A new code of political ethics is pronounced," lamented the *Utica Herald*, "a new theory of Government has been discovered. It is not a Republic, but a Despotism we are living under. The Constitution is not a chart of freedom, but an instrument of Bondage. The object of the Government is not to protect the liberties of the People, but to further the interests of Slavery. It is not Freedom that is national, but Slavery."[74]

The Dred Scott Decision was a major turning point along the road to civil war. As opposed as they were to the extension of slavery to the territories, or the very existence of slavery in the South, the thought of being forced to accept slavery in their own states, as remote as that may have been in actuality, filled Northerners with an explosive combination of fear and rage. "Much as I abhor war," Gerrit Smith declared, "I nevertheless believe, that there are instances when the shedding of blood is unavoidable."[75] To Joshua Giddings in Ohio, Smith wrote in 1858, "The slave will be delivered by the shedding of blood — and the signs are multiplying that his deliverance is at hand."[76] Nor were these words hollow, for Smith was in regular contact with the catalyst of the Kansas conflict, John Brown. As early as February, 1858, Brown wrote to Franklin B. Sanborn to share his belief that Smith was ready to "go in for a share in the whole trade."[77] This simple phrase meant that Smith was interested in joining a new conspiratorial group later known as the "Secret Six." Dedicated to the abolitionist's mission of eliminating all slavery from the nation, six men — Dr. Samuel Gridley Howe, Rev. Theodore Parker, Thomas Wentworth Higginson, George Luther Sterns, Sanborn and Smith — joined together to pool their influence and money to support a new effort by Brown to effect the elimination of the national evil — by force if necessary. In the summer of 1858, Smith confirmed to Sanborn his support of Brown, stating: "For several years I have frequently given him money towards sustaining him in his conquests with the slave-power. Whenever he shall embark in another of these contests I shall again stand ready to help him; and I will begin with giving him a hundred dollars. I do not wish to know Captain Brown's plans. I hope he will keep them to himself."[78] To Thaddeus Hyatt, Smith wrote: "We must not shrink from fighting for Liberty — and if Federal troops fight against her, we must fight against them."[79] Clearly, Smith had come a long way since his early days in the relatively conservative colonization movement. His influence on national affairs was about to take a very serious turn.

On October 16-18, 1859, with the moral and financial support of Gerrit Smith and the other members of the "Secret Six," John Brown led eighteen men who invaded Harper's Ferry, Virginia, capturing the United States arsenal located there by armed force. Calling upon the local slave population to arise and seize its freedom, Brown planned to distribute arms from the arsenal to the slaves that he anticipated would rally to his appeal. This plan to arm slaves, arousing long-held fears of slave rebellion, sent a shock throughout the South. Malevolent editorials vied with venomous oratory in Congress and throughout the South to excoriate Brown, the abolitionists, and the North in general. Similarly, Brown's execution by the State of Virginia on December 2 led to an outburst of sympathy among anti-slavery circles for the new martyr to the cause, including a heated meeting at Gerrit Smith's home in Peterboro in January 1860 to protest the execution.[80] Brown's precipitate action widened the North-South divide more than any previous event, elevating the forthcoming national election in 1860 to even greater importance.

With partisans of both North and South in no mood to compromise, the Democrats, the only really major national party, found themselves unable to agree upon a candidate acceptable to enough delegates to gain the nomination. In frustration, with each faction unwilling to trust a candidate from the opposing section of the country, Northern Democrats reconvened in a separate meeting to nominate Stephen A. Douglas from Illinois, while their Southern counterparts put forward John C. Breckinridge of Kentucky. The Republicans met in Chicago where the major contenders for the nomination were unable to claim a majority of the votes, eventually giving the nod to compromise candidate Abraham Lincoln. In an attempt to forestall civil war, moderates, largely from the border states between North and South, formed the Constitutional Union Party to nominate John Bell on a platform that promised to solve the slavery controversy through Constitutional amendment. A fifth faction, the tiny remnant of the Liberty Party, met in Syracuse to nominate Gerrit Smith for the presidency. By now reduced to insignificance as a political party, the die-hard radicals clinging to the Liberty banner remained unwilling to join the ranks of the Republicans, a party they still believed to be insufficiently committed to the anti-slavery crusade.[81] Though he would play no role on the national scene through his candidacy in 1860, Gerrit Smith, his small band of Liberty Party loyalists, and the greater anti-slavery population of Oneida County had already made significant contributions to the development of the crisis about to sunder the Union.

In July, Smith hosted a mass meeting at his home to speak to the faithful.

> Church of Peterboro! Be true to your own God at the approaching Election. He is not your God, who would have men vote for candidates who are in favor of a white man's Party, and of excluding the black man from suffrage and citizenship. For you God "made of one blood all nations," and is impartial and loving toward them all. Is not your God, who would have men vote for candidates in favor of seizing the poor innocents, as they fly from the pit of slavery, and of casting them back into it. For your God would have the ruler do justice to the "poor of the people, save the children of the needy, and break in pieces the oppressor," His rulers, in making report of their administrations, can say as the Buchanans and Pierces have never said, that they "break the jaws of the wicked, and plucked the spoil out of his teeth." He is not your God, who would have men vote for candidates who recognize a law for slavery. For a law for slavery is a greater and crueler absurdity than a law for murder. Every right-minded man would see his children in the grave rather than in the chains of slavery.[82]

The campaign that summer and fall was spirited, the "Wide Awakes" parading noisily through cities and small villages alike in their blue capes and blue hats,

The Mohawk "Wide Awakes" rallied on behalf of Abraham Lincoln during the heated 1860 election campaign. *(National Archives)*

shouting their praise for the Republicans and "Honest Abe," the Illinois "Railsplitter." Not to be outdone, the "Little Giants," decked out in red clothing and headgear, proclaimed near and far the virtues of Democrat Stephen A. Douglas. When the votes were counted, Oneida County went for Lincoln; yet, many people, fearing the possibility of war, voiced little support for the more radical abolitionists whom some labeled "troublemakers."[83] Smith replied to the accusations in November 1860, shortly after the election: "Some of these Abolitionists are blamed for entertaining, as did their sainted brother, James G. Birney, so small a hope that the voters of our country will bring slavery to a peaceful end through the ballot-box. ... Our speeches and writings for a quarter of a century, show that we look for a speedy termination of American Slavery. But our growing fear, in the light of our growing knowledge of American voters, is, that the termination will be violent instead of peaceful. It will come in some way in God's providence, and it will come soon."[84]

From the activist, participatory revivalism of Rev. Charles G. Finney that sparked "The Second Great Awakening," to Gerrit Smith's moral and financial support of John Brown's violent zealotry, Oneida County was deeply involved in the development of abolitionism on the national level, and as such, played a significant role in the impending conflict. In *The Burned-over District: The Social and Intellectual History of Enthusiastic Religion in Western New York, 1800-1850*, Whitney Cross concluded that "No other section of the country would throughout the years before the Civil War prove to be so thoroughly and constantly sensitive to antislavery agitation."[85] Gerald Sorin, in his study *The New York Abolitionists: A Case Study of Political Radicalism* asserted that "The New York abolitionist leaders were radical. They held ideas which were radical in substance—specifically, immediate emancipation and political and economic equality for blacks. They led a social movement and participated in agitation for direct action which would eventuate in freedom for blacks and a society of racial brotherhood; and ultimately they experienced a total commitment to abolitionism."[86] Chief among these leaders were those in Oneida County. "Abolitionism in Utica and its environs was sparked by some of the nation's most important advocates of immediatism," concluded Edward Magdol in his book *The Antislavery Rank and File: A Social Profile of the Abolitionists' Constituency*.[87]

With the election of Abraham Lincoln, secession began. On April 12, 1861, South Carolina artillery opened fire on Fort Sumter, a United States installation in Charleston harbor. In response to the new crisis, Gerrit Smith again hosted an assemblage in Peterboro. "We are assembled, my neighbors, not as Republicans, nor Democrats, nor Abolitionists—but as Americans," he began. "And we are assembled to say that we are all on the side of the Government; and that it must be upheld at whatever expense to friend or foe. ... The end of American Slavery is at hand."[88] The time for peaceful solutions had passed. Soon, "Father Abraham" would call upon Oneida County to send its sons to shed their blood to accomplish what revivalism, rhetoric and politics could not.

---

[1]Edward Magdol, *The Antislavery Rank and File: A Social Profile of the Abolitionists' Constituency* (New York: Greenwood Press, 1986), 22; Emerson Klees, *Underground Railroad Tales With Routes Through the Finger Lakes Region* (Rochester: Friends of the Finger Lakes Publishing, n.d.), 95.

[2]Richard L. Manzelmann, "Revivalism and Reform," in *The History of Oneida County* (Utica: Oneida County, 1977), 54; quote from Helen Wessel, ed., *The Autobiography of Charles G. Finney* (Minneapolis: Bethany House Publishers, 1977), 9, 10; Milton C. Sernett, *Abolition's Axe: Beriah Green, Oneida Institute, and the Black Freedom Struggle* (Syracuse: Syracuse University Press, 1986), 32.

[3]Manzelmann, 54; Sernett, *Abolition's Axe*, 32; Magdol, 24; quote from Gerald Sorin, *Abolitionism: A New Perspective* (New York: Praeger Publishers, 1972), 45.

[4]Sorin, 44-45; Magdol, 25; Manzelmann, 54-55.

[5]Manzelmann, 54; Sernett, *Abolition's Axe*, 32, 80; Magdol, 24; C. S. Griffin, *The Ferment of Reform, 1830-1860* (New York: Thomas Y. Crowell Company, 1967), 24.

[6]Keith J. Hardman, *Charles Grandisson Finney, 1792-1875, Revivalist and Reformer* (Syracuse: Syracuse University Press, 1987), 273.

[7]Rev. Charles B. Austin, *Historical Discourse, Delivered Before the Presbyterian Church, at New York Mills, N.Y., September 10, 1876* (Utica: T.J. Griffiths, Printer, 1877), 22-23; Helen Wessel, ed., *The Autobiography of Charles G. Finney* (Minneapolis: Bethany House Publishers, 1977), 124-25; Rev. Charles G. Finney, *Memoirs of Rev. Charles G. Finney* (New York: A. S. Barnes & Company, 1876), 183-84.

[8]Ernest J. Savoie, "The New York Mills Company 1807-1914, A Study of Managerial Attitudes and Practices in Industrial Relations" (Ithaca, NY: Cornell University, M.S. Thesis, September 1955), 47; Austin, *Historical Discourse*, 23; *Walcott Memorial Presbyterian Church*, 17.

[9]Manzelmann, 54; Magdol, 24.

[10]Manzelmann, 53.

[11]Sernett, *Abolition's Axe*, 33; Manzelmann, 57.

[12]Manzelmann, 57; Sernett, *Abolition's Axe*, 160n; quote from Sorin, 49.

[13]Magdol, 22; Sorin, 67, quote from 70; Sernett, *Abolition's Axe*, 4-12, 83; Leonard L. Richards, *"Gentlemen of Property and Standing": Anti-Abolition Mobs in Jacksonian America* (New York: Oxford University Press, 1970), 85.

[14]Magdol, 22; Richards, 85, quote from 86.

[15]Sorin, 90; Sernett, 36.

[16]Daniel E. Wager, *Our Country and Its People: A Descriptive Work on Oneida County, New York* (Boston: Boston History Company, 1896), 312. See also Peter Jarvis, "Abolitionism in Oneida County," unpublished ms., Oneida County Historical Society (1968), 2.

[17]*Circular of the Executive Committee of the Whitestown and Oneida Institute Anti-Slavery Societies* (Utica: William Williams Press, n.d.), 3; Jarvis, 2.

[18]Richards, 86.

[19]Richards, 87.

[20]"Defensor," *The Enemies of the Constitution Discovered, or, An Inquiry into the Origin and Tendency of Popular Violence* (New York: Leavitt, Lord & Co., 1835), 74; see also Richards, 87.

[21]"Defensor," 62; see also Richards, 87.

[22]Jarvis, 3.

[23]"Defensor," iii.

[24]Everts and Fariss, *History of Oneida County, New York* (Philadelphia: J.B. Lippincott & Company, 1878), 295; "Defensor"; Jarvis, 3.

[25]"Defensor," 60-61.

[26]"Defensor," 66; Richards, 90.

[27]"Defensor," 137-38.

[28]Richards, 69, 140, 143; Magdol, 26.

[29]Richards, 136, 139; Magdol, 22.

[30]*Utica Observer*, October 21, 1835; *Utica Whig*, October 21, 1835; "Defensor," 88; Richards, 91; Magdol, 22; Klees, 95.

[31]Klees, 94-95; Charles A. Hammond, *Gerrit Smith: The Story of a Noble Life* (Geneva, NY: Press of W. F. Humphrey, 1908), 8; Edward J. Renehan, Jr., *The Secret Six: The True Tale of the Men Who Conspired with John Brown* (New York: Crown Publishers, Inc., 1995), 15.

[32]Klees, 95; Hammond, 9, 13.

[33]Sernett, *Abolition's Axe*, 42-43; Hammond, 25.

[34]Sernett, *Abolition's Axe*, 43; Klees, 95.

[35]"Defensor," 157; Klees, 95.

[36]Hammond, 30; Sorin, 51; Klees, 94.

[37]Magdol, 23, 43; Alice Hatcher Henderson, "The History of the New York Anti-Slavery Society" (Ann Arbor: University of Michigan, Ph.D. dissertation, 1965), 25, 109, 111, 401.

[38]Magdol, 44; Sernett, *Abolition's Axe*, 44, 165n49; Milton C. Sernett, *North Star Country: Upstate New York and the Crusade for African American Freedom* (Syracuse: Syracuse University Press, 2002), 32, 40-41.

[39]Magdol, 44; Jarvis, 4.

[40]Magdol, 23.

[41]Magdol, 23, 43, 55, 113n2; Henderson, 25, 401; Sorin, 49; Eric Foner, *Free Soil, Free Labor, Free Men: The Ideology of the Republican Party Before the Civil War* (New York: Oxford University Press, 1978), 74; *The Friend of Man*, August 4, 1836; National Archives, Record Group 233, HR 25A-H1.8, petition from New York Mills regarding slavery in the territories.

[42]Sernett, *Abolition's Axe*, 40, 160n; Sorin, 49.

[43]Sernett, *Abolition's Axe*, 160n; Foner, 109; Sorin, 49-50.

[44]Sernett, *Abolition's Axe*, 52, 58

[45]Sernett, *Abolition's Axe*, 49, 52, 54-55.

[46]Sernett, *Abolition's Axe*, 59; quote from Sorin, 114.

[47]Sorin, 104, 116; Sernett, *Abolition's Axe*, 55.

[48]Sorin, 104; Sernett, *Abolition's Axe*, 55.

[49]Klees, 96; Renehan, 17; Hammond, 38-39.

[50]Lawrence J. Friedman, "The Gerrit Smith Circle: Abolitionism in the Burned-Over District," *Civil War History*, Vol. 26, No. 1 (March 1980), 18.

[51]Friedman, 25.

[52]Friedman, 29.

[53]Friedman, 23, 27, 30; Manzelmann, 56; Sernett, *Abolition's Axe*, 136; Goodell quote from Sernett, *North Star Country*, 120-21; Smith quote from Sorin, 78.

[54]Sernett, *Abolition's Axe*, 112; Hammond, 36; Foner, 302; *National Party Conventions 1831-1972* (Washington, DC: Congressional Quarterly, 1976), 25.

[55]George W. Clark, *The Liberty Minstrel* (New York, 1846); Milledge L. Bonham, Jr., "A Rare Abolitionists Document," *The Mississippi Valley Historical Review*, Vol. 8, No. 3 (December 1921), 267, 269-271.

[56]Sernett, *Abolition's Axe*, 114.

[57]Foner, 81; Sernett, *Abolition's Axe*, 109, 117; Stewart Mitchell, *Horatio Seymour of New York* (Cambridge, MA: Harvard University Press, 1938), 68; letter, Smith to Salmon P. Chase, May 31, 1842, Gerrit Smith Papers, Syracuse University.

[58]Sorin, 113; Sernett, *Abolition's Axe*, 55.

[59]*National Party Conventions*, 25; Sernett, *Abolition's Axe*, 117; Sernett, *North Star Country*, 118.

[60]Sorin, 75.

[61]Friedman, 28; Sorin, 88. First quote from Sorin, second from Friedman.

[62]Sernett, *Abolition's Axe*, 124; Sorin, 50; *National Party Conventions*, 27-28; Rush Welter, *The Mind of America 1820-1860* (New York: Columbia University Press, 1975).

[63]Magdol, 107, 123; unidentified newspaper clipping, September 1909, Oneida Historical Society.

[64]Alfred R. Conkling, *The Life and Letters of Roscoe Conkling, Orator, Statesman, Advocate* (New York: Charles L. Webster & Company, 1889), 30.

[65]*National Party Conventions*, 29, 31; Renehan, 17, 61; Hammond, 56-57, Greeley quote from 54.

[66]Jarvis, 5.

[67]*Utica Morning Herald*, June 15, 1854.

[68]*Utica Morning Herald*, June 16, 1854.

[69]Magdol, 107, 123; Klees, 97; Richard L. Manzelmann, *The History of Oneida County* (Utica: Oneida County, 1977), 55.

[70]Jarvis, 7; *Utica Herald*, May 24, 1856.

[71]Chester G. Hearn, *Companions in Conspiracy: John Brown & Gerrit Smith* (Gettysburg, PA: Thomas Publications, 1996), 41, 49; Friedman, 36.

[72]Hearn, 41.

[73]Foner, 302-303; Sorin, 115.

[74]*Utica Herald*, editorial March 10, 1857, 2. See also Jarvis, 9.

[75]Quote from Hearn, 53.

[76]Hearn, 54.

[77]John Brown to Thomas Sanborn, February 20, 1858, quoted in Hearn, 53.

[78]Quoted in Hearn, 55.

[79]Hearn, 41, 49; Friedman, 36.

[80]Foner, 138.

[81]Hammond, 27; Foner, 303; Renehan, 11.

[82]Quoted in Hammond, 102.

[83]Hammond, 65.

[84]Hammond, 111.

[85]Whitney Cross, *The Burned-over District: The Social and Intellectual History of Enthusiastic Religion in Western New York, 1800-1850* (Ithaca: Cornell University Press, 1950), 226.

[86]Gerald Sorin, *The New York Abolitionists: A Case Study of Political Radicalism* (Westport, CT: Greenwood Publishing Corporation, 1971), 3.

[87]Magdol, 43.

[88]Hammond, 183.

CHAPTER 3

"A TIME TO TRY MEN'S SOULS"
THE 14TH NEW YORK VOLUNTEERS ON THE PENINSULA

by

Cheryl A. Pula

As the first infantry regiment organized in the county, the 14th New York State Volunteers came into existence as the First Oneida County Regiment. It originated on April 15, 1861, when just three days after the Civil War began with the shelling of Fort Sumter in Charleston, South Carolina, and just one day after the fort fell to the Confederates, President Abraham Lincoln called for 75,000 volunteers to put down the rebellion. That same night, a meeting of prominent citizens and officers of the Utica Citizens Corps, a volunteer militia unit first organized in 1808, approved a motion offered by M. Henry Barnard which offered to formalize Utica's support for the national government.

> Whereas, It is the duty of every citizen to respond promptly to the call of his country for aid, therefore;
> Resolved, That the Utica Citizen Corps hereby tender their services to the Governor of this State as volunteers to join any force that may be raised to meet the demand of the General Government for forces against the traitors in the South.
> Resolved, That the Corps will be ready to march at 48 hours notice, fully armed and equipped.[1]

Recruitment and fund raising for what was billed as the "Volunteer Battalion of Central New York" began immediately, and five days later some $8,000 had already been subscribed for the regiment.[2] Men from the Utica Citizens Corps and other nearby militia units were soon joined by volunteers from other parts of the county. Eventually, five of the regiment's ten companies would be recruited mostly in Utica: Company A composed of men from the Utica Citizens Corps under Colonel James McQuade; Company B, known as The Continentals, under the command of Capt. William Brazie; Company C, the German Lafayette Rifles, under Capt. Frederick "Fritz" Harrer was the German Lafayette Rifles; Company D commanded by Capt. Michael McQuade; and Company E, the Seymour Light

Artillery, commanded by Capt. Lewis Michaels. The remaining five companies were raised mostly outside of Utica, or even outside the county. Company F commanded by Capt. Charles Muller, a store clerk, hailed from Boonville; Company G under Capt. Charles Skillen, was from Rome and nicknamed the Gansvoort Guards; Company H with Capt. Samuel Thompson was from Syracuse; Company I commanded by Capt. Horace Lahe, a newspaper foreman for the Lowville *Journal and Republican*, was from the Lowville area; and Company K under Capt. William Seymour was from Hudson.[3]

Though excitement ran high and most residents of the county supported the president's call for troops, some were not so supportive as reflected in the following article written by E. Prentiss Bailey, editor of the *Utica Observer*:

Col. James McQuade of Utica
(Donald Wisnoski)

Of all the wars which have disgraced the human race, its has been reserved for our own enlightened nation to be involved in the most useless and foolish one. What advantage can possibly accrue to any one from this war...? Does any suppose that the millions of free white Americans in the Southern States ... can be conquered by any efforts which can be brought against them? Brave men, fighting on their own soil...for their freedom and dearest rights, can never be subjugated. The war may be prolonged until we are ourselves exhausted, and become an easy prey to military despotism or equally fatal anarchy; but we can never conquer the South. Admit...that they are rebels and traitors; they are beyond our reach. Why should we destroy ourselves in injuring them?[4]

The editor's misgivings notwithstanding, recruiting continued at a fever pitch with the ranks swiftly filling. Company commanders met and elected James McQuade their colonel. The eldest of nine children, he had been born on April 27, 1829. He attended school at a Catholic college in Montréal, Québec, Canada, were he became a scholar of Latin and French. He then returned to Utica to study

Capt. Lewis Michaels
(Donald Wisnoski)

law at the firm of Spencer and Kernan, but gave up the pursuit of law to enter the banking business. This led him into politics with election as Assistant Clerk of the Assembly, a position he held from 1852 to 1854. Returning to Utica from Albany, he went into business with his brother selling spices and coffee, but several years later sold out his part of the business. In 1859, he was elected to the New York State Assembly on the Republican ticket, but served only one year before being defeated for re-election by Francis Kernan. When the Civil War began, he was head of the Utica Citizens Corps.[5] The lieutenant colonelcy went to Charles H. Skillen from Rome, a crockery merchant originally from Amsterdam, who was promoted from captain of Company G.

Preparations moved forward quickly. Men arrived from all over the county, donations provided comforts and necessities for those who enlisted, and families began to face the reality of separation. On April 23 the new soldiers marched through the streets of Utica to the New York Central Freight Station where, "amid scenes of wild enthusiasm of tears and cheers," they left for Albany shortly after midnight. On April 24, the *Utica Observer* raved "Such a day as this our city had never before seen."[6]

Upon reaching the capital, the Oneida County men were formally accepted into Federal service for two years as the 14th New York State Volunteer Infantry with the nickname of "The Corps Regiment," after the Utica Citizens Corps which formed its Company A. The old Citizens Corps was composed mostly of men of Irish ancestry, while other companies included men of other groups such as the Germans who predominated in Company C, and thirty-three Welsh recruits who came from the village of Remsen. The 14th New York officially mustered in on May 17, 1861. On the 21st and 23rd uniforms were issued to the men and on the 24th "a delegation of ladies from Utica presented the regiment with silk national colors."[7]

Billeted in a large building at 797 Broadway, it soon became evident that the food in the army was not what they were used to at home. Said David Ritchie,

> Supper was not so good as it should have been. We had nothing but bread and cold scraps of beef, tough as leather; the former without butter. Inasmuch as Mr. Roeselle ... gets fifty cents a day for our board, we feel that he is making too much money out of the volunteers, who claim that they should have plenty of good, plain food, at least. Several complained today that the meat at dinner was tainted and that it made them sick.[8]

Charles Muller of Boonville
(Donald Wisnoski)

Not everyone in the regiment had the same problem. The Germans of Company C took their meals not in a field kitchen, but a local German restaurant.[9] Life for the rest improved when the regiment moved to quarters outside of the city at what was formerly the Albany Industrial School.[10] There the food took a decided turn for the better according to John Trolan of Company E:

> We have met the enemy and they are ours! ... Instead of being fed like swine, we are once more used as men. Instead of being obligated to eat cat food that would be nauseating to the veriest pauper in existence, we are provided with that which is wholesome, and entirely satisfactory to the brave defenders of their country's flag.[11]

If some had problems with the food, the men quickly found that being issued a uniform was not an exact science, but rather a matter of take what you could get. Drummer William "Billy" Harrer described the process:

> The way clothing was given out was great. The commissary Sergeant got up on a box and threw out the clothes, fit or no fit...The boys would exchange with each other, and thus secure what would fit...such pantaloons never before were made by any tailor, either in New York or in Paris. They were big enough for Jumbo.... None of the boys would exchange with me, so I took out my knife, and cut off about 10 inches on the legs.... They were a sight; or rather, I was when in them.[12]

C. B. Merbine.
(Donald Wisnoski)

The daily routine consisted of drilling and guard duty until the regiment was moved to Camp Morgan outside of the city. While there, the men found camp life quite boring and many wanted to return home to Utica. Some even deserted, but were returned to the regiment where their fellow comrades in arms quickly learned the punishment meted out to deserters. The men in question were literally tarred and feathered and drummed out of the camp.[13]

One of the duties the men performed while in Albany was to escort the mortal remains of Colonel Elmer E. Ellsworth to their final resting place. Ellsworth had been a member of the famed 11th New York Infantry, known as the Fire Zouaves because most of the regiment had been New York City firemen. On May 24th, Ellsworth and some of his troops crossed the Potomac River from Washington, D.C., to Alexandria, Virginia, where a local hotel, the Marshall House, had been flying a Confederate flag that was visible from the White House. Ellsworth and his men marched to the hotel where the colonel rushed up the stairs to haul the offensive flag down. Ellsworth succeeded in doing so, but while leaving the hotel with the rebel banner in his hands he was shot and killed by the hotel's proprietor, James Jackson, who was himself then shot by Corporal Francis Brownell of Troy, New York. Ellsworth, who had been a personal friend of President Lincoln, was sent back to Albany for burial, and the Oneida County unit was given the honor of escorting his body from the capitol building in Albany to a boat which would take it home for burial in Mechanicville.[14]

On June 14 orders arrived for the 14th New York to leave at 3:00 PM on June 17 for the seat of war. The following day the men were issued 1845 model rifles, and on the appointed date, 740 strong, they marched down State Street, then across to Broadway to the steamboat landing on the Hudson River where they were reviewed and addressed by Gov. Edwin D. Morgan who promised the married men in the regiment that if they did not return from the war their families would be not be forgotten and would receive financial aid.[15]

Loaded aboard the steamer *Henry Andrews*, the troops embarked for New York City, sailing down the Hudson to the accompaniment of fireworks and cannon salutes from every town and hamlet along the way.[16] Upon its arrival in New York, the regiment was greeted by the Sons of Oneida, a group of ex-Oneida

County natives living in Brooklyn and New York. The *New York Times* of June 17, 1861, described the welcoming committee:

> The Fourteenth Regiment will reach the city by Tuesday's morning boat from Albany. At the landing it will be received by some three hundred natives of Oneida County, new residents in New York ... it may be remarked that such an astonishing number of Oneida-born folk has been discovered in our midst, as to warrant the belief that more residents of this metropolis date from that county then from any other in the United States. Measures have already been taken to form a permanent association of the New-York Sons of Oneida.[17]

Drummer William Harrer
(With Drum and Gun in '61)

In New York the men marched to the Washington Parade Grounds where they received half a day of rest and forty rounds of ammunition. On June 19 the Society of the Sons of Oneida presented the regiment with an elegant state color made by Tiffany and Company to match the national flag they received in Albany.[18] The *New York Times* described the new regimental colors:

> A very beautiful regimental standard for this regiment was furnished by Tiffany & Co., on Saturday, to the order of gentlemen of our City. It is of the dimensions prescribed by State military regulations—-six feet by six and a half, and its material a rich, dark blue silk, heavily tinged in yellow. The staff is of lancewood, mounted in fire-gilt, tipped with a silver spear-head, and so constructed as to fold together when not in use. The device of the flag, elegantly embroidered, represents the military arms borne by our New-York contingent, the shield containing in one half the State arms, and in the other the bars of the Federal coat. Over the shield is the State crest, the eagle perched upon the globe, and beneath it a graceful garter inscribed *Excelsior.* Under this motto is the Regimental designation, Fourteenth Regiment, New-York Volunteers.[19]

The *Times* went on to describe the regiment,

> The Fourteenth Regiment ... is mainly composed of Oneida county men, Utica, Rome, and other towns of the neighborhood, contributing companies. One company, and one that is sure to be efficient, however, is made up entirely of stalwart Welshmen, whom the storm of war had seduced from their farms on the hill-sides of Steuben.... The Colonel commanding is James McQuade, of Utica, till now Captain of the well known "Citizen's Corps," of that city.... The

Col. Edward F. Jones, a native of Utica, led the 6th Massachusetts when it was attacked by a mob in Baltimore.
(Donald Wisnoski)

above named company, which was organized in 1836 ... has long held a most honorable position among the independent military organizations of the State, and now, volunteering for the war, worthily flanks a regiment, of which it has been in some manner the nucleus.... The Fourteenth is made up of serviceable material, its members generally being well-to-do specimens of the farming population of Oneida ... it is perhaps in better marching order than any corps as yet numbered in the Empire State quota.[20]

On the following day the regiment boarded cattle cars at the New Jersey Railroad Station for the trip to Washington, D.C. En route they had to pass through Baltimore, Maryland, where on April 19, the 6th Massachusetts Infantry had been attacked by a mob of Confederate sympathizers. As a border state, Maryland had citizens that backed both the North and the South, but the largest city, Baltimore, was a hotbed of pro-Confederate feelings. When the Massachusetts regiment arrived in the city, its commander, Colonel Edward F. Jones, a former Utican, was warned by railroad officials that there could be trouble. Rumors had been circulating that the residents would try to obstruct the movement of Union troops through the city. Jones ordered his men to load their weapons, but they were under orders not to fire unless they received specific instructions to do so. Meanwhile, citizens of the city, after learning that the troops had been warned, set up blockades along the local rail lines the regiment would have to use to transfer from one railroad station to the other. This forced the Bay Staters to march to the Camden Street rail station. While doing so, they were attacked by a mob throwing bricks and rocks. Four soldiers were killed, and the troops were ordered to fire on the attackers, killing a dozen. The incident quickly became known as the Pratt Street Riot.[21]

When the New Yorkers arrived in Baltimore, the same tense feeling still prevailed. Having to follow the same route to the Camden Street station as the Massachusetts regiment, the Oneida County men were forced to proceed through the city with fixed bayonets which proved enough to discourage any incidents and the regiment was unmolested as it made the move through Baltimore.

The regiment made the remainder of the trip to Washington, D.C., uneventfully by rail, arriving in the nation's capital on June 20, 1861.[22] There, it was invited to the White House by none other than President Abraham Lincoln. The invitation was accepted, and the president had coffee and ham sandwiches sent to them. While they were enjoying the repast, the president settled himself on the White House veranda and read a newspaper.[23] The food consumed, the regiment then proceeded to their quarters on, ironically, 14th Street. The men did not fully appreciate the nation's capital. In fact, other than the public buildings and its name, they did not like it at all. David Ritchie observed:

Gaius Jones
(Oneida County Historical Society)

> The best thing about this city is its name, next its memories, and finally its public buildings. Aside from these three points, the town is contemptible. It is lousy with Secessionists and is the den, the very lair of swindlers. Soldiers are cheated here most unmercifully. They are charged exorbitant prices for everything, especially in the line of hotels.... No one can pass through the meshes of the town and come out with a particle of filthy lucre clinging about his person.[24]

Most of the men believed the general consensus in the North as a whole, that the war would not last long and they would soon be free to go home. David Ritchie wrote home that it was difficult to realize there was even a war on, as they were camped literally within sight of the enemy but felt they were not in any more danger than they had been back home in Oneida County. They were very optimistic that the conflict would be of short duration. Said Ritchie,

> How the enemy can hold out much longer with such a force pouring in as there is now I cannot see. There are over 50,000 men in and around Washington—a force twice as large as the Secessionists have within 100 miles. In addition to this force another almost as large is gradually approaching in the west, thus hemming in the enemy by slow but sure degrees.[25]

The regiment caught the eye of General Winfield Scott on July 4 when a large parade took place along with an inspection of New York State troops. As the Fourteenth passed by the reviewing stand under the eyes of Scott and no less a personage than President Lincoln, Scott told the president that the Oneida County boys were a "fine marching regiment."[26] The same day, the regiment visited the U. S. Capitol, which was still under construction, but was impressive nonetheless. In the evening, they were treated to a Capitol tradition, a huge fireworks display.

The "First Oneida" encamped at Camp Douglas at Meridian Hill, Virginia, in July, until the 22nd of that month when it was assigned to the 1st Brigade, 2nd Division, Army of Northeastern Virginia, under the command of General William Tecumseh Sherman. With the new assignment it moved to Fort Corcoran near Arlington Heights, only a few hundred yards from the former home of Robert E. Lee overlooking the Potomac River across from the city of Washington. Sherman must have been impressed by the Oneida County regiment because in August he chose it from among all the regiments under his command to be reviewed by Prince Louis Napoleon of France. The prince voiced the opinion that the troops were an "intelligent and fine looking body of men."[27]

Shortly thereafter, Sherman's confidence in the regiment was nearly destroyed when many members stated they had enlisted for only three months service, not two years. They nearly revolted over the issue, asserting that the government could not make them serve past August 17. Officers sent to Washington to investigate ascertained that all members of the regiment had indeed enlisted for two years and were legally bound to serve until May 1863. Even so, it took a great deal of persuasion to make the discontented companies finally realize they were in for two years. The Oneida County regiment was not the only group that disputed its term of enlistment. Several other New York regiments also believed they had enlisted for only a few months instead of years. It was later found that much of the confusion had arisen because newspapers "back home" had been trying to dissuade more men from joining the Federal cause. A major factor had been William Cunningham,[28] a reporter for one of the Utica newspapers, who stated publicly that he believed the war had gone far enough, that there was need for compromise between North and South, as well as a dividing line between the two sections of the country. He went on to say that he would do everything in his power to get all of the Oneida County regiments back home. He was arrested.[29]

During its service outside Washington, the First Oneida observed the retreat of the Federal army after the Battle of First Bull Run in late July, had a brief skirmish at Balls Cross Roads, Virginia, on September 14, and another brief encounter with rebels at Widow Childs' House, Virginia, on October 14. The regiment spent the remainder of the year near Fort Corcoran. In March 1862 it was transferred to the 2nd Brigade, 1st Division, Third Corps, Army of the Potomac, after a general reorganization of the Federal army. Commanded by Brigadier General George W. Morell, the brigade also included the 4th Michigan, 9th

The 14th New York formed at Miner's Hill, Virginia
(Oneida County Historical Society)

Massachusetts, and 62nd Pennsylvania.[30]

Some men had no difficulty adapting to military life, while others experienced problems being away from home. Most, if not all, of the men had never been away from home before, or at least not more than a few miles from home. While some compensated by playing cards, making friends and other activities, there were those who could not adjust. One such individual was a North woodsman named Henry Lee. Billy Harrer, a drummer in the regiment, explained:

> We had in our company the biggest man in the regiment. His name was Lee; born and bred in the North Woods, in the Adirondack mountains, a hunter and a trapper—a genuine woodsman. He must have been six feet six in height, broad shouldered, muscular, heart as big as his great frame, gentle, kind, a true child of nature. He enlisted in Utica.... He was every inch a man. The whole regiment looked up to him in more senses than one. And this remarkably great man got homesick! He was reported sick. The doctor could not see nothing wrong in his physical condition. He moped ... would talk to no one. Every day found him weaker. He fell away in flesh ... wasted to a mere skeleton ... finally his gentle spirit took flight ... and we reverently laid him away ... with the church at Falls Church ... in Virginia .... Reared in the majestic forest ... used to communion only with kindly nature, the noise, the sin, the cruelty, the unnaturalness of everything about him—these were too much for him. Homesickness killed him.[31]

That same month, March 1862, marked the beginning of what would be Major General George Brinton McClellan's first campaign as the commander of the Army of the Potomac. "Little Mac," as he was called, fancied himself another Napoleon. The general was known as a superlative organizer and had managed to raise the morale of the Federal army by making sure they were paid regularly, received adequate food and clothing, and through constant drilling, reviews and other events designed to give them pride in themselves. His men adored him.

McClellan proposed a campaign which he visualized as an amphibious operation, sailing his troops aboard ship from Alexandria down to Fortress Monroe, Virginia, to bypass the main Confederate army around Manassas Junction, then proceeding up the York Peninsula to capture Richmond. The Army of the Potomac numbered approximately 121,500 infantry, 44 batteries of artillery, 1,150 wagons and over 15,000 horses, plus tons of other supplies.[32] On St. Patrick's Day, March 17, the 14th New York moved in "good spirits," the men singing as they marched, to Alexandria, Virginia. There the men boarded the transport *Nellie Baker* for the trip down the Potomac to Fortress Monroe. The Oneida County regiment was part of four corps that McClellan planned to use in his grand campaign. After disembarkation on March 24, it marched several miles to Hampton Village, which it found in flames. According to William Harrer, "we landed at Fortress Monroe, and marched some three miles out, going through a town called Hampton, which was all in flames…. The negroes along the way told us the Hamptonians were all rich slave holders … and … rather than let the town fall into our possession, each man had fired their own house with his own hand, and then made off to Yorktown to join the Confederate army."[33]

Ten days later, on March 27, the First Oneida moved out as part of the advanced guard of McClellan's whole army as he began his movement toward Richmond. For the next few days the men skirmished with rebels as the Southerners withdrew slowly before the Union army until the Confederates reached some protective breastworks at Howard's Bridge. Ordered to charge the position, the 14th New York drove the Confederates from cover, capturing two with only "slight loss." The prisoners were Germans from a Mississippi regiment, but they proved unhelpful and would not tell the Yankees anything.[34]

On April 5 the regiment encountered another small Confederate force dug in at the intersection of the Warwick and Yorktown Roads, but another charge again sent the rebels into retreat. The Army itself continued on to Yorktown in a driving rain. The Oneida County men skirmished daily until April 8 when they pitched their tents in a peach orchard near Yorktown. Despite these early successes, the advance ground quickly to a halt when McClellan's army ran into a well-prepared Confederate defensive line manned by 13,000 troops under Brigadier General John B. Magruder. The Union general ordered his men to prepare for a siege of historic Yorktown.[35] William Harrer described work on the siege lines:

> The regiments from Maine and others who knew how to handle the axe were ordered to the woods. They cut down saplings … and wove them into baskets about four feet high, having neither bottoms nor covers. These baskets were carried by other regiments to the front. Other regiments, with shovels, were at hand, ready to set them in line and fill them with earth. One night's labor set up the first line of … breastworks…. How many such baskets do you think it would take to make a protection six feet high and four feet wide? Our line was 13 miles in length.[36]

Every twenty or so feet an opening was left for mounting siege guns. While the breastworks were being constructed, the Federals were in danger from rebel sharpshooters, who took delight in shooting Union officers. To keep from being a target, McClellan would tour the front wearing a private's uniform. Those building the works were also harassed, noted Harrer:

> During the day by the smoke, and at night, by the fire, he could tell the instant ... the enemy's gun was fired. When he saw it he would shout, "Down!"... and every man would fall flat on the earth with his nose in the dirt. The shell would burst, kill or wound one or two, and the work would go on again until the next "down" was called ... it kept on day and night for 10 days in succession. That was a time to try men's souls.[37]

The 14th New York was stationed between Batteries 3 and 7 of the Union line, with the front line being commanded by Colonel McQuade, who had moved up to brigade command when Gen. Morell moved up to division command. With McQuade's elevation, command of the 14th New York devolved onto Lt. Col. Charles H. Skillen. On May 4, during a dress parade, the rebels began shelling the Federals. By 2:00 P.M. the firing from both sides was horrendous. Joining in the fray were several Federal gunboats from the nearby river. After three hours of intense fire, at approximately 5:00 P.M. the rebels sent out three soldiers bearing a white flag of surrender. Yorktown was given over to Union forces. The surrender was greeted with shouts and cheering from the 14th New York.[38] Drummer Harrer commented on the fall of the city, including a visit from President Lincoln and an entourage of onlookers:

> Up to May 4, no drum had been heard for many days; but now the bands were playing, and great was the joy over the fall of Yorktown. Here we again saw President Lincoln. He came sauntering along on an old black nag, in that same old stove-pipe hat, and with a lot of Washington ... accompanying him. It seemed to us that these Washington patriots were always to the front when the enemy was fleeing. They fought with their chins.[39]

Before the Federal siege lines were completed, the Confederate army began a withdrawal back toward Richmond. The two armies engaged briefly outside another historic Virginia town, Williamsburg, with the Federals emerging with a tactical victory, but the rebels escaped to continue their withdrawal. To stop the enemy's retreat, McClellan ordered an amphibious flanking movement at Eltham's Landing, but this proved ineffective. The Federal navy then attempted to reach Richmond by sailing up the James River, but nothing came of this effort either. With the lull in action, the 14th New York enjoyed a brief respite of camp life, but did not find it conducive to good health. The beef ration they received was so tough that it could not be softened even when boiled in water. Camp guards had to be constantly on the watch for rebel sharpshooters, several of whom were able to target members of the regiment with fatal consequences. After several men on each side had been hit, both Federals and Confederates could see little purpose to the occasional deaths and agreed to a temporary local truce. The pickets took advantage of the uneasy calm to trade with one another, the Federals meeting their rebel counterparts in the "no man's land" between the lines to procure a plug of good Southern tobacco in exchange for coffee. One enterprising member of the Oneida County regiment named Reinhardt traded for some leaf tobacco which he took back to camp and fashioned into cigars that he sold to his fellow comrades in arms for a tidy profit.[40] But tobacco and coffee were not the only things that passed through the lines in the lull between battles. Runaway slaves came through, usually under the cover of darkness, to seek freedom. The Federals put them to work as laundrymen and cooks. William Harrer was impressed by the fact that the escaped slaves seemed very religious, praying every day for the souls of the masters they left behind.[41]

HANOVER COURT HOUSE

The respite in camp ended as quickly as it began when Gen. Fitz John Porter ordered a reconnaissance in force to uncover the Confederate positions in the vicinity of Hanover Court House. The brigade fell in at 7:00 AM on May 27 in a pouring rain and took to the roads. The rain lasted until about noon, when it was replaced by oppressive heat and humidity. Col. McQuade reported the marching difficult because of the condition of the roads and the brigade's position at the end of the column behind the supply trains. When firing erupted ahead, McQuade pushed the brigade forward "as expeditiously as possible," but arrived at the front after the rebels had retired. Soon, however, a messenger arrived from the corps commander, Gen. Porter, reporting that Gen. John H. Martindale's command was in danger of being attacked from the rear. Although the men were greatly fatigued by the strenuous ten hours of marching they had already done, McQuade "appealed to them to hurry to the support of their comrades, and they obeyed with the utmost alacrity."[42] "Think of it," one participant wrote, "each man loaded with eighty or one hundred pounds, marching sixteen or eighteen miles in the mud, slipping every step, clothes soaked with rain, [and] fighting a battle after such a march."[43]

In the van of the movement, Lt. Col. Skillen met Gen. Morell near the Kinney Farm some two miles from Hanover Court House. The general immediately ordered him to rush the 14th New York forward across a wheat field about 600 to 800 yards wide to relieve the 2nd Maine and 44th New York which had nearly exhausted their ammunition and were under immediate threat of being overrun by Gen. Lawrence O'B. Branch's Confederate brigade comprised of the 7th, 18th, 28th, and 37th North Carolina regiments. Skillen ordered his command into column by companies, then rushed the laboring men across the muddy field and into the woods on the other side just as the rebels launched an assault aimed

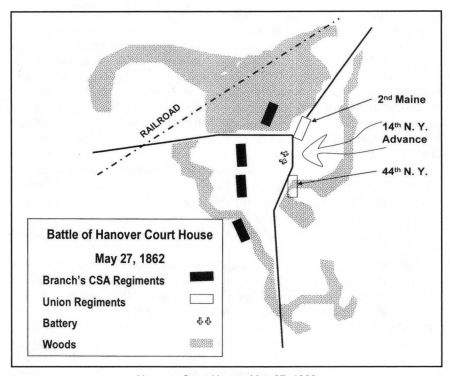

Hanover Court House, May 27, 1862

at capturing Martin's Battery (Battery C, Massachusetts Light Artillery). The men went quickly into line of battle under what Col. Samuel W. Black of the 62nd Pennsylvania, following the New Yorkers, described as "a very fierce fire." Arriving just in time to support the battery and the threatened regiments, Skillen ordered a destructive fire by battalion, followed by "brisk and well-sustained file firing" that forced the rebels to abandon the field. Skillen then received orders to cease fire and rush to the support of Griffin's Battery (Battery K, 1st U.S. Light Artillery), which the 14th New York did without further engagement.[44]

The Battle of Hanover cost the regiment four men seriously wounded and three lightly wounded. "I take pride and pleasure in stating that both officers and men under my command behaved with admirable courage and coolness during the entire battle," wrote Skillen in his official report following the fight.[45] In a letter to a friend, however, he betrayed other feelings:

> Don't wish to be in a battle … it is horrible: the booming of the cannon and the rattle of small arms are loud enough, but the yells of the combatants, the groans and shrieks of the wounded, the terrible mutilations of those who are

killed ... are some of the scenes of a battle; and then to have the care of a regiment on one's hands, not knowing whether they will stand fire or run away, adds
to the other horrors. I look and feel ten years older than I did one year ago. But
if God spares my life to reach home, I shall feel very thankful.[46]

In its first major combat action, the 14th New York acquitted itself well. In
his report of the action, Gen. Morell wrote that the 14th New York was ordered
into the woods where a "severe battle was evidently raging" to a position

> where the firing was heaviest, and there found General Martindale with the
> Second Maine resisting the principal attack of the rebels. The men were almost
> exhausted, their ammunition was nearly expended, yet they were manfully hold-
> ing their ground against superior numbers, when the Fourteenth New York
> Volunteers came to their relief and took the fight off their hands. And it was time,
> for the gunners had been driven from their pieces, the remnant of the Twenty-
> fifth New York had broken and been reformed at a distance to the rear, and the
> right wing of the Forty-fourth New York had given way. It was the turning point
> of the fight. The Second Maine with drew, the Fourteenth New York Volunteers
> opened fire, and the enemy began to give way.[47]

Gen. Martindale, in his own report of the action, commented both on the desperate situation his troops faced and the arrival of the 14th New York:

> The battle had now lasted quite an hour, and although the center of my line
> was broken under a cross-fire which was entirely destructive and insupportable,
> still the Second Maine on the right, I believe every man, and the largest body of
> the Forty-fourth New York, with the lieutenant-colonel and major, on the left,
> maintained their ground without flinching. It is now disclosed that they were
> assailed by four times their number. The ammunition was nearly exhausted, as
> was reported to me by Major Chaplin of the Second Maine, but the two pieces
> of artillery, which rested in battery without a gunner and within less than 200
> yards of the enemy on the right, did not induce a man of them to come from the
> shelter of the woods in which he was covered.
> Re-enforcements at length arrived under the command of the commanding
> general of the division and the corps. The Fourteenth New York, of Morell's
> brigade, commanded by Colonel McQuade, was in advance, and approached the
> position of the Second Maine. By orders of the commanding general of division,
> Lieutenant-Colonel Skillen, commanding the Fourteenth, formed his regiment
> with great promptitude agreeably to my directions, and moved to the relief of the
> Second Maine.[48]

Col. Charles Roberts, commanding the 2nd Maine, was equally lavish in his
praise.

> My ammunition being nearly exhausted, many of my men having fired
> away their 60 rounds, I anxiously looked for re-enforcements, when finally I
> espied a regiment, the New York Fourteenth, under Lieutenant-Colonel Skillen,
> coming to our relief. Then such a shout arose from my command that the enemy,

wavering, gradually commenced to fall back, the Fourteenth getting upon the ground and opening, and a shell or two from one of Captain Griffin's guns stationed in the rear dropping among them, and a force on their left advancing, they finally retired and the rout was perfect.[49]

With the rebels defeated, McClellan continued his advance on Richmond. After moving his supply base from White House Landing to Harrison's Landing on the James River, on June 25 he began a general advance on the Confederate capital. By this time, the main Confederate army under Gen. Joseph E. Johnston had marched from its positions around Manassas Junction to the battlefields east of Richmond, where it joined Magruder's force from the Peninsula, along with other arriving reinforcements, in defense of the city. As McClellan advanced, by the end of May his army reached the Chickahominy River. Gen. Erasmus Keyes' Fourth Corps crossed first, providing Johnston with an opportunity to strike his isolated corps at Fair Oaks before the balance could come to its aid. At the opposite end of the Union line, Porter's Fifth Corps played no direct role in the fighting during which Johnston was seriously wounded. In his place, Pres. Jefferson Davis appointed his military advisor, Gen. Robert E. Lee.

THE SEVEN DAYS BATTLES

While Lee settled in as the new commander of the rebel forces defending Richmond, both he and McClellan received reinforcements. McClellan also adjusted his forces by moving all of the troops south of the Chickahominy except for Porter's Corps which was left north of the river to link up with forces under Gen. Irwin McDowell that had been ordered to move from the Shenandoah Valley to report to McClellan. On June 25, McClellan struck Lee's lines at Oak Grove, drove in the rebel pickets and occupied their positions, but darkness soon called a halt to the assault. Meanwhile, Porter's Corps on the Union right flank remained isolated north of the Chickahominy with only some cavalry to support it. Lee planned to take advantage of this by striking the exposed flank with a force more than twice its size including some 47,000 troops under Gens. James Longstreet, A. P. Hill, and Daniel Harvey Hill, along with an additional 18,500 under Gen. Thomas Jonathan "Stonewall" Jackson.

Lee's careful planning for the attack went swiftly awry as Jackson's flanking force fell hours behind time and the individual unit attacks were badly managed. Nevertheless, Confederate pressure forced Gen. John Reynolds's Union division to fall back from its positions along Beaver Dam Creek, endangering the Union right flank. Brig. Gen. Charles Griffin assumed command of what had been Morell's Brigade at about 2:00 PM on June 26, and within an hour was ordered forward with his men, including the 14th New York, to support Reynolds on the right flank. They arrived about 5:30 PM, went into position, and four companies became involved in skirmishing, losing one man killed and three wounded.

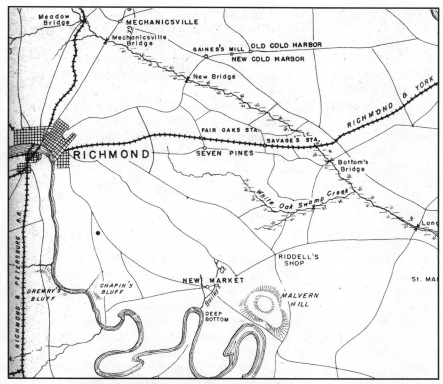

Seven Days Battles *(West Point Atlas of American Wars)*

Darkness, however, soon halted the action. That night, McClellan ordered Porter's Corps to retire to the vicinity of Gaines's Mill and establish a new defensive line. Lee followed, determined to make another attempt to crush Porter's exposed Corps while the Confederates still held a numerical advantage.[50]

Porter located his new line skillfully along a large plateau some forty to eighty feet in height that was known locally as Turkey Hill. Protected on its northern and western edges by Boatswain Swamp, the thick surrounding woods limited the Confederate's potential routes of approach, while the generally clear plateau allowed for the weight of Union artillery to be added to the defense. Porter arranged his defense with Morell's division facing generally west on the left and Gen. George Sykes's division on the right facing north. Gen. George A. McCall's division formed the reserve. With slightly more than 27,000 men available, Porter was about to be the focal point of some 54,300 Confederates that Lee was to hurl against his lines. Although Porter had planned to construct defensive abatis to protect his front, no axes were available so the front line lacked significant obstacles to the rebel approach other than the swampy ground.[51]

The men of the 14th New York slept in the woods that night, lying on the damp ground without cover or blankets. At daybreak, they marched along the road to Gaines Mill, arriving around 7:00 AM. Within two hours they were in line of battle near the Watts family farm. Gen. Morell arranged his line with Butterfield's Brigade on the far left, followed to the right by Martindale's and Griffin's Brigades, the latter linking with Sykes's Division. The front was covered by skirmishers from Col. Hiram Berdan's U.S. Sharpshooters under Lt. Col. William Y. W. Ripley. Griffin arranged his brigade with the 9th Massachusetts on the right, the 14th New York in the center, and the 4th Michigan on the left. The 62nd Pennsylvania was held in reserve. The rebels appeared about noon led by Brig. Gen. Maxcy Gregg's Brigade of five South Carolina regiments, followed by the rest of Maj. Gen. A. P. Hill's "Light Division," five more brigades from Georgia, Virginia, North Carolina, and Tennessee, with a regiment each from Alabama and Louisiana.[52]

Gregg launched a fierce attack that fell mostly on the 9th Massachusetts, which remained steady and repulsed the initial assault. On the far left, however, the Michigan regiment began to waver when pressed by another attack, but soon recovered and held its position. A brief lull ensued, but soon Gregg's brigade attacked again, supported by Branch's North Carolinians. Amid the chaos that ensued, the 1st South Carolina Rifles pressed home a bayonet attack on a Massachusetts battery, but were met and thrown back by Duryea's Zouaves, the 5th New York Infantry. Losses were high among the rebel regiments, but on they came, pressing into Griffin's defenders. In the 14th New York, the right flank was especially raked by enemy fire, but as Griffin observed, it "nobly and repeatedly drove him back at the point of the bayonet."[53] Another attack staggered the line about 2:30 PM, the smoke hanging so heavily and the crash of battle so loud that Lt. Col. Skillen found it hard to make himself seen or heard by his men. To better direct his troops men, Skillen climbed atop a hemlock log, but his new position was too conspicuous and before long a rebel ball ripped into the left side of his chest. Nearby men quickly fashioned a stretcher out of two muskets and a blanket to carry Skillen to a field hospital, but he died on the way.[54]

The lieutenant colonel was not the regiment's only casualty. Men fell on every side, some writhing with painful wounds, others still in death. In Company C, Captain Frederick "Fritz" Harrer stood encouraging his men until shot through the left knee. His brother, drummer William Harrer, described the incident:

> My noble brother, our captain, was shot through the leg, the left knee being shattered and mangled dreadfully. From that wound he died within three days. All I could hear around me was, "Oh! Oh! Oh! Oh!" when the brave men were hit by the merciless lead which brought them down. There was no whining, no nervous yelling, nor hysterical screams of agony, only that involuntarily "Oh! Oh! Oh!" as they fell.[55]

The wound proved mortal. Capt. Harrer was buried at Savage's Station, Virginia, while Skillen was brought back to New York State and interred in Amsterdam. Another who fell was Abraham Squires. Two weeks before the battle he had written home to Utica: "The Battle of Richmond ... has not yet taken place.... If it shall be my fate to fall in the act of sustaining the 'stars and stripes,' so be it.... If I should get shot in the coming battle, you can draw my pay and bounty, but I hope I shall be spared to draw it myself."[56]

The 62nd Pennsylvania moved forward to support the 9th Massachusetts and the right flank of the 14th New York, momentarily thrown into confusion by Skillen's loss. Though taking serious losses, the Oneida County men held. They held again at 5:30 when a fourth rebel attack threatened their position. But at 6:30, a fifth enemy attack led by fresh troops—Col. Evander M. Law with the 4th Alabama, 2nd and 11th Mississippi and 6th North Carolina; Brig. Gen. John Bell Hood with the 1st, 4th, and 5th Texas, 18th Georgia, and Hampton's South Carolina Legion—rolled up troops to Griffin's left. The 4th Michigan and the left flank of the 14th New York were caught in a deadly crossfire at the same time that fresh rebels pressured their right flank. Under increasing pressure from both flanks, the lines began to waver, men began to fall back before the onslaught. Griffin ordered a retreat.[57]

As Billy Harrer retired, he thought of those being left behind, the dead and wounded, including his brother, and he felt tears fill his eyes. As they retreated, Confederates fired at them across the open plateau, but with the rebels now out in the open the Federal artillery decimated the attacking waves with canister. As the New Yorkers reached the far side of the field, Col. McQuade rushed forward, seized the colors, and waved them back and forth above his head. "Rally on the colors, men," he yelled as loudly as he could, "I'll stand by you to the last!" The men rallied to their colonel. Forming behind an artillery battery, they were soon joined by reinforcements from Gen. Henry W. Slocum's division from Gen. William B. Franklin's Sixth Corps who helped to steady the new line. A countercharge by the new troops blunted that last rebel attack. Once again darkness soon ended the day's bloodshed. The Federals lost 6,837 men, but had held. Lee lost 7,993. His plan to destroy Porter's Corps had once again failed.[58]

Following the desperate battle, McClellan issued orders for the Army of the Potomac to continue its retreat. Heavy skirmishing took place on June 28 as the rebels followed the retiring Federals, nipping at their heels. The armies clashed at Savage's Station on the 29th and White Oak Swamp on the 30th with Lee launching repeated attacks that were all beaten back, but at the end of each day McClellan chose to continue the retreat. By the evening of June 30, the Union army was falling back on positions occupied by Porter's Corps on Malvern Hill. The position was naturally strong, a wide plateau rising gradually some 130 feet above the surrounding area, and skillful engineers made it even more imposing by placing some 250 guns on its slopes, most with clear fields of fire over the

approaches the Confederates would have to use. But the position also had the
James River in its rear, giving many the impression of a "last ditch" defense.[59]

Col. McQuade led the 14th New York away from the field at Gaines's Mill
on the afternoon of June 28, crossing the Chickahominy River at Alexander's
Bridge before camping for the night near the Trent farm. On the 29th, the march
continued on to Savage's Station, then across White Oak Swamp to Britton's farm
where the regiment again bivouacked for the night. At dawn on the 30th, the regiment continued its march over Turkey Bridge along the Quaker Road, and on
toward Malvern Hill, but just after the men stopped to rest about 10:00 AM orders
arrived to backtrack to provide support against a threatened rebel attack.
McQuade pushed the regiment forward in support of the 9th Massachusetts and
62nd Pennsylvania ahead of him. Held in reserve, the regiment suffered one man
slightly wounded by artillery fire but was otherwise unengaged. The men slept
with their arms throughout the night to be ready for any eventuality.[60]

Early the next morning orders arriving shifting the 14th New York into
defensive position with the rest of the Union army on Malvern Hill. Gen. Morell
established his headquarters at the J. H. Mellert residence with his division holding the far left of the Union line. Morell assigned Griffin's Brigade to the left of
his line, and Griffin in turn deployed his men with the 14th New York and a section of Battery C, 1st Rhode Island Light Artillery on the left of his line forming
the extreme left flank of the Union position. McQuade took position between the
road to Richmond and the Mellert house, facing west. His men had been given
the very important and difficult assignment of protecting the army's flank from
being turned. Should it fail, the entire position on Malvern Hill might become
untenable forcing a disastrous retreat. No sooner had the men arrived in their
position than rebel artillery opened fire. Federal guns responded and throughout
the early afternoon shells arched back and forth across the fields as the two sides
sought an advantage. Fortunately for McQuade and his men, most of the rebel
shells were directed elsewhere leaving the 14th New York in relative safety. Their
luck would not last.[61]

Late that afternoon Lee launched his army in a direct assault on the Union
position, with Griffin's Brigade the first to be hit. Across the open wheat field
rushed Brig. Gen. Ambrose Wright's brigade—the 3rd, 4th, and 22nd Georgia, 1st
Louisiana, and 44th Alabama—supported by the brigades of Brig. Gen. Lewis A.
Armistead and Brig. Gen. William Mahone. The U.S. Sharpshooters opened a
lively skirmish fire, then fell back to Griffin's line which opened a deadly fire on
the rebel advance. McQuade's Oneida County men fired and reloaded as quickly
as possible. Supported by massed artillery, they created a deadly field of fire that
broke up the Confederate attack. David Winn in the 4th Georgia later tried to
describe to his wife the "desperate charge," and what it was like to be on the
receiving end of this well-directed fire: "It is astonishing that every man did not
fall; bullet after bullet too rapid in succession to be counted ... shell after shell,

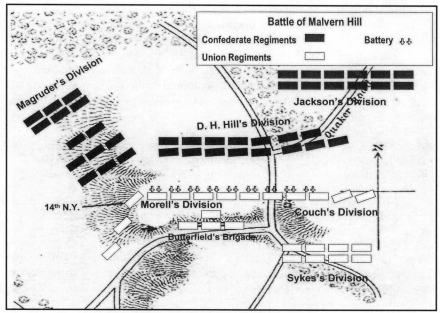

The 14th New York at the Battle of Malvern Hill

illuminating the whole atmosphere, burst over our heads, under our feet, and in our faces." Not a single rebel made it to within three hundred yards of the Federal position.[62]

Next to rush to the assault was Mahone's brigade containing the 6th, 12th, 16th, 41st, and 49th Virginia, but the crossfire of artillery and infantry fire tore their ranks apart as it had Wright's brigade before it. A quiet settled over the field, but soon the Confederates launched another attack on the right of the Federal line, meeting with no more success than their earlier assaults on left. While this new attack was unfolding, Lt. Col. Ripley, in charge of the sharpshooters, sent an urgent message to Gen. Morell informing him that a large Confederate force was making its way under cover of the woods and the dense smoke toward a ravine leading around the left flank and rear of the Union position. Sensing the immediate danger, Morell sent an aide with an order for McQuade to rush the 14th New York to the threatened flank, and another to Major Francis A. Schoeffel to move his 13th New York to a position where he could support McQuade.[63]

The 14th New York quickly changed front, moving to its left to confront the rebel column about to attack up the hill leading to the Crew house. While the Confederates launched yet another doomed assault on the main Union line, the men from Oneida County were left to contend with the threat that might unhinge the entire Union line. Seeing the bluecoats before them, the rebels charged up the hill toward McQuade's men who opened an effective fire that drove them back. Rebel sharpshooters began to take a toll on the regiment, but a second attack was beaten back, then a third in what Gen. Morell called "a sharp engagement." Griffin, in his official report of the action, noted that the 14th New York was "exposed to a most deadly fire, which it withstood without flinching during the entire engagement, repulsing the enemy three times."[64] Harrer described the scene in his memoirs:

> The enemy ... advanced a massive line of infantry to storm our position. But it was in vain. Our boys nobly held their ground and about nightfall began to drive their opponents before them. They who had advanced so threateningly began to fall into confusion. The 600-pounders from the gunboats roaring and smashing through the woods after the fleeing foe added terror to their flight. No one of the Confederate generals, nor all of them together, could rally their army.[65]

In the confusion of the rebel retreat, William Bettinger, a farmer from Germany serving as a musician, noticed a Confederate soldier with a musket on his shoulder some distance ahead of him. Harrer described what happened next:

> Now for a piece of strategy, thought he [Bettinger], worthy of putting on record. Bettinger sprang to his feet, yelled to the soldier to throw down his gun, and ran at him with his fife held out like a pistol, covering him. "Down with your gun; you are my prisoner." And the fellow, terrified, thinking the fife was a revolver, lost no time in laying down his gun. Billy took him prisoner to the headquarters nearby.[66]

The 14th New York held its position until about 2:00 AM the following morning when it was ordered to retire. Despite the severe defeat inflicted on the Confederates, Gen. McClellan had once again decided on retreat, essentially ending his Peninsula Campaign. During the course of the Seven Days Battles, the regiment suffered three officers and thirty men killed, nine officers and 167 men wounded, one officer and fifteen men captured, for an aggregate loss of 225. In the wake of the desperate engagements, Col. McQuade, as the sole surviving colonel in the brigade, became its commander for the next eighteen months. Gen. Morell recognized McQuade's steady leadership with a recommendation that he be promoted to brigadier general. Gen. Porter concurred, forwarding his own recommendation for the promotion.[67]

At McClellan's direction, the 14th New York retired to Harrison's Landing on the James River where the Army of the Potomac established its new camp. The men hated Harrison's Landing. Continual rain turned the place into a mud hole, the roads nearly impassable and the ground so soggy that they could not even pitch their shelter halves because the tent pins would not stay in the ground. It was difficult to build fires for warmth, as what little wood they could find was damp and difficult to burn. The men were tired and hungry, most having run out of food days before. Latrines overflowed, causing the camp to smell like a huge, outdoor privy. Flies and mosquitoes invaded the camp, leaving the men infested with lice, their lives completely miserable. Morale declined, until finally a new supply of fresh meat and vegetables arrived, along with new uniforms, allowing the men to get rid of their lousy clothes, which they promptly burned.[68]

ANTIETAM, FREDERICKSBURG, CHANCELLORSVILLE

Following the Peninsula Campaign, Gen. Robert E. Lee determined to take advantage of McClellan's retreat by moving his Confederate Army of Northern Virginia north to menace Washington, D.C. The result was a clash with Gen. John Pope's Federal Army of Virginia on the plains around Manassas, the Second Battle of Bull Run. Fearing for the safety of the capital, President Lincoln ordered the withdrawal of McClellan's force back to the defense of Washington. In response to this, in August the 14th New York began a general movement toward the historic towns of Williamsburg and Yorktown, from whence it had begun its campaign up the Peninsula. The men marched east, away from Richmond, to Newport News where they boarded transports for Aquia Creek on August 20. From there, they boarded a train to Fredericksburg, then marched on to Falmouth in the oppressive heat and humidity of the Virginia summer. With many of the smaller creeks dry, the men ran out of fresh water and had to get by with whatever they could find. William Harrer described one incident when the thirsty men found a small pool of water by the roadside. "The water was like yellow paint and filled with thousands of tadpoles and little frogs. But no difference. 'Water! Water!' was our cry, and water we were glad to get, no matter how bad it was. But, as Christian Scherer got the last dip out of it, there he saw in the bottom of the hole a dead snake about seven feet long. But this is nothing. In the soldier's life everything goes."[69]

Though in the general vicinity of Manassas around the time of the Second Battle of Bull Run, the regiment did not take part in that engagement. When Lee used his victory there as an opportunity to invade Maryland, the 14th New York followed along in pursuit with the Army of the Potomac. Fortunately for the men, the regiment was kept in reserve for most of the deadly Battle of Antietam on September 17, advancing only later in the day to support the right flank after the most serious of the fighting had already concluded. Drummer Harrer described their brief encounter, along with his own personal reflections on the nature of civil war: "We advanced as skirmishers and soon came to hot fighting. We took some prisoners, among them the whole regiment from New Orleans, known as the Louisiana Tigers. I had a sister married in New Orleans, and I thought perhaps her husband was among them.... Such was the war of the rebellion.

Politics—politics was what did it. The father was against the son, brother against brother, brother-in-law against brother-in-law, and that was one of the hardest features of the unnatural conflict."[70]

Following Antietam, Pres. Lincoln removed McClellan from command, replacing him with Major Gen. Ambrose P. Burnside. In November, word circulated that Lincoln had proclaimed a national day of thanksgiving. For the 14th New York, it was a bittersweet occasion. When the appointed day arrived, November 27, Harrer reported that "We had one hardtack per man—no coffee, no sugar, no pork—only the lonely, only hardtack. The boys grumbled ... 'This is not much of a Thanksgiving day.'"[71]

In December, Gen. Burnside determined to attack the Southern army at Fredericksburg, Virginia. Lee's Confederates were entrenched on Marye's Heights with a commanding view of the town and the surrounding area. Just in front of the hill was a sunken road bordered by a stone wall. Behind the wall Lee had stationed infantry, and on the hill above were several batteries of artillery. In the face of these strong positions, Burnside sent several waves of Union infantry across a wide open plain in a vain attempt to break the rebel lines. The 14th New York, along with another Oneida County regiment, the 146th New York (Fifth Oneida County Regiment), watched the developing battle from a vantage point across the Rappahannock River. At 3:00 PM on December 13 the two New York regiments crossed a pontoon bridge to the Fredericksburg side of the river where they made their way through the town itself toward the battlefield. While there, they came under heavy enemy fire that killed several men. "As our time of enlistment was now nearly expired," wrote Harrer, "and I had come out all right through so many battles, I prayed to God to save me once more if it should be His good will to do so, and I would fast every Friday and think of His mercy to me."[72]

Burnside ordered thirteen separate assaults, none of which came within fifty yards of reaching the rebel positions. Casualties were appalling. Luckily for the 14th New York, as the time for its turn came near, Burnside's staff finally convinced him of the folly of further attacks. They were to be spared the slaughter, but they were not spared the aftermath of battle. Even though it was Virginia, it was the coldest winter in memory for that area. The men spent the night across from the heights without proper winter clothing, shivering, listening to the pitiful cries of the wounded who still lay on the field before the stone wall.[73]

A month later, Burnside decided to move the army westward along the Rappahannock to outflank the rebels. Days of cold winter rain intervened, turning the roads into quagmires and ending the campaign. Harrer recalled the scene:

> ... such a rain! Really such a down-pour ... has not been on earth since the days of Noah's flood.... I never got another such a soaking as that in all the days of my life.... The farther we marched through it the deeper and deeper we sank in the mud, mud, mud, until we fairly got stuck.... We saw most wretched sights— batteries and wagon-trains up to the hubs in mud. One battery I shall never for-

get—16 mules attached to one piece of artillery, pulling to get it out—but of no use. The poor mules and horses were wickedly abused. All the thrashing and yelling accomplished nothing toward extricating the wagons. The animals, with their loads, only sank deeper and deeper in the mud. The everlasting pouring down of the rain on men and beasts kept on. We were hopelessly stuck in the mud, the bottomless, shoreless sea of mud, the mud of old Virginia, the sticky, dirty, dreadful mud, and the enemy about us and making us a by-word and a jest by erecting huge boards with placards painted on them thus: Burnside's Army Sticking in the Mud.[74]

In the spring of 1863, after the disastrous Mud March in January, Burnside was replaced as commander of the Army of the Potomac by Major Gen. Joseph "Fighting Joe" Hooker, who instituted a reorganization of the army. The changes left the 14th New York in the Fifth Corps, now commanded Major Gen. George Gordon Meade. Hooker planned to make a movement much like Burnside envisioned—move west along the Rappahannock, then cross the river to gain the rear of the Confederate army and force Lee to come out into the open and attack so the Union forces would benefit from being on the defense. Hooker, of course, planned for better weather. He also drilled the army through the spring months, made sure the troops were paid promptly, provided new uniforms and improved rations, and in other ways sought to raise morale. With the army's health and confidence restored, Hooker began his campaign on April 27. Leaving about half of his army at Fredericksburg to demonstrate and hold Lee's army in position, Hooker marched three corps west along the Rappahannock.

With Col. McQuade leading the brigade, coupled with the death of Lt. Col. Skillen, command of the 14th New York fell on newly promoted Lt. Col. Thomas M. Davies. By the end of April, the regiment had less than a month remaining in its enlistment. The men were looking forward to anticipating going home. When orders came to move out on yet another campaign, few looked forward to the experience. Reluctantly, they joined the marching columns headed west, reaching Hartwood Church that same evening. By evening of the 28th the regiment reached Kelly's Ford on the Rappahannock River, which it crossed on the following day. Continuing their march, the men crossed the Rapidan River at Ely's Ford, eventually arriving in the vicinity of the small crossroads known as Chancellorsville on the morning of April 30. About 4:00 PM orders arrived for the brigade to march to Banks's Ford on the Rappahannock to support Brig. Gen. James Barnes's brigade, but after three miles another order arrived for the brigade to return to its original position where it went into camp for the night.[75]

On May 1, Hooker began an advance toward the Confederate rear near Fredericksburg. McQuade's brigade led the advance of Griffin's division which was to provide support for Gen. George Sykes's division engaged near Salem Church. Before McQuade could become involved, orders arrived from Hooker to break off the engagement and retire to their earlier positions. The 14th New York again retraced its steps that night, marching to the vicinity of Stout's Mills where it went into position to the right of Gen. Andrew A. Humphreys' division on the left the Union line. On the following day, May 2, the 14th New York received orders to dig fortifications which it, and other units, did throughout the day.[76]

On the night of May 1-2, Gens. Lee and Jackson devised a plan for Jackson to hit the exposed right flank of Hooker's army with some 30,000 troops. On the early evening of May 2, Jackson unleashed the assault, triggering a major engagement over the next two days. The 14th New York remained in position, listening to the increasing sounds of furious fighting, until about 4:30 AM on May 3 when it moved to a new position to the right of the White House. Around 4:00 PM on May 4, Griffin ordered McQuade to advance his

Lt. Col. Thomas M. Davies
(Donald Wisnoski)

brigade on a reconnaissance. The 4th Michigan advanced as skirmishers, with the balance of the brigade in support, but the force returned to its positions when the Confederate lines were uncovered, the purpose of its original reconnaissance.[77]

Although all of the Confederate attacks had been repulsed after the initial surprise assault, on the evening of May 5 Hooker decided to withdraw his army back across the Rappahannock. The brigade crossed on the morning of May 6. Ironically, on the eve of its service coming to an end, the 14th New York failed to get the word to join the retreat. The regiment appeared to be cut off from the new Federal lines. McQuade's quick thinking saved the day. Discovering a narrow, unmapped little road that he thought could be used to extract the regiment from its perilous predicament, the colonel asked the men if they were willing to follow him through the woods and across an open field in a bid to reach friendly lines.[78]

Billy Harrer described what happened:

> As soon as the first gray, glimmering of dawn appeared, the command was repeated in whispers ... to follow the colonel double-quick. This run I shall never forget. It was a race for freedom, for liberty, for life. The colonel had discovered ... an obscure road ... and he made up his mind that if we did not get out by this road before daylight we, in the last day of our service, the day on which the term of our enlistment expired ... we would be captured and sent as prisoners to Andersonville or Richmond to die there like dogs as our comrades who had been captured were dying.[79]

Hooker's campaign was over; another Union failure. Mercifully, the 14th New York lost only three men slightly wounded in its last campaign. On May 12, William Harrer and his drummers beat reveille for the last time. Their stint in Federal service was over.

The 14th New York returned in triumph to Utica on May 20, 1863, only five minutes before the arrival of veterans of the 26th New York, the Second Oneida County Regiment, also returning at the end of its service. The appreciative citizens provided a reception that had been planned for several weeks. Relatives, friends, and neighbors from Utica, Rome, and the surrounding towns and villages had taken up collections to decorate the city for the occasion and to purchase home cooked meals for the returning men, their first in two years. The two regiments disembarked and formed up in Bagg's Square, adjacent to the station. There, Mayor Charles Wilson officially welcomed them home. Then, the men marched to Broad Street where Ward Hunt spoke about the service of the 14th New York, followed by C. H. Doolittle who spoke about the 26th New York. Col. McQuade gave a short speech in appreciation of their welcome home.[80] Children sang patriotic songs, and a parade formed on lower Genesee Street including the veterans of the two regiments, the 45th Militia Regiment, the Utica Cavalry Company, the Utica Fire Department, and several local bands. Onlookers were sobered to see the regimental colors, so beautiful when the men marched off to war, now faded, tattered, torn, hanging almost in shreds. The 14th's standard bore no less than thirty-three bullet holes. The parade concluded, and everyone retired to a banquet in Chancellor Square.[81]

The regiment mustered out of the service on May 24. Until then, the men were housed in the Oneida County Court House. Awaiting their final discharge, they soon found their money was no good in Utica and the surrounding towns. Wherever they went, no shopkeeper, saloonkeeper, or merchant would accept payment for anything the returning soldiers wanted. Upon his return to Utica, Col. McQuade finally received his well-deserved promotion to brevet brigadier general, and later to major general. He became one of the co-founders of the Loyal Legion, as well as the George Washington Post of the Grand Army of the Republic (G.A.R.). In 1879, he was selected to be Department Commander of the G.A.R. of New York State.[82]

Though no longer in the army, McQuade did not sit back and bask in his past fame. He was elected mayor of Utica twice, both as a Republican and a Democrat. He also acted as postmaster of the City of Utica, then served two terms as the Quarantine Commissioner of the Port of New York. He was a presidential elector for the Democratic ticket in 1868, and again in 1876, later serving as Secretary for the Electoral College. In 1872, he was appointed manager of the State Lunatic Asylum, a position he held until his death on March 25, 1885. He was buried in St. Mary's Cemetery on Mohawk Street in Utica.[83]

During its two years in Federal service, the 14th New York suffered sixty of its men killed in battle, 194 wounded, and sixteen missing. Forty-two also died of disease, while seven became prisoners of war. The 14th suffered a total of three hundred and nineteen casualties. The regiment served nobly and with honor. But the good people of Oneida County had not seen the end of sending their sons, husbands, and relatives off to fight in the fratricidal conflict. Four other regiments would follow them as the war escalated to even more terrible heights.

———————

[1]*Utica Citizens Corps* (Utica, NY: Utica Citizens Corps Veterans Ass'n., 1938), 20.

[2]New Century Club, *Outline History of Utica and Vicinity.* Utica, NY: L.C. Childs and Sons, 1900, 22.

[3]New York State Military Museum and Veterans Research Center, *14th Regiment, New York Volunteer Infantry, Historical Sketch From the 3rd Annual Report of the Bureau of Military Statistics,* http://www.dmna.state.ny.us, 1; *Utica Citizens Corps*, 23.

[4]Howard Thomas, *Boys in Blue From the Adirondack Hills,* Prospect, NY: Prospect Books, 1960, 13.

[5]*New York Times,* obituary of James McQuade, March 26, 1885; *Utica Citizens Corps,* 21, 23.

[6]William Harrer, *With Drum and Gun in '61: A Narrative of the Adventures of William Harrer of the Fourteenth New York State Volunteers in the War for the Union from 1861 to 1863.* Greenville, PA: The Beaver Printing Company, 1908, 5; *Utica Citizens Corps,* 22.

[7]*Utica Citizens Corps,* 23.

[8]Norman L. Ritchie, ed., *Four Years in the First New York Light Artillery: The Papers of David F. Ritchie* (Hamilton, NY: Edmonston Publishing, Inc., 1997), 2.

[9]Harrer, *With Drum and Gun in '61,* 5.

[10]Thomas, *Boys in Blue From the Adirondack Foothills,* 19.

[11]Thomas, *Boys in Blue From the Adirondack Foothills,* 19.

[12]Harrer, *With Drum and Gun in '61,* 6.

[13]Harrer, *With Drum and Gun in '61,* 6.

[14]*Utica Citizens Corps,* 27.

[15]Harrer, *With Drum and Gun in '61,* 7; *Utica Citizens Corps,* 23.

[16]Ritchie, *First New York Light Artillery,* 5; *Utica Citizens Corps,* 23.

[17]*New York Times,* "Local Military Movements," June 17, 1861, 9.

[18]Thomas, *Boys in Blue From the Adirondack Foothills,* 21.

[19]*New York Times,* "Local Military Movements," June 17, 1861, 9.

[20]*New York Times,* "Local Military Movements," June 17, 1861, 9.

[21]Maryland Online Encyclopedia, http://www.mdoe.org/riots_balt_1861.html.

[22]Frederick Phisterer, *New York in the War of the Rebellion* (Albany: Lyon Publishers, 1912), Vol. 2, 1901.

[23]Harrer, *With Drum and Gun in '61,* 8.

[24]Ritchie, *First New York Light Artillery,* 7.

[25]Ritchie, *First New York Light Artillery,* 6.

[26]Ritchie, *First New York Light Artillery,* 8.

27Ritchie, *First New York Light Artillery,* 10; *Utica Citizens Corps*, 24.

28Thomas, *Boys in Blue From the Adirondack Foothills,* 32.

29Ritchie, *First New York Light Artillery,* 11.

30New York State Military Museum, *14th Infantry Regiment*, 1; *O.R.*, Series I, Volume XI, Part 1, 684; *Utica Citizens Corps*, 24.

31Harrer, *With Drum and Gun in '61*, 26; Lee's full name is found in *Utica Citizens Corps*, 23.

32Wikipedia, www.wikipedia.org/wiki/Peninsula_campaign, *Peninsula Campaign,* 4-5; *Utica Citizens Corps*, 24.

33Harrer, *With Drum and Gun in '61*, 35.

34Harrer, *With Drum and Gun in '61*, 36; *Utica Citizens Corps*, 24.

35*Utica Citizens Corps*, 24.

36Harrer, *With Drum and Gun in '61*, 37.

37Harrer, *With Drum and Gun in '61*, 38.

38Harrer, *With Drum and Gun in '61*, 41; *O.R.*, Series I, Vol. XI, Part 1, 400.

39Harrer, *With Drum and Gun in '61,* 41.

40Harrer, *With Drum and Gun in '61*, 44.

41Harrer, *With Drum and Gun in '61*, 44.

42*O.R.*, Series I, Vol. XI, Part 1, 698, 700-01, 717-18, 721.

43Thomas, *Boys in Blue From the Adirondack Foothills*, 62.

44*O.R.*, Series I, Vol. XI, Part 1, 717-18, 720-21; Alexander S. Webb, *The Peninsula: McClellan's Campaign of 1862* (Edison, NJ: Castle Books, 2002, reprint of 1881 edition), 93.

45*O.R.*, Series I, Vol. XI, Part 1, 720-21.

46Thomas, *Boys in Blue From the Adirondack Foothills,* 62.

47*O.R.*, Series I, Vol. XI, Part 1, 699.

48*O.R.*, Series I, Vol. XI, Part 1, 705.

49*O.R.*, Series I, Vol. XI, Part 1, 709.

50*O.R.*, Series I, Vol. XI, Part 2, 271, 312.

51Stephen W. Sears, *To the Gates of Richmond: The Peninsula Campaign* (New York: Ticknor & Fields, 1992), 213-14; Thomas, *Boys in Blue From the Adirondack Foothills*, 65.

52*O.R.*, Series I, Vol. XI, Part 2, 272-73, 313; Sears, *To the Gates of Richmond*, 223, 387.

53*O.R.*, Series I, Vol. XI, Part 2, 313.

54*O.R.*, Series I, Vol. XI, Part 2, 313.

55Harrer, *With Drum and Gun in '61*, 49.

56Thomas, *Boys in Blue From the Adirondack Foothills*, 69.

57*O.R.*, Series I, Vol. XI, Part 2, 273; Sears, *To the Gates of Richmond*, 241, 386.

58Harrer, *With Drum and Gun in '61*, 52; New York State Military Museum, *14th New York Infantry, Historical Sketch*, 1-2; Thomas, *Boys in Blue From the Adirondack Foothills,* 66-69; Sears, *To the Gates of Richmond*, 249.

59Sears, *To the Gates of Richmond*, 310.

60*O.R.*, Series I, Vol. XI, Part 2, 274, 313-14.

[61]*O.R.*, Series I, Vol. XI, Part 2, 274-75; Webb, *The Peninsula*, 154.

[62]Sears, *To the Gates of Richmond*, 324-25, 390; *O.R.*, Series I, Vol. XI, Part 2, 314.

[63]*O.R.*, Series I, Vol. XI, Part 2, 275, 315; Webb, *The Peninsula*, 166.

[64]Thomas, *Boys in Blue From the Adirondack Foothills*, 72; *O.R.*, Series I, Vol. XI, Part 2, 275, 315; Webb, *The Peninsula*, 166.

[65]Harrer, *With Drum and Gun in '61*, 61.

[66]Harrer, *With Drum and Gun in '61*, 62.

[67]*O.R.*, Series I, Vol. XI, Part 2, 276-78, 315; *O.R.*, Series I, Vol. LI, Part 1, 107; Thomas, *Boys in Blue From the Adirondack Foothills*, 72; *New York Times*, obituary of James McQuade, March 26, 1885.

[68]Thomas, *Boys in Blue From the Adirondack Foothills*, 74.

[69]Harrer, *With Drum and Gun in '61*, 73.

[70]Harrer, *With Drum and Gun in '61*, 82.

[71]Harrer, *With Drum and Gun in '61*, 85.

[72]Harrer, *With Drum and Gun in '61*, 87.

[73]Thomas, *Boys in Blue From the Adirondack Foothills*, 112-113.

[74]Harrer, *With Drum and Gun in '61*, 95-96.

[75]*O.R.*, Series I, Vol. XXV, Part 1, 275, 517.

[76]*O.R.*, Series I, Vol. XXV, Part 1, 275, 517.

[77]*O.R.*, Series I, Vol. XXV, Part 1, 518.

[78]*O.R.*, Series I, Vol. XXV, Part 1, 519.

[79]Harrer, *With Drum and Gun in '61*, 109.

[80]Thomas, *Boys in Blue From the Adirondack Foothills*, 140.

[81]Thomas, *Boys in Blue From the Adirondack Foothills*, 141; New Century Club, *Outline History of Utica and Vicinity*, 26.

[82]*New York Times*, obituary of James McQuade, 1885.

[83]Harrer, *With Drum and Gun in '61*, 80.

CHAPTER 4

"A MOST DISASTROUS DAY"
THE LIFE AND DEATH OF THE EMPIRE BATTERY

by

James S. Pula

Enthusiasm for enlistment ran high throughout the North in the wake of the firing on Fort Sumter. Oneida County was no different. Even as the 14th New York marched off to war, men were busy enlisting in other units or planning for new organizations. Within the 14th itself, one of those with ambitions for his future, even as the regiment marched off to war, was its quartermaster, Thomas H. Bates. On July 31, 1861, he received authority from the War Department to organize a battery of "flying artillery." With his authorization in hand, he submitted his resignation and began the trip home to recruit.[1]

Arriving in Utica, Bates immediately set to work organizing what would become Battery A, 1st New York Light Artillery, also known as the "Empire Battery." Most of the recruits hailed from Utica, Edmeston, Little Falls, Phoenix, Clinton, Burlington, South Brookfield, New Berlin, Jordan, Sauquoit, Bridgewater and Sherburne. Bates offered the quartermaster position to David F. Ritchie who held the same position in the 14th New York. Other officers included Lt. George P. Hart and Lt. Thomas H. Crego.[2]

The battery was officially organized at Utica and mustered in on September 12, 1861. On October 22, the men gathered in Chancellor Square for an inspection and dress parade before "a great crowd of ladies and gentlemen, who could not frame compliments sufficient to express their admiration of the artillerymen."[3] On the following day, as the men prepared to leave, Bates was presented with a "splendid sabre" and the Rev. Dr. Daniel G. Corey offered a prayer "for their success in battle and safe return." According to David Ritchie, the goodbye was quite emotional, "young women were not abashed to be pressed and kissed and men were not unashamed to weep."[4]

Arriving by train in Elmira on October 23, the Empire Battery was inspected by General R. B. Van Valkenburg and assigned to Colonel Guilford D. Bailey's 1st New York Light Artillery. The following day it boarded another train for Washington, which it reached on November 1 and went into camp behind the

Capitol Building on East Capitol Street. For Quartermaster Ritchie, arriving in Washington with a new unit for the second time that year, it was a time of reflection:

> There is nothing about the clash of arms inspiring enough to capture me, although I am engaged in this conflict heartily enough. I love my friends and home too much—and that fact explains my presence here. I had rather follow some peaceful occupation than scheme to destroy the lives of my brother men, however much they may have transgressed the laws of God and man. Now, however, I esteem it my duty to be where I am.[5]

David F. Ritchie *(Four Years)*

The Empire Battery was assigned to Camp Barry where it would remain until March 1862. As the season was already advanced, the officers and men quickly began designing a more permanent camp than their canvas shelters, assuming they would be in "winter quarters" for some time. Captain Bates arranged for the purchase of lumber for flooring and two large iron stoves for the battery to cook its food.[6] As Ritchie described it in a letter to the Utica *Morning Herald,*

> For a week the mechanics of the Empire Battery—and they are neither few nor poor—have been busy. The sound of the hammer, the saw and the mallet have been heard from early morn till dewy eve, and behold the result: Our camp is now a village of 150 inhabitants. The street is wide, and on either side are the dwellings, of uniform height, size and style. They are built of wood as high as the cornice; the roof is of canvas, the same that was formerly used for tents. Perhaps you will get a more accurate idea of the improvement we have made when I say that for each tent there has been built an oblong frame 7 1/2 x 10 feet square, five feet high and just the size of the base of the tent itself. This frame is boarded and bottomed tight. The tent is then set on the top of the open frame or box, and then secured so that it forms an excellent roof, and the whole makes quite a house. It will be seen that by this means the occupants of each tent gain 375 feet. And more important that the extra room is the increase in the warmth and general comfort of the

men. There is now room in each tent for three berths to be built on one side, each berth of sufficient magnitude to accommodate two sleepers. At one end or side may be placed a small stove, leaving space for a table, several camp stools, etc., etc., and "room for company" besides. A number of the tents are already furnished with stoves, while others are fitted out with ingeniously contrived fireplaces, with a chimney built outside the tent a little below the surface of the ground, and opening into the apartment. This latter makes one of the most comfortable arrangement imaginable. It is much like an old-fashioned fire-place, and is full, as pleasant to sit by the camp, as it is now arranged, presents quite a unique appearance, and is the admiration of all who visit us. It is entirely a company enterprise, and the expense is assessed on each member. Each tent is occupied by six men. ... As for the Empire Battery, it is made comfortable, and we can now afford to wait and see what would have been done, or what would not have been done, for us, if we had not done it ourselves.[7]

At Camp Barry, Bates had an opportunity to begin drilling his men. They were immensely proud of the new brass light 12-pounder field pieces they received from the government, and some credited their Representative, Roscoe Conkling, for helping them obtain brand new guns. Popularly known as the "Napoleon," the piece could fire solid shot, shells, spherical case or canister, with a 2.5 pound charge propelling a solid shot to a range of 1,680 yards. It was most effective when used against assaulting infantry columns which it could rake with deadly canister up to a range of 300 yards. Each gun, or "tube" as artillerymen called them, weighed 1,200 pounds. Each piece in the six-gun battery was worked by nine men, a sergeant (chief of the piece), corporal (gunner), and seven privates. Of the latter, two served at the limber issuing and distributing ammunition, one carried the ammunition to the gun, and the other four actually worked the piece. Each two guns were organized as a section commanded by a lieutenant, with three sections comprising the battery under the command of the captain.[8] Lt. George P. Hart commanded one section, Lt. Thomas H. Crego another, and Lt. David F. Ritchie the third.

One of the highlights of camp life that fall was a review by Gen. George B. McClellan accompanied by a large number of spectators who arrived by carriage, horse, or on foot to view the ceremonies and catch a glimpse of the commanding general. More personal enjoyment came when friends from the 14th New York and 26th New York, camped nearby, visited the battery to renew acquaintances and share news from home. Thanksgiving also provided an opportunity for a celebratory meal and socializing, but for the most part the late fall and winter were accompanied by the boredom of camp routine, drill, and the cold, wet, dismal weather of the season. "It is raining today," Ritchie wrote to the folks back home, but, cozily seated as I am by a good fire inside my little white house, it does not make a dreary sound, pattering on the taut canvas overhead. I rather like the music played by the liquid drops upon my housetop. There is something martial about it, for I can fancy it the tread of any armed elfish host, marching, marching, marching—per chance to bring back to their allegiance some "seceded" State or States in the wide dominions of beautiful Queen Mab.

It is not unpleasant, I assure you, "the rain on the roof" of a canvas tent, with the fancies it awakens in the brain, especially if you feel a little drowsy, and the tent don't leak, I could easily sit this rainy afternoon and dream away several hours down here in camp, listening to the rain and wondering what policy the Queen of the Fairies would pursue in suppressing the treason of her rebellious elves; picturing the "form and feature" of her warrior "McClellan," and her rebel gnome "Beauregard," numbering her forces, and reviewing her strength. But the conviction that there are many in the land of the "loyal" North" who watch with eager eye for every scrap of intelligence from the tented field, where almost every one has a brother or son, father, lover or friend; constrains me, to return to things of reality.[9]

Reality returned in late March 1862 with preparations for beginning the next campaign. Leaving Washington, the battery marched smartly down Pennsylvania Avenue, turned onto 14th Street, and then marched to Meridian Hill where it was assigned to the artillery brigade attached to Brigadier General Silas Casey's 2nd Division of the Fourth Corps under Brigadier General Erasmus D. Keyes. There the men were reunited with Col. Guilford Dudley Bailey who commanded the artillery brigade.[10] A West Point graduate who was born in Martinsburg, New York, in 1834, Bailey was experienced, having served in the 2nd U.S. Artillery on the western frontier and in Kansas and Texas. When the war began and his commanding officer in Texas surrendered to Confederate authorities, Bailey refused the order to capitulate and instead escaped along with Captain George Stoneman, taking their guns with them to Union territory. After serving in the relief of Fort Pickens near Pensacola, Florida, he organized the 1st New York Light Artillery of which he was appointed colonel.[11]

Battery A received orders to move out on March 28, marched to Alexandria, Virginia, on the Potomac River and boarded ship for Fortress Monroe. Like the 14th New York before it, the Empire Battery was to be part of General George B. McClellan's massive transfer of the Army of the Potomac to the York Peninsula for his campaign against Richmond. The battery landed near Fortress Monroe on April 1 to find "The weather is mild and pleasant and peach trees are in blossom. Oysters and sutlers are plenty as blackberries, the former very cheap, the latter very dear."[12]

Five days after landing Bates led his men off in the wake of McClellan's advance. The weather quickly took a turn for the worse with heavy rains lashing the column, turning the roads into a reddish muddy quagmire that impeded horses, wagons, limbers and guns. Fog obstructed the view. The tents had not caught

Col. Guilford Bailey (*USAMHI*)

up with the column, leaving the men with only their oilcloth ponchos as protection from the rains. A cold east wind soon arose, making life more uncomfortable, while food and forage gave out because wagons could no longer navigate the impassable pathways. Ritchie, was not alone in voicing complaints. "George B. McClellan is called by some the 'Young Napoleon' but the only reason I can see for giving him that name lies in his dissimilarity to the Old Napoléon. The title sounds ironical."[13]

After more than two weeks, the weather abated somewhat. On the 18th, the Empire Battery covered 17 miles, arriving for the night near Warwick Court House. After a rest, the men continued their trek on April 22, moving to a position between the York and James Rivers, still following in the wake of the front lines. "The march led us over bottomless bogs and stumpy clearings," Lt. Ritchie wrote, "through unfathomable mudholes, sullen streams and across noisy corduroys."[14] When they finally halted for the night, music from a nearby rebel band filtered through to their campsite.

May 4 found them on the march again, through thick pine forests that shielded their movement but also forced them to keep to the roads with their guns and wagons. The Confederates knew this, so they planted torpedoes—what we today would call mines—all along the way to make the advance as costly as possible. Anyone stepping on one of the buried pressure devices would cause a deadly explosion. Ritchie echoed others when he labeled the contraptions "an act of cowardice and barbarism."[15] The following day it rained again, bringing with it a return of the slippery, clutching mud. As they gingerly felt their way forward, the sounds of battle echoed back to them from Williamsburg, but they arrived too late to take part in the engagement. That evening the men camped in a wheat field, soaked to the bone, cold, hungry, with nothing to separate their reclining forms from the soggy ground.[16]

Continuing their march toward the York River, the men passed along fields and earthworks where the Battle of Williamsburg was fought. "The ground was strewn with dead horses, cannon balls and small arms. All day Tuesday and Wednesday parties were busy burying the dead and as we left on our march from Williamsburg we heard them firing parting volleys over the remains of their comrades."[17] The scenes were sobering, the marching slow. Two days took them only fifteen miles to a position near the Chickahominy River. After a brief rest, they resumed their march at 3:00 AM on May 14, reaching New Kent Court House a little after sunrise on a warm spring morning. Further marches over the next few days took them to Baltimore Crossroads and on until they camped on the farm of the widow Susan Rawson which General Casey appropriated for his headquarters since the widow had fled to Richmond.[18]

May 20 brought their first action when rebel artillery fired shells close by without causing any casualties. Bates opened fire with about twenty rounds of shell and shrapnel. After the brief encounter, Bates limbered up to continue his march to the Chickahominy where the battery crossed the river on pontoons at Bottom's Bridge, marched to near Seven Pines and went into camp on the evening of May 30. Throughout that night, the camp was swept by what Gen. Erasmus Keyes described as a "raging a storm the like of which I cannot remember. Torrents of rain drenched the earth, the thunderbolts rolled and fell without intermission, and the heavens flashed with a perpetual blaze of lightning."[19]

Under Keyes direction, the Fourth Corps, moved out along the Williamsburg Road, passed the small crossroads called Seven Pines, and halted about a mile beyond the crossroads. With pickets reporting the enemy but a short distance ahead beyond a growth of woods, Keyes ordered his men to dig entrenchments, fronted by abatis and rifle pits. Gen. Darius Couch's division went into place at Seven Pines, with Gen. Silas Casey's division thrown forward to man the front-line positions. Casey's regiments went into line on both sides of the Williamsburg Road. In addition to the infantry entrenchments, they constructed a small, pentagon-shaped redoubt not quite as tall as a man. Casey planned to use the redoubt as an artillery position, manning it with Battery A, 1st New York Light Artillery. Three of the battery's guns went into position in the redoubt under Lt. Hart, while the other three, lacking room in the earthwork, unlimbered outside and to the left of the entrenchment under the command of Lt. Ritchie.[20]

The field surrounding the redoubt was about three-quarters of a mile wide. Casey's division deployed in advance of the redoubt with Captain Joseph Spratt's Battery H, 1st New York Light Artillery, forward and to the right of the redoubt and supported by Brig. Gen. Henry M. Naglee's brigade. Slightly forward of Battery A in and around the redoubt, Casey stationed the brigade of Brig. Gen. Henry W. Wessels in the center of the Union line and that of Brig. Gen. Innis N. Palmer on the left. Behind the redoubt, in position near Battery A, Casey placed Capt. Butler Fitch's 8th New York Independent Battery.[21]

Throughout the morning, reports came in of Confederate troops arriving in large numbers. At one point, Lt. James B. Washington, an aide of Confederate commanding officer Gen. Joseph E. Johnston, blundered into Union lines and was taken prisoner. The presence of Washington, and reports of sizeable Confederate movements, convinced Casey that the rebels were about to launch an attack. Sometime after 11:00 AM, Union pickets reported the Confederates approaching through the woods fronting the Union lines.[22]

While Gen. Casey checked the positioning of his troops and examined the intelligence reports he was receiving, the men in the Empire Battery settled into their new positions. The morning passed peacefully, allowing them to brew coffee, play cards, or otherwise pass the time. As Lt. Ritchie sat writing a letter home around noon, two artillery rounds suddenly passed over his head landing behind the battery. Aroused from their leisure, the artillerymen jumped to their feet and rushed to their guns.[23] Casey quickly sent the 103rd Pennsylvania forward to reinforce the picket line, while ordering the rest of his division to stand to arms. The general then ordered Spratt's Battery H to use its four three-inch rifled guns to throw shells over the intervening woods into the area where the Confederate buildup had been reported. Within a few minutes, firing from the woods increased and the Pennsylvanians came tumbling back in some disorder followed closely by a massive wave of Confederates.[24]

In and around the redoubt, the artillerymen sprang into action as the scattering of musketry in the woods grew quickly into a crescendo of volleys. A few wounded men passed the battery on their way to the rear, while an occasional musket ball, an overshoot from the firing lines to their front, zipped through the air. Col. Bailey spurred his horse over to Battery A, entered the back of the redoubt, and ordered Bates to open fire into the woods. Bates turned to his gunners, yelling the order over the din of the distant musketry. The concussion of the opening shot had not yet dissipated when one of the seemingly random musket balls found Capt. Bates horse, narrowly missing the battery commander who was standing but a foot away. Although they could not yet see the rebels, the gunners could see smoke arising from the wood line which they used as their target. As the field pieces came alive, "thundering forth their stern music," Lt. Ritchie thought to himself that "the sharper din of the musketry suggests thoughts of closer quarters and imminent risks."[25]

Leading the Confederate attack was Gen. Daniel Harvey Hill's division including the brigades of Brig. Gen. Robert E. Rodes, Col. George B. Anderson, Brig. Gen. Samuel Garland, Jr., and Brig. Gen. Gabriel J. Rains. They were supported later in the engagement by Brig. Gen. John Bell Hood's brigade. Hill's division, when deployed in line of attack, extended beyond both flanks of Casey's force which allowed it to quickly enfilade the Union line. The 6th South Carolina and the Palmetto Sharpshooters swiftly made their way through the woods on the federal right and began firing into the flank and rear of Naglee's brigade. Losses mounted quickly. Rebel sharpshooters targeted the horses in Spratt's battery to prevent removal of the guns that were now endangered. Caught in the crossfire,

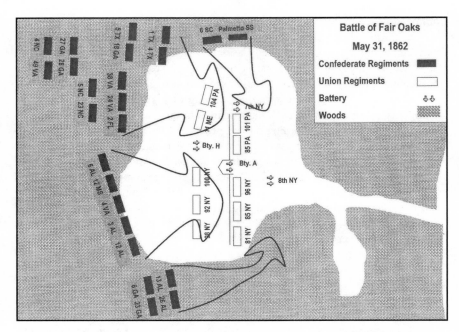

Naglee's regiments began to fall back. Spratt hurriedly limbered his guns, but one had to be abandoned for lack of horses to remove it.[26]

As Union troops on the right fell back, jubilant Confederates rushed from the woods in pursuit. "Suddenly Battery H ceases fire and presently we see their pieces hurrying toward the rear. What can it mean?" Lt. Ritchie later recalled thinking. "Our infantry too is falling back. What troops are those advancing from the woods with banners flying? It does not seem possible but true it is—*that is the rebel flag!*"[27] With the Confederates now in plain sight across the open field, and Union troops out of the way to their front, Col. Bailey immediately ordered the gunners to switch to murderous canister. As he stood by one of the Empire Battery's guns observing the result, a musket ball struck him in the temple splattering blood about the area. Nearby, Cyrus Covey of West Edmeston was working his gun inside the redoubt when another ball smashed through his brain, killing him instantly. Edward Howard of Phoenix, a rider, stood next to his team behind the battery when a rebel marksman put a ball into his groin and a buckshot into his head.[28]

Across the field, attacking rebels out in the open suffered even more. Leading the assault against the redoubt were the brigades Rodes and Garland. Rodes's men led the attack across a gently rising ground *en échelon* with the 6th Alabama under Col. John B. Gordon stepping off first followed by the 12th Mississippi, 5th Alabama, and 12th Alabama. Before the day was over the regiment would lose every field officer and 59 percent of the 632 men it took into action. Its colonel was saved only when his horse was shot from under him, landing next to him as an impromptu cover from Union fire. In Garland's brigade, Lt. Col. Louis Pyles led the 2nd Florida across the open field "under heavy fire from the enemy troops and artillery." Suffering heavy losses, Garland ordered a charge on the guns that were raking his men with deadly canister even at some 400 yards distance. Pyles fell seriously wounded, Major George Call was killed, and the 2nd Florida lost 46 percent of the 435 men it brought into action.[29]

"How long can this last?" Ritchie wondered. "It seems as though we were knocking a thousand men out of existence every second."[30] But all was not well despite the slaughter endured by Rodes's and Garland's brigades. To the right, Naglee's brigade, having been flanked, was in retreat while Spratt was busy saving his three remaining rifled guns. To the left, Rains brought his four regiments—the 13th and 26th Alabama and 6th and 23rd Georgia—onto the exposed Union flank where they took position behind a fence line and raked the federals with an accurate fire at close range. Gen. Casey rode up yelling "Give them double charges, boys! Give them double charges!" As Adjutant William Rumsey of Watertown fell wounded, double charges of canister swept the field, but could do nothing to prevent the flanking fire reaching the battery from Rains's position. Rebel marksmen began targeting the exposed battery horses behind the redoubt, the dead animals acting as anchors in their harnesses while the wounded beasts shrieked in pain as they flailed about unable to escape their restraints.[31]

The double charges of canister quickly depleted the remaining supply of ammunition. Gen. Naglee approached and requested fire placed on the Confederates pursuing his brigade as it withdrew, but he no sooner arrived than rebel marksmen shot his horse from under him. He quickly remounted a battery horse to continue directing the fight. Nearby, Major David H. van Valkenburg, who succeeded Bailey in command of the 1st New York Light Artillery, fell mortally wounded leaving the artillery without a field officer. Naglee quickly assumed command of the guns in his immediate area, but by then the Empire Battery had lost some sixty horses and men were beginning to fall as marksmen worked themselves in behind the redoubt. With the infantry in retreat, it was obvious to Naglee that the position could no longer be held. He ordered the artillery removed to prevent its capture.[32]

With few horses left, Bates found himself with no means of removing the guns. Naglee estimated that three to four of the six houses on each piece had been killed or wounded, making it impossible to remove either the stricken animals or the artillery. Convinced that nothing more could be done, he ordered the guns spiked and abandoned. To the front, rebel infantry pressed within 75 yards of the battery, while to the left Alabama marksmen were within an easy range of 80 yards. The pieces were abandoned as the men scrambled to the rear, but they were not spiked. The guns and caissons were all lost. "It was a most disastrous day," Ritchie wrote. "We lost all our camp equipage, personal baggage—everything

Officers of the 1st New York Light Artillery. Seated, Col. Guilford D. Bailey. Standing, from left, Major David H. Van Valkenburg, Major Luther Kieffer, 1st Lt. and Adj. William Rumsey, Lt. Col. Henry E. Turner, Major Charles S. Wainwright. Bailey and Van Valkenburg were killed and Rumsey was seriously wounded at the Battle of Fair Oaks. *(USAMHI)*

except what we had about us."[33]

The end of the engagement did not result in an end to the fighting. Pens took over once the guns were silent. In the official report of the engagement that he sent to Secretary of War Edwin M. Stanton, Gen. George B. McClellan wrote that "Casey's division, which was in first line, gave way unaccountably and discreditably."[34] Such a severe and public reprimand from the commanding general immediately brought forth a barrage of indignant correspondence from the division's officers. Casey complained to McClellan about the "injustice" done to his men, while Naglee demanded a court of inquiry. Gen. Keyes, the corps commander, endorsed both and forwarded them to McClellan. The commanding general replied, through his assistant adjutant general, that a formal inquiry would have to wait because of the ongoing campaign, but he would have his inspector-general "make a preliminary investigation." The inspector general's report concluded that the division had faced overwhelming numbers and held its position well until flanked, but had become disordered in its retreat. Some had behaved very well, others had not behaved well. "In this division," the report concluded, "there are many worthy of praise for good conduct who suffer for the bad conduct of others."[35]

Ritchie complained that McClellan's report "treated us shamefully," a sentiment no doubt held by others. "We are hoping that our battery will be again united and furnished with more guns and permitted to cope with the rebels under its former proud title of Empire Battery," Ritchie wrote. "I know of no reason why we should not have more guns as there are plenty of them in the Washington Arsenal."[36] But it was not to be. Perhaps it was the fact that the guns had not only been lost, but had not been spiked that soured higher authority on the battery. Captain Bates was sent home to Utica to reorganize the unit, but on June 15, 1862, the remaining officers and men were divided between other commands. Lt. Hart found himself assigned to the 8th New York Independent Battery along with forty former members of Battery A. Lt. Crego and 63 men went to the 7th New York Independent Battery and Lt. Ritchie took fourteen with him into Battery H, 1st New York Light Artillery.[37]

Bates returned to Utica where he recruited men to reconstitute Battery A. When completed, it was assigned to the Artillery Camp of Instruction near Washington, D.C., from January to June of 1863. Reassigned to Maj. Gen. Franz Sigel's Division in the Department of the Susquehanna, it was engaged in skirmishes at Chambersburg, Pennsylvania on July 4 and again on July 30. Thereafter, it served at various posts in Pennsylvania, all of which were removed from the front. It mustered out and the men were honorably discharged at Elmira on June 28, 1865, having lost four men killed and mortally wounded, all on that fateful day at Fair Oaks, and nine men by disease during the course of its service. For the Empire Battery, active combat, for all practical purposes, ended on a fire-swept Virginia field when the war was barely a year old. The same could not be said for the other organizations raised in Oneida County.

---

[1]Norman L. Ritchie, ed., *Four Years in the First New York Light Artillery: The Papers of David F. Ritchie* (Hamilton, NY: Edmonston Publishing, Inc., 1997), 9; Frederick H. Dyer, ed., *A Compendium of the War of the Rebellion* (Cedar Rapids, IA: Torch Press, 1908), 1388; Frederick Phisterer, ed., *New York in the War of the Rebellion, 1861-1865* (Albany: J. B. Lyon Company, 1912).

[2]Norman L. Ritchie, ed., *Four Years in the First New York Light Artillery: The Papers of David F. Ritchie* (Hamilton, NY: Edmonston Publishing, Inc., 1997), 9; Dyer, *Compendium*, 1388; Phisterer, *New York*.

[3]Ritchie, *Four Years*, 9, 16-17; Dyer, *Compendium*, 1388; Phisterer, *New York*.

[4]Ritchie, *Four Years*, 18; *Utica Morning Herald & Daily Gazette*, October 22, 1861.

[5]Ritchie, *Four Years*, 18.

[6]Ritchie, *Four Years*, 18-19.

[7]Dyer, *Compendium*, 1388; Ritchie, *Four Years*, 19.

[8]Ritchie, letter to the Editor of the Utica *Morning Herald*, November 27, 1861.

[9]Philip Katcher and Tony Bryan, *American Civil War Artillery 1861-1865 (I) Field Artillery* (Oxford, England: Osprey Publishing Ltd., 2001), 4, 14, 16, 21; Ritchie, *Four*

Years, 35; Mark Adkin, *The Gettysburg Companion: The Complete Guide to America's Most Famous Battle* (Mechanicsburg, PA: Stackpole Books, 2008), 149-51.

[10]Ritchie, letter to the Editor of the Utica *Morning Herald*, November 27, 1861.

[11]Ritchie, *Four Years*, 34; Dyer, *Compendium*, 1388; Phisterer, *New York*.

[12]Roger D. Hunt, *Colonels in Blue: Union Army Colonels of the Civil War. New York* (Atglen PA: Schiffer Military History, 2003), 35; obituary, *New York Daily Tribune*, June 5, 1862.

[13]Ritchie, *Four Years*, 35-36.

[14]Ritchie, *Four Years*, 37-38.

[15]Ritchie, *Four Years*, 41-42.

[16]Ritchie, *Four Years*, 44.

[17]Ritchie, *Four Years*, 45.

[18]Ritchie, *Four Years*, 45-46.

[19]Ritchie, *Four Years*, 49-51.

[20]Ritchie, *Four Years*, 50-53; *O.R.*, Series I, Vol. XI, Part 1, 872-73.

[21]*O.R.*, Series I, Vol. XI, Part 1, 872-73; *O.R.*, Series I, Vol. XI, Part 1, 913; Ritchie, *Four Years*, 58.

[22]Ritchie, *Four Years*, 58; Webb, *The Peninsula*, 101.

[23]*O.R.*, Series I, Vol. XI, Part 1, 913; Sears, *To the Gates of Richmond*, 121.

[24]Ritchie, *Four Years*, 58.

[25]*O.R.*, Series I, Vol. XI, Part 1, 874, 913.

[26]Ritchie, *Four Years*, 58-59.

[27]Stephen W. Sears, *To the Gates of Richmond: The Peninsula Campaign* (New York: Ticknor & Fields, 1992), 126; Alexander S. Webb, *The Peninsula: McClellan's Campaign of 1862* (Edison, NJ: Castle Books, 2002, reproduction of 1881 publication), 104.

[28]Ritchie, *Four Years*, 59.

[29]Ritchie, *Four Years*, 56-59; Webb, *The Peninsula*, 105; *O.R.*, Series I, Vol. XI, Part 1, 919.

[30]*O.R.*, Series I, Vol. XI, Part 1, 971-72; Sears, *To the Gates of Richmond*, 128; Zack C. Waters and James C. Edmonds, "'It Is No Use Killing Them': The 2nd Florida Infantry Flaunts its Fortitude in the Company of Virginians," *America's Civil War*, Vol. 23, no. 3 (July 2010), 54.

[31]Ritchie, *Four Years*, 59.

[32]Ritchie, *Four Years*, 60; Sears, *To the Gates of Richmond*, 128; Webb, *The Peninsula*, 105; *O.R.*, Series I, Vol. XI, Part 1, 918-19.

[33]Ritchie, *Four Years*, 60-61; Webb, *The Peninsula*, 105; *O.R.*, Series I, Vol. XI, Part 1, 918-19.

[34]Ritchie, *Four Years*, 61, 63; *O.R.*, Series I, Vol. XI, Part 1, 923; Webb, *The Peninsula*, 105.

[35]*O.R.*, Series I, Vol. XI, Part 1, 749.

[36]*O.R.*, Series I, Vol. XI, Part 1, 750-53.

[37]Ritchie, *Four Years*, 57, 66.

[38]Ritchie, *Four Years*, 1388; Phisterer, *New York*.

CHAPTER 5

"FOR THE SUPPORT AND VINDICATION OF OUR NATIONAL FLAG"

THE 26TH NEW YORK VOLUNTEER INFANTRY

by

Robert Tegart

Only six days after the South Carolina authorities opened fire on Fort Sumter, the April 18 edition of the *Clinton Courier* reported that Captain William H. Christian of Utica, a veteran of the Mexican War, had begun forming a volunteer battalion of four companies "for the support and vindication of our National Flag."[1] Volunteers came from all parts of Oneida County, with long processions winding their way along the various routes to Utica to enlist in what would become the 26th New York Volunteer Infantry. Popularly referred to as the "Second Oneida" since it was the second infantry regiment recruited in the county, the new volunteers were greeted with cheers and festivities in each village they passed. In Clinton, white-haired veterans of the war of 1812 wearing cockade hats led the procession through the village accompanied by the martial music of the Clinton Cornet Band and the occasional roar of saluting cannon. When a company from Hamilton under Capt. George Arrowsmith passed through the village on April 29, the *Courier* reported excitedly that it appeared some of the townspeople were "somewhat excited by potent beverages but all appeared to be brim full of patriotism and fight."[2]

In Utica, Col. Christian took up residence at the Sherwood House from where he began organizing and drilling the incoming volunteers in the local armory. As the initial contingent of seventy men began to grow, Christian established a formal headquarters in the Utica City Hall, while drilling moved to the more spacious Chancellor's Square on Bleecker Street, an elegant 3.4 acre Victorian park whose walkways were adorned with elm trees, flowers, and fountains. This quiet park, intended to host concerts, celebrations, and peaceful Sunday picnics, became the center of the initial military training the new soldiers would receive.[3] Men arrived from all parts of Oneida County and the surround-

Col. William Christian
(Donald Wisnoski)

Lt. Col. Richard H. Richardson
(Donald Wisnoski)

ing area, with some eventually joining the regiment from as far away as Monroe, Seneca, and Tioga Counties. Richard H. Richardson mustered in as lieutenant colonel, with Gilbert S. Jennings of Rochester filling the role as major. Although most companies contained a mix of men from various locations, in general Companies A, B, C, and E were recruited at Utica, Company D at Hamilton, F at Whitestown, G and H (originally intended for the 13th Regiment) at Rochester, I at Oriskany, and K at Candor. Although most of the men hailed from the towns and villages of Oneida County, the regiment also included recruits from Chenango, Herkimer, Madison, Monroe, Seneca, and Tioga Counties.[4]

TABLE 1: RECRUITMENT AREAS OF VARIOUS COMPANIES[5]

Co.	Where Recruited	By Whom Recruited	Org'ize	Accepted
A	Utica, Oneida County	Capt. M. Casselman	May 1	May 1
B	Utica, Oneida County	Capt. Geo. A. Blackwell	April 25	May 1
C	Utica, Oneida County	Capt. David Smith, Jr.	April 25	May 3
D	Hamilton, Madison Co.	Capt. George Arrowsmith	April 28	May 7
E	Utica, Oneida County	Capt. Anthony Brendle	May 6	May 7
F	Whitestown, Oneida Co.	Capt. Ezra F. Wetmore	April 26	May 3
G	Rochester, Monroe Co.	Capt. Gilbert S. Jennings	April 24	May 2
H	Rochester, Monroe Co.	Capt. Thomas Davis	May 2	May 2
I	Oriskany, Oneida County	Capt. John H. Palmer	May 10	May 13
K	Candor, Tioga County	Capt. James B. Caryl	May 14	May 14

Major Gilbert Jennings
(Donald Wisnoski)

Capt. George Arrowsmith
(USAMHI)

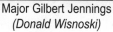

Since the unit had not yet reached the minimum number to be mustered into service, the government would not provide the normal clothing, housing, rations, or equipment that volunteer units received once they entered into federal service. Until they were officially sworn into service, their needs had to be met by the generosity of the local governments and private citizens. When the number of volunteers exceeded 500, Utica's mayor brought the matter before the Common Council which decided to house two companies in City Hall and to identify other space that could be used if necessary. Another company was quartered in a tavern on the far side of the bridge over the Mohawk River in Deerfield, with all three companies authorized to take their meals at different hotels with a committee of citizens picking up the bill. Three other companies were located "elsewhere," receiving their meal at their own quarters. Citizens also pitched in to provide food in "liberal quantities."[6]

Indeed, the local communities treated their favorite sons as heroes. In addition to the food and accommodations, village governments and private citizens presented the men with all types of soldierly items. On April 27, the mayor of Rome presented a sword to Colonel Christian. The Union Cricket Club presented a revolver to George White who served in the unit, while the management and employees of the Curtiss Machine Shop in Utica presented a revolver to James Cook of Captain Ezra Wetmore's Company and the printers of Utica gave a Bowie knife and revolver to J. Edward Robinson, also of Wetmore's Company. Not to be outdone, A. B. Clark, a mill owner in Clarks Mills, gave revolvers to about twenty volunteers from his area.[7]

Its recruiting goal now met, Col. Christian finally received orders on May 3 for the unit to leave for Elmira the following day. Part of the troops were to entrain for Canandaigua where they would make connections for Elmira, while the balance were to travel to Geneva where they would board a steamer for the trip down Seneca Lake to Watkins Glen where they could board another train for Elmira. When the appointed hour arrived, the *Utica Daily Observer* reported "They marched to the depot headed by the Utica Brass Band and accompanied by a large crowd of men, women, and children. At the depot they were assigned cars which they entered midst the cheers and earnest farewells of the men and tearful good-byes of the women. ... [A]s the train moved off the band played and the crowds gave three rousing cheers while the volunteers waved their handkerchiefs, hats, and flags and seemed to be in fine spirits."[8]

Camp Chemung

Labeled the "Queen City of the Southern Tier," Elmira was a busy canal town of about 15,000 people at the terminus of the Chenango Canal. The intersection of several major railroads led to its selection, along with Albany and New York, as one of the military rendezvous sites for the state. As the regiments poured into Elmira's Erie Railroad depot, hundreds of men tumbled out of the rail cars, formed into ragged lines, and marched off to their quarters. Most of the units arrived still clad in civilian dress. As their number increased rapidly with each arriving train, and with the new barracks as yet incomplete, finding accommodations became difficult leading to the use of every available billet including old factories, homes, public halls, and churches. Companies A, B, and F of the 26th were assigned quarters in a church and took their meals at the Revere House, while Company E settled into quarters over a store in Water Street and took their meals at the Franklin House. The main camp was located on the site of the state fair grounds. Consisting of forty acres of land about a mile from the village, it was named Camp Chemung for the Chemung River flowing through Elmira. It consisted of three separate camps known as Barracks No. 1 (located in what was "Arnot Field" south of Washington Avenue and east of Lake Street), Barracks No. 2 (located in the old Fifth Avenue Ward near the Northern Central Railroad Shops), and Barracks No. 3 (located on West Water Street above Hoffman Street). When completed, the barracks could accommodate about 3,000 troops. The mess room could seat 1,200-1,500 men at a time and the bakery could produce 6,000 loafs of bread per day. The camp operated throughout the war, later becoming a prison for captured Confederate soldiers.[9]

The 26th was assigned, along with the 13th Regiment from Rochester, to Barracks Number 3, or the Williamsport Barracks as it was sometimes called. Reports on the quality of the new barracks varied, one observer referring to them as roughly put up buildings resembling an "Irishman's shanty" while another volunteer correspondent described the new barracks as: "Ten buildings one for each company, are erected upon a line with the barracks of Colonel Quinby's Regiment, constructed with rough boards, with tight roofs, and in every respect comfortable. Each building is about 90 by 60 feet, has a stove, with two tiers of bunks on either side, each bunk intended for two soldiers and each soldier has a clean, comfortable straw mattress. The Captains and lieutenants have a room for their own use on one side, in the front part of the building."[10]

Although the men were now housed, they remained without uniforms or other military equipment. Capt. George Blackwell published a call for assistance in the *Utica Observer*, explaining that "The volunteers are much in want of underclothing, such as shirts &c. Most of them came here with only one shirt expecting to get their uniforms and other clothing on arriving at this place. In this they have been disappointed and now they are sadly in want of clothing. If the ladies of Utica have anything of the kind to send, they can do so to Captain Blackwell, Company B."[11] The ladies responded with boxes containing all sorts of supplies from clothing to havelocks to food. Churches in the Utica area formed groups, Union Societies and Sewing Associations sprang up, and women's groups from Manchester and Clarks Mills sent "Home-made woolen socks, flannel bandages ten inches wide and a yard long, towels, pocket handkerchiefs, and small bags, each containing thread, woolen yarn, needles, &c for mending."[12] The ladies of Hamilton sent four barrels of "numerous luxuries in the form of eatables and clothing," while those of Clinton responded with a large box of clothing.[13]

On June 11, Lt. William Averell arrived in Elmira as mustering officer in charge of the camp. He noted that there were 5,422 officers and men in camp forming seven regiments. The 26th New York Volunteer Infantry, now officially mustered, had been supplied with arms, equipment, uniforms, and tents. Averell reported the 26th was in good order, had fine discipline considering the short time they had been in service, and therefore would be ready to take to the field at short notice. However, despite Averell's comments, discipline was not always respected. A correspondent to the *Rochester Union* wrote: "We had a little difficulty this morning with company A and company B of the Utica regiment. They took breakfast after us, and for some reason were dissatisfied and commenced destroying the tables. They tore one all to pieces. Maj. Terry immediately called out our entire regiment to quell the disturbance and we soon arrested the ringleaders and placed them in the guardhouse. Company B then commenced the same thing, but the man who made the first move was immediately arrested and quiet was soon restored."[14]

In early June a group of prominent Uticans journeyed to Elmira to present the regiment with a flag. As the news of the impending visit spread throughout the camp, squads of men scattered in all directions to collect evergreen boughs and other bouquets to decorate the camp. In a very short time it took on a festive appearance with rows of cedar boughs in front of the barracks, flagstaffs ornamented with wreaths, and decorations forming mottoes placed on buildings. One soldier described it as "a regular Fourth of July." On June 9, Judge Smith of Oneida and William Lewis of Utica presented the colors to Colonel Christian before the regiment and a crowd of local spectators. The *Utica Daily Observer* told its readers that "The flag is a beautiful one, 8 x 5, of fine banner silk, with a bright yellow fringe, with which the cord and tassel correspond. The staff is of rosewood and is jointed. The ferule is of silver, and the head of the staff is ornamented with a guilt ball on which an eagle is perching. The cost of the colors was $125."[15]

Thomas Davis
(Donald Wisnoski)

Less than a week later, on June 14, Christian received orders that the regiment would be transported to Washington, D.C., within the next few days. Upon hearing the news, the men broke ranks and cheered wildly, hung their hats on their bayonets, and began to march around the parade ground. Over the next few days officers noted that the men seemed to train in earnest, no doubt in anticipation of moving to the front. Quartermasters issued rations and ammunition to the regiment, along with new caps and shoes. On their final night in Elmira, the men, led by their colonel, marched past the barracks of other regiments and through Elmira, all along the way cheered by their fellow soldiers and townspeople.[16]

ON TO WASHINGTON

The 26th New York left Elmira at 10:15 AM on June 20, 1861, aboard a train consisting of fifteen passenger cars and five freight cars pulled by two steam locomotives. Although it was a rainy morning, a large group of citizens from Elmira were on hand to wave, yell, and shed some tears for the soldiers as the train pulled away. Their first stop was in Williamsport, Pennsylvania, where they paraded through the streets and were given a picnic dinner by local civic groups. It seemed as if every inhabitant of the town was on hand to visit with them. As they lined up to get back on the train every man was presented with a cigar. The train rolled on into the night straight through Harrisburg and in the gray light of morning entered Maryland. The troops were now in slaveholding territory and everyone sat alertly to watch for those vile secessionists whom they expected would look like Jefferson Davis. Reaching Baltimore, they formed up to march

John Jennings
(Donald Wisnoski)

through the streets to another rail terminal where they would board a train for Washington. Well aware of the violence that had erupted between a Massachusetts regiment and the local populace, the Oneida County men marched nervously through the streets in grim silence, making no reply to comments from the crowd and accepting no refreshments or water from them for fear of poisoning. Fortunately, with the exception of a few remarks and hisses from some bystanders, there was no sign of violence.[17]

Two days after it left Elmira, the regiment arrived in Washington having little or no sleep or rations since its departure. Without any opportunity for rest, the men were ordered to fall in and march under the broiling Washington sun to Meridian Heights, a hill about three miles from the city. It was a difficult march for men both tired and unused to lengthy marches. Several were overcome with the heat and fell out. By the time the regiment arrived at its destination it was late evening and the men, too tired to set up their tents, simply lay down and rolled themselves up in their blankets to sleep.[18]

As newcomers to the seat of war, the Oneida County men experienced a certain amount of nervousness facing the unknown in the presence of the enemy. Alerts were frequent as jittery pickets fired on shadows, causing the regiment to turn out for many false alarms. But despite the tenseness, many were able to explore the wonders of the nation's capital, take a swim in the Potomac River, or enjoy a panoramic view of the city from the unfinished dome of the Capitol Building. Yet all was not without controversy. Some confusion existed during the original mustering of the regiment, leading some to believe they had enlisted for three months and some for two years. To add to the confusion, five companies had been initially reported as enlisted for three months, although their certificates read two months and the muster rolls read two years. Although the adjutant verified that two years was the correct term, not everyone agreed. When the regiment received its pay in August, some men insisted their service had expired, a few even deserting and heading for home. The issue was finally settled, although not to the liking of many, when Col. Christian read before the regiment a letter from Assistant Adjutant General A. D. Ruggles, dated July 25, which stated: "I am directed to say that all the New York two year regiments are to be considered as in the service of the United States for that period. Among these are the 12th

Volunteers, Colonel Walrath, the 13th Volunteers, Colonel Quinby, the 19th, Colonel Clark, the 21st, Colonel Rogers, the 26th, Colonel Christian, which were originally three months regiments."[19] This was soon followed by Special Orders No. 325 dated August 2, 1861.

> His Excellency the President of the United States, desiring the further services of the Twenty-sixth regiment N. Y. S. V., and having made requisition upon the Governor of this State therefore, Colonel Christian is hereby directed, on the expiration of the term for which such regiment was mustered into the service of the United States (August 21, 1861), to report his command to the Adjutant General of the United States army, for duty under the order of the United States Government for the remainder of the term of the enlistment of the regiment into the service of the State of New York.[20]

ACTIVE DUTY

The days of relative comfort at Camp Vernon, just south of Alexandria, ended in late July when Gen. Irwin McDowell led the newly recruited army south to end the rebellion. As the First Battle of Bull Run raged to the south on July 21, the 26th New York received orders to pack three days' rations and march to Alexandria where it would board a train for Fairfax Station. There the regiment joined Col. John McCunn's brigade along with the 15th, 25th, and 37th New York. Marching toward the raging battle, the men could hear the dull thud of cannon fire and the sharp rattle of musketry, but before they arrived the issue was settled in favor of the Confederates.[21] Maneuvering to cover the Union retreat, Col. Christian wrote that "Every road leading from the scene is crowded with returning troops. They came by squads, by companies, by regiments. Blackened faces and tattered uniforms designate those who suffered most severely."[22] Capt. George Arrowsmith described the scene in more detail: "All parts of the North were represented in the rout—Zouaves with their gay uniforms torn, dirty and blood-soiled, soldiers without shoes, some without guns or knapsacks, ... some without eyes, some without ears, and others with various flesh wounds, riding, limping or running—such was the picturesque procession which went along the road all yesterday afternoon.... I really think the rebel general is very foolish not to attack us today. Most of the regiments are completely demoralized, and are crossing the river in crowds."[23]

Following the disaster at First Bull Run, President Lincoln and Secretary of State William Seward visited the regiment and had a lengthy meeting with Col. Christian. Soon after, Gen. McDowell was replaced with Gen. George B. McClellan who spent the remaining weeks of summer and the fall months reorganizing the defeated army. New regiments arrived, incompetent officers were weeded out, and a new emphasis on discipline promoted greater professionalism, while a better supply system increased morale and rifle drills were added to marching and drilling to ensure that the men knew how to use their weapons effectively. A typical day began with reveille at dawn, roll call, an hour of drill, and cleaning the camp before breakfast at 7:00 AM. The balance of the morning would then be filled with guard duty and more drill, with the main meal at noon. Further drilling by company and regiment filled the afternoon, followed by the sounding of retreat at sunset and tattoo, or "lights out," at 9:00 PM.[24]

For the most part, the fall passed without interruption except for a reconnaissance and skirmish at Pohick Church, about twelve miles from Alexandria, in October. Since rebel cavalry had been plundering and intimidating pro-Union farmers in the area, Col. Christian received orders to lead a detachment of 300 infantry and a company of cavalry to capture the enemy forces, estimated at about 50 men. Christian placed Capt. Arrowsmith in charge of the operation, with orders to encircle the enemy to prevent them from fleeing. Arrowsmith advanced his force quickly, surprising the rebel cavalry which was using the church for shelter. When men from the 26th advanced, the rebel pickets fell back on the church, spreading the alarm that the Yankees were coming. The Confederates reacted quickly, leaving the warm meal they were about to consume to establish a defensive line. But before they could take their positions, Arrowsmith gave the order to "Fire." The first volley unhorsed several Confederates, forcing the rest into a hasty retreat across an open field to a fence where they dismounted. After firing several ineffective shots, the rebels remounted and continued their retreat, leaving their breakfast to be enjoyed by Arrowsmith's men.[25]

Although successful in its first encounter with the enemy, Arrowsmith had not followed orders to surround the rebel force, thus allowing most of the group to escape. Gen. Henry Slocum, to whose command the 26th belonged, was furious at Arrowsmith's failure to follow instructions, pronouncing the entire expedition an utter failure. "What is still more annoying to me and disgraceful to my command," reported Slocum, "is the fact that instead of being marched back to camp in good order, a large portion of the command was allowed to disband beyond our line of pickets, and, as might have been anticipated from such a proceeding, this force sent to operate against the troops of the enemy was converted into a band of marauders, who plundered alike friend and foe."[26] Slocum was so angry that he sought and obtained permission from McClellan to initiate a court of inquiry into Col. Christian's handling of the operation, but the issue was eventually dropped. As a result, however, Slocum questioned Christian's ability to command and the regiment acquired a reputation as a poorly disciplined unit. Soon thereafter the 26th was transferred from Slocum's command to Gen. James S. Wadsworth's command defending Washington.[27]

The regiment remained in the vicinity of Alexandria for the rest of 1861 continuing its duty in defense of the nation's capitol. During this time the men were put to work on the fortifications, constructing a bombproof and strengthening the

The 26th New York formed outside Fort Lyon
(National Archives)

works at Fort Lyon, while also receiving training on the fort's artillery pieces. William E. Bowen, in Company E described his experience in a letter home: "I am working at carpenter work on fort building barracks for winter the government pays the carpenters one dollar per day so I get me thirty nine dollars a month now we are going to live in the fort this winter."[28]

The arrival of Christmas brought a welcome suspension of normal activity as the men celebrated the holiday with a feast of oysters and turkey, while "singing and music was the order of the day." A correspondent wrote to the *Clinton Courier* that "I should very much like to spend New Years in Clinton, but as I cannot I must be content with wishing it may be a happy New Year to all. I trust another New Years Day will see the war ended that we may all spend it at home."[29] When New Year's Day arrived, the Central New Yorkers, unused to the southern climate, marveled at the "very warm weather for January," much more like spring than winter. "Most of the Boys sat up to watch the in coming of the New Year," reported one soldier, "and the band played all night making sleep simply impossible." Col. Christian's wife hoisted the "glorious Stars and Stripes" over the fort followed by "an impressive and short speech" by the Chaplain, Methodist Rev. Dr. Daniel W. Bristol, following which the men celebrated New Year's Day with target shooting, ball playing, wrestling, and other diversions.[30]

By early February a feeling of impatience pervaded the camp. Z. W. Sanford wrote that "Time, immortal time rolls on, and still the inactivity of the 'Army of the Potomac.' Thousands now lie in the 'tented field' exposed to the inclemency of a cold wet winter, and also liable to contagious diseases so incident to a long continuance of camp life, which is far worse and more to be dreaded than trusting to fate and fortune on the battle field. We are ready, willing and anxious to fight, and would like to see an aggressive and Napoleonic campaign, which would infuse new enthusiasm in the army, and render a soldier's life less obnoxious.... If this wet weather continues, the sickness and mortality will be fearful."[31]

The longer the men remained in the crowded camp, disease continued to take its deadly toll. Men were dying from the poor living conditions, exacerbated by three weeks of very wet weather that created mud so thick that drills and training had to be suspended. Everyone was anxious to leave the unhealthy camps.[32] Their wishes came true with the onset of spring. Determined to take Richmond in one bold stroke, Gen. McClellan planned to lead the Army of the Potomac south through Chesapeake Bay by ship to Fortress Monroe on Virginia's York Peninsula, bypassing the main Confederate army and placing the Federals in position to march directly on the Confederate capital. At the same time, other Union forces were to move up the Shenandoah Valley to deny its rich farmlands to the rebels. Meanwhile, in an attempt to divert Union troops from the Richmond campaign, Southern leaders dispatched Gen. Thomas J. "Stonewall" Jackson to the Shenandoah Valley to dispute the Federal forces there in the hope that a victory would force the North to divert troops to that theater of operations. Jackson's success in the valley had the desired result. The War Department immediately ordered Federal troops sent to reinforce the Shenandoah Valley in response to a series of stunning rebel victories by Jackson's undermanned army.

Called from its winter quarters, the 26th New York was one of the units ordered to pursue Jackson's army. Originally leaving Fort Lyon on May 3, the regiment sailed aboard a steamer down the Potomac River some thirty miles to Aquia Creek. From there it marched overland some fifteen miles to Fredericksburg on May 10. Meanwhile Jackson began to advance north, hitting the Union forces at Front Royal on May 23, defeating a force of about 800 men under Col. John Kenly. With continued Confederate successes in the Valley, Union forces around Fredericksburg received orders to head back north again to meet the threat posed by Jackson's advance. The 26th quickly marched back to Aquia Creek on May 25, returning to Alexandria by steamer. On the following day the regiment crowded onto a train west to Manassas Junction. Two days later the men were issued new rations and forced marched along the Manassas Gap Railroad from Manassas Junction west towards Front Royal. Covering about 50 miles in three days, they arrived at Front Royal on June 1. They moved so quickly that by the third day of the march they outdistanced their supply lines, forcing them to exist on hardtack and coffee. On the third night the warm weather gave way to cold rain, obliging the men to sleep under wet blankets since their tents were miles behind among the supply wagons.[33]

Rain drenched the area for three days, swelling the creeks and rivers, destroying some of the bridges, and making movement difficult at best.

Nevertheless, the regiment captured several stragglers from Jackson's command. On June 3 orders arrived for two companies to escort prisoners to the army headquarters. William Bowen described the rebels as "a rough set of men dirty and ragged they wear gray uniforms." George Arrowsmith, who spoke with some of the Southern officers, found them to have a "dogged resolution to fight to the last" and commented that "their knowledge of the country and the mountain roads, and their superior advantages for obtaining and giving information of our movements" provided them with great advantages.[34]

On June 18 the regiment was ordered to move by rail back to Manassas Junction where it was to go into camp. During the early summer of 1862 it had traveled over 500 miles, with some estimates ranging as high as 1,000 miles, endured fatiguing marches and cold wet nights out in the open, but had not fired a shot against the enemy. Back in camp it spent the rest of June with a routine of daily drills and inspections. Once again, impatience appeared. Except for the brief skirmish at Pohick Church, the regiment had yet to "see the elephant." Like most who had yet to experience the horrors of war, the men were anxious to move south to end the rebellion once and for all.

SECOND BULL RUN

Following the defeat of McClellan's army on the Peninsula, Gen. Robert E. Lee led the Confederate Army of Northern Virginia north in a race to threaten the capital at Washington, D.C., before McClellan's army could arrive from the Peninsula to bolster its defenses. The other Federal force, the Army of Virginia under Gen. John Pope, included the 26th New York—along with the 94th New York, 88th Pennsylvania, and 90th Pennsylvania—as part of Brig. Gen. Zealous B. Tower's 2nd Brigade, 2nd Division, Third Corps, Army of Virginia. Its mission was to protect the capital by interposing itself between Lee's army and Washington until McClellan's troops arrived. Gen. Nathaniel Banks' Second Corps of Pope's army ran into Jackson's portion of Lee's army at the Battle of Cedar Mountain on August 9. As the fighting unfolded, Gen. James B. Ricketts' division, including Tower's brigade and the 26th New York, rushed forth as reinforcements.

The 26th arrived on the field as darkness was falling, taking up a position on the right of the Union line. The men quickly set up a camp in a grove of trees, but the night passed with little sleep since repeated outbursts of artillery fire kept them on edge. Charles McClenthen in Company G wrote that the Union artillery "opened on them with such a perfect shower of shot and shell that an ordinary thunderstorm would be but a 'tempest in a teapot' compared to it." It was, he thought, "a splendid sight and as we seemed to be perfectly safe we enjoyed it hugely."[35] The "splendid sight" turned sickening the following morning when daylight revealed the horrible carnage of mutilated and dismembered bodies.

Though they had still not seen the "elephant," they had now witnessed first hand what they might expect the first time they did.

Following Cedar Mountain, the "Second Oneida" marched to Rappahannock Station, then on to Culpepper, Brandy Station, and Warrenton as the two armies maneuvered for position. Tired and hungry from the constant marching, they frequently came under hostile artillery fire, while small units from the regiment occasionally fought skirmishes with rebel cavalry. Assigned as the last unit in the brigade's column, the men also suffered from constant clouds of thick dust kicked up by the marching feet of the hundreds of men in the regiments that preceded them. As they marched, some men broke ranks to forage for food and tobacco among the houses and barns along the route of march.[36]

During the long marches, with the attending stress of imminent combat, questions began to arise about Col. Christian's leadership qualities. Gen. Tower began to suspect that Christian was not up to the task, which was perhaps one reason he assigned the 26th the last position in the line of march. Within the regiment, some officers also began to have doubts. Many observers noticed favorably the personal leadership of Gen. James P. Ricketts. "Wherever the danger was greatest," Charles McClenthen wrote, "there he might be seen, glass in hand, keenly watching the movements of the enemy, and giving his orders with that coolness which only brave men exhibit."[37] But the same circumstances that animated Ricketts seemed to cloak the colonel. "Where is Christian?" became an ever more frequent question as the booming of artillery echoed across the ranks. "It was becoming apparent that the stress and strain of forced marches and battle were taking a toll on Christian's ability to command," wrote McClenthen.[38]

August 27 brought orders for a forced march to Thoroughfare Gap to oppose Confederate Gen. James Longstreet's forces that were trying to link up with Lee and Jackson. The rapid march in sweltering heat proved brutal. By the end of the day the men were "completely tired and worn out, disheartened and suffering from hunger, many could not, and others would not try to keep up; but would lie down and try to obtain a little rest in every corner of the fence and under every tree along the road." They spent the night, according to McClenthen, "supperless as usual," but by the time they arrived in position Longstreet had successfully traversed Thoroughfare Gap and was marching on Manassas Junction.[39]

Twelve days of almost continual marching without adequate rations or shelter brought the regiment to the old battlefield of Bull Run. Many of the men were now barefoot, without overcoats, tents, or blankets. To McClenthen they were like "automatons without life or spirit" who dropped to sleep where they halted and soon awoke to the command to fall in and move off. The "officers and men alike were ragged, dirty, and worn almost to skeletons from hunger and fatigue."[40]

The morning of August 30 found the regiment encamped with Tower's brigade on the rolling fields where the previous year the armies had clashed at

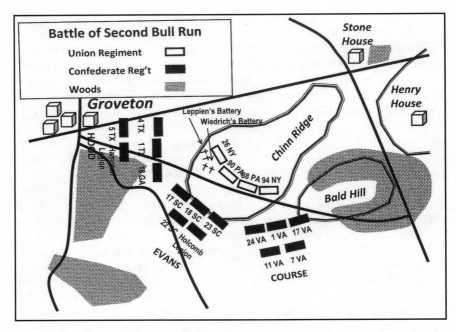

First Bull Run. Rousing their tired bodies early, the men downed a hasty break-fast before being ordered, along with Brig. Gen. Abram Duryée's brigade, to move to the center of the Federal line. Arriving in their new position, the men lay sweating upon the ground exposed to 100-degree temperatures for several hours.

As they lay there, about 4:00 PM Gen. Longstreet's rebel corps launched a crushing assault on the far left of the Union line held by only two brigades under Col. Nathaniel McLean and Col. Gouverneur K. Warren. Warren's men, the first to be hit, were quickly overwhelmed leaving McLean's Ohio brigade alone to face the waves of Confederates. McLean clung tenaciously to Chinn Ridge, throwing back two Confederate assaults before being forced back by a third assault, losing over a third of his men in the process. Costly though it was, McLean bought thirty minutes that Gen. Pope put to good use rushing reinforce-ments to his exposed flank.

The first units ordered forward were Tower's brigade and Col. Robert Stiles's brigade, also from Ricketts' division. The 26th fell into line and rushed off at the double quick, but without its colonel. As the regiment moved toward the sound of the firing, Col. Christian, who was apparently suffering from a serious cold and had complained of the heat during the day, complained again to the regimental surgeon, Dr. Walter B. Coventry, who helped Christian from his horse, laid him under a shady tree, and covered him with a blanket. As the men hastened past their prostrate leader, they caught their last glimpse of him until after the engage-ment. Lt. Col. Richard H. Richardson led the men forward to Chinn Ridge.[41]

Surgeon Walter Coventry
(Donald Wisnoski)

Lt. John Kingsbury
(Donald Wisnoski)

Arriving at the front at the double-quick about 4:30 PM, the 26th New York went into line on the left flank of Tower's brigade in support of McLean's brigade and Capt. George Leppien's 5th Maine Light Artillery battery to its front, both of which were threatened with being overrun. The two companies on the left of Richardson's command opened fire, but the rest of the regiment, being masked by the Union troops to its front, was forced to withhold fire.[42] What happened next was described by Adjutant William Bacon, a graduate of Hamilton College and the son of Judge William J. Bacon of Utica.

> We came up in beautiful style by the flank amidst a shower of shot and shell, and were ordered to a hill on the left of center, to support the 5th Maine Battery, which was being placed in position. The gunners had just unlimbered and loaded when the regiment in front broke, and came running towards the battery. Before the battery had time to fire on the rebels, they were within five rods of it. The gunners delivered one fire right in the face of the enemy, then turned with the horses and caissons, and ran straight into our ranks, while the broken regiments rushed upon us at the same time.[43]

Corp. John Williams of Company F recalled the same scene:

> Before we had time to look around us, the first thing we saw was one of the regiments on top of the hill coming to an about face, and tearing down the hill a little faster than the regulation allows for a double-

Adjutant William Bacon   Fife Major Sam Benedick
(Donald Wisnoski)   (Oneida County Historical Society)

quick, running right into our left wing and breaking it, and a battery ran
right into our right wing and broke that also.[44]

The rapid retreat of the 5th Maine's caissons and supporting infantry through
the partially formed ranks of the 26th threw the regiment into immediate confusion. Richardson, Bacon, and the other officers raced about trying to restore
order, but by the time the fugitives cleared the regiment, the pursuing
Confederates of Brig. Gen. Micah Jenkins' and Col. Eppa Hunton's brigades were
fast approaching their position, attacking Tower's remaining brigade from three
sides, seriously wounding Gen. Tower and decimating the brigade with deadly
enfilading fire. With Tower's wounding, Col. Christian became the senior officer
in the brigade, but in his absence an organized brigade defense was difficult.

Confederate fire ripped through the 26th's hastily reformed ranks, increasing
the confusion as men began to fall. One of the deadly balls smashed Charles
McClenthen's musket in his hands, but he quickly discarded it, picking up another from the ground. "I tell you," he later wrote home, "that was a hot place the
bullets and cannon and shell all mixed together."[45] One of the bullets cut into
Thomas Francis's leg, while another wounded John Hughes. "It seemed awful to
hear the roar of muskets and cannon and to hear the groans of wounded men,"
McClenthen wrote, "the man next to me on my right was shot dead. Sometimes
you had to walk on the dead."[46] Lt. John Kingsbury recalled that "the rebels
opened fire from two sides. They had us flanked with a cross fire of artillery."[47]
To McClenthen, it was "as heavy and galling fire as ever has been poured upon

any body of troops during the war; shot, shell, grape and canister with a heavy enfilading fire of musketry, it seemed that every arm and all the projectiles known to modern warfare had been let lose upon us at once."[48]

But worse was to come. Tower's brigade was being outflanked on the left and orders soon arrived for Richardson to face his men left and double quick to the support of the hard-pressed 94th New York on the brigade's left flank. Swept by fire from front and flank, the 26th suffered terribly. The color sergeant fell wounded, as did most of the color guard. Three times the colors fell, but each time someone stepped forward to pick them up. Gradually the line began to disintegrate under the weight of renewed Confederate attacks and the loss of nearly a third of its number. Down went the colors once again as the line began to break, men turning for the rear by one and twos. A confused melee broke out around the fallen colors. Into the swirling mass raced Corp. Paul McClusky of Clinton, who seized the banner from the ground, determined to rescue the regiment's honor.[49]

Adjutant Bacon looking over the scene, saw the colors move to the rear and immediately felt a sense of "mortification, shame, indignation, all commingled."[50] Turning his horse, he yelled out to the men, trying to rally them to stand firm. Lt. Col. Richardson, Captain Norman W. Palmer, and others were also conspicuous in their efforts to stop the retreat. At the base of the hill, near a line of trees, Capt. James Caryl of Company K brandished one of the regimental colors, imploring men to rally. Responding to their efforts, Corp. McClusky halted, waving the colors he had rescued to encourage others to rally. And rally they did, forming a new line at nearly a right angle to the brigade, facing to the left flank where Confederates continued to exploit their overlap of the Union position. "For a while we made a desperate stand, although flanked on the left, and subjected to a most severe and deadly fire, completely enfilading us," Adj. Bacon recalled.

> I was standing by cheering the men on as well as I knew how, when suddenly, amidst the peculiar whistle of the minie balls, I heard a quick "thug" and felt a sharp pain in my left leg, just above the ankle. Looking down, I saw that I was wounded how severely I could not tell. I tried to step on my left foot, but found the pain severe enough to prevent my bearing my full weight on that leg. Seeing that the regiment was now wholly disorganized, and my presence could be of no further avail, I walked backward from the field with my sword still drawn and my face to the enemy, until I was entirely out of range, when I turned about and moved slowly away.[51]

The regiment held its new position for some twenty to twenty-five minutes, running low on ammunition, until it received orders to retire with the survivors of Tower's brigade.[52] Major Gilbert Jennings recalled that the regiment held its new position until it was ordered to retire after losing about one third of its strength in killed and wounded. "We then retreated to the other side of the woods," he recalled, "reformed our regiment, and were advancing again when we were ordered by General McDowell to retreat to Centreville and encamp for the night."[53] The 26th had been engaged from about 4:30 PM until 6:00 PM when it was ordered to retreat. Lt. Col. Richardson later reported the regiment's loss at 118 killed and wounded, and 55 missing "who have not been accounted for since the action."[54] Many of the latter lay dead upon the field. A later accounting placed the loss at four officers and fifty enlisted men killed in action and another two officers and 87 men wounded, as well as 25 men missing.

Gen. John Pope, who commanded the Union forces at Second Bull Run, wrote in his official report that

> Tower's brigade "was pushed forward into action in support of Reynolds' division, and was led forward in person by General Tower with conspicuous skill and gallantry. The conduct of that brigade, in plain view of all the forces on our left, was especially distinguished, and drew forth hearty and enthusiastic cheers. The example of this brigade was of great service, and infused new spirit into all the troops who witnessed their intrepid conduct."[55]

Col. Christian reappeared about 7:00 PM, remaining with the regiment for about half an hour and, as described by McClenthen, "enjoined upon us to take good care of the colors (which did not seem to me in much danger)."[56] The colonel then left in search of the rest of the brigade which he now commanded. On the march back to Centreville, the officers and non-commissioned officers of the 26th held a council to discuss Colonel Christian's ability to command. Some officers expressed the belief that he was no longer effective, physically ruined, and, with his sudden recovery just as the battle was ending, a disgrace to the Regiment. A vote was taken to ask Gen. Ricketts to remove Christian from command, but when the ballots were counted the motion was voted down. Christian would continue in command.

ANTIETAM

With the defeat at Second Bull Run, the 26th New York retreated with the rest of the army toward Washington, D.C. Meanwhile, Gen. Lee moved his Confederate army northwestward, taking advantage of the Northern disorganization to capture the Federal garrison at Harper's Ferry and launch an invasion into western Maryland. Lee's plan was to continue into southern Pennsylvania, forcing the Union Army of the Potomac to come out of its entrenchments around Washington to do battle in the open field at a time and place of Lee's choosing. Fortunately for the North, however, a copy of Lee's secret orders for the campaign was apparently lost, ending up in a field where it was discovered by some Indiana infantrymen. Recognizing the importance of their find, the Hoosiers sent the document up through channels, giving Gen. George McClellan, by the end of the day, a complete picture of the plans and disposition of the rebel army. Once convinced of the authenticity of the document, McClellan ordered his army into motion to try and defeat Lee in detail before he could consolidate his forces.

The 26th New York left its camp on September 6, 1862, marching into Maryland where it reached Mechanicsville on September 11. At Cookesville it turned west, marching through Coopersville and Poplar Springs, crossing the Monocacy River, and arriving at Frederick on September 13. On the following day, orders arrived for Ricketts' division, including Christian's brigade, to march to South Mountain some eighteen miles away.[57] Turner's Gap at South Mountain offered one of the few major routes through the mountains that would allow McClellan to interpose his army between the scattered elements of Lee's command. Given its strategic importance, a force of Confederate infantry had been assigned to prevent Union troops from using it to move west. Inevitably, the two forces soon clashed.

As the men of the 26th New York neared South Mountain late in the day, the now-familiar rattle of musketry, punctuated by the heavier booming of artillery, reached their ears, informing them that the conflict had already begun. Rushed forward about 5:00 PM, the regiment received orders to relieve the 14th Brooklyn which had already been in action for about three hours. Lt. Colonel Richardson wrote in his after action report that the regiment quickly formed into line of battle on the right flank of the brigade and began advancing up the slope. They found the rebels of Col. Joseph Walker's South Carolina brigade in a strong defensive position, firing on them from a cornfield and brush atop the hill. Richardson led the men forward, advancing uphill toward a fence running along a tree line at the top of the hill. Soon he became aware of Confederate infantry in line behind a fence running through the cornfield. Richardson quickly shouted orders to his command, pouring a destructive volley into the rebels. Return fire revealed other rebel positions, with the two opposing forces settling down to an exchange of fire that lasted until nightfall finally brought it to an end.[58]

As the sun began to rise the next morning, skirmishers looked in vain for the Confederates who had quietly slipped away during the night. In a letter home, William Bowen wrote that the regiment found about 300 dead or wounded rebels lying about the ground.[59] Soon Richardson received orders to march, leading the regiment off along the dusty roads to Keedysville, Maryland, where it camped for the night, the men cleaning their arms and equipment while speculating over their evening campfires about where their next adventure would take them.

On September 16 the regiment received orders to march, heading off toward the small town of Sharpsburg, Maryland, located between a northward bend in the Potomac River on the west and Antietam Creek to the east. The men fell in around 3:00 PM for a relatively short eight-mile march that brought them across Antietam Creek. By 8:30 PM they were nearing Sharpsburg when they came under rebel artillery fire. As it was getting dark, the men were ordered into camp in what would soon become famous as the North Woods to wait for morning. Jittery pickets frequently interrupted their sleep with sporadic gunfire, but since it was obvious that battle would soon be joined it is problematic whether any of the men enjoyed a truly restful sleep.

The men were roused from their sleep at 4:00 AM on September 17. Formed into line of battle with the rest of the brigade, Col. Christian, leading the brigade, ordered them forward in the direction of the East Woods about a half mile away. The 26th New York advanced on the far left of Christian's brigade, which held the extreme left flank of Ricketts' division, which formed the extreme left of Gen. Joseph Hooker's First Corps. Thus, the 26th New York held the far left flank of the Union advance. As soon as the men emerged from the North Woods, Confederate artillery opened on the exposed lines. Christian ordered a halt, keeping the brigade in line but moving no closer to the enemy. Gen. Ricketts, commanding the division, noticed the delay in Christian's advance and sent a staff officer riding over to get the brigade moving. On the insistence of the staff officer, Christian ordered the brigade forward once again, riding behind the 26th New York which he maneuvered in a strange zigzag pattern, apparently in an attempt to avoid the artillery fire. All it accomplished was to expose the men to the rebel guns for a longer time. "First it was 'forward' then by the 'left flank' then 'forward,' then by the 'right flank,' 'forward,' left oblique,' etc.," complained one eyewitness, "until we thought they were making a show of us for the benefit of the Rebel artillery. Many of our men fell."[60]

Finally reaching what they thought would be the relative cover of the East Woods, the men found themselves in an artillery crossfire that continued to pound the regiment. Again Col. Christian faltered, allowing his brigade to come to a halt amid the shelling. A staff officer appeared with orders to push on, but Christian appeared confused. The officer ordered the troops forward, but as they advanced from the East Woods into an adjoining cornfield Christian suddenly muttered that he had enough of the shelling, jumped from his horse, and headed to the rear. Lt. William H. Halstead in Company C remembered that the entire regiment watched as the colonel went "ducking and dodging his head and go crouching along" to the rear.[61] Later it was reported that as he fled to the rear he shouted to the advancing troops that the battle was lost and the army was in full retreat. Whatever the exact circumstances, the troops would never forget or forgive Christian's actions that deadly September morning.[62] With little option, he tendered his resignation on September 19 and returned to Utica.

While the colonel moved in one direction, Lt. Col. Richardson led the 26th New York forward into the cornfield on the Samuel Mumma farm. Rebels from Col. Isaac Trimble's Georgia brigade appeared to the front, some 350 yards dis-

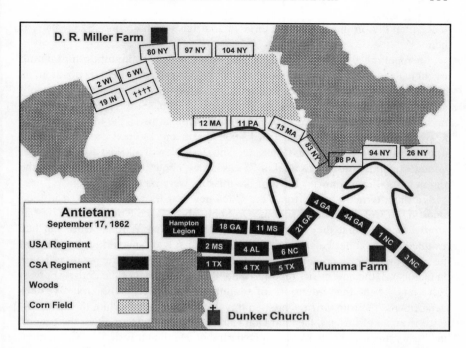

Antietam
September 17, 1862

USA Regiment

CSA Regiment

Woods

Corn Field

tant, when Richardson gave the order to open fire. The regiment poured a devastating fire into the enemy flank, each man then loading and shooting as quickly as they could while return fire zipped overhead, rustled through the corn, or struck flesh with a dull thud. Volley after volley swept across the deadly field until after about thirty rounds the order was passed to cease firing to conserve the rapidly diminishing ammunition. Meanwhile, Confederate reinforcements arrived in the form of the Georgia and North Carolina infantry of Gen. Roswell Ripley's brigade.[63]

Probably believing the Northerners to be faltering as their fire slackened, the Confederates advanced out over the open ground in at attempt to break the Union line. Seeing the enemy approach, Richardson again opened fire, with the two enemy forces trading volleys across the open farmlands. When one of the color bearers of the 26th fell, Charles Cleveland of Company C stepped forward, seized the fallen banner, and bore it forward until wounded three times. He would later receive the Medal of Honor for his heroism. Soon the rebel lines wavered, then began to retire, the survivors retreating behind a fence dividing the cornfield. "Our regiment fought for two hours and twenty minutes," recalled William Bowen, until "all our cartridges was all gone so we could not do anymore so we had to go off but we did kill them fast we could see them fall by dozens and so did our men. The men all around me were killed and wounded and there I was all alone sometime but that did not scare me so I came out all right it is a tough sight to see men lay on the ground for three or four days with no one to take care of them."[64]

In repelling the attack, the 26th had exhausted its ammunition, prompting urgent calls to the rear for resupply. Meanwhile, the regiment held its position, its ammunition exhausted, subjected to artillery and long-range musket fire it could not return. Soon, however, reinforcements arrived, replacing the 26th and allowing it to retire some distance to be resupplied. Antietam was the bloodiest single day of the Civil War with more than 12,000 Union and 13,000 Confederate casualties in killed, wounded, and missing. The 26th New York lost five killed, 41 wounded, and 29 missing, a total of 75 casualties, about one-third of the men the regiment took into action.[65] Most of the missing were never seen again.

In the aftermath of the fight, the Utica newspapers were restrained in their reporting of Col. Christian's actions. On September 22 the Utica *Daily Observer* simply reported that they had received a dispatch that William Christian had resigned and Colonel Peter Lyle of the 88th Pennsylvania would replace him, at the same time expressing confidence that Lyle would ably fill the position. Later, on October 2, the newspaper reported that "the late Colonel of the 26th went west yesterday with the intention of connecting himself with the Western Department."[66] From Utica, Christian traveled to Cincinnati, Ohio, to seek assistance from an old friend, General Don Carlos Buell, only to find that the general had been transferred to the Western Department. He then traveled to Washington, D.C., St Louis, Indianapolis, and Chicago offering his services at a reduced rank and without pay only to find that no one was interested. When the 26th was mustered out in May of 1863, Christian was in Harrisburg, Pennsylvania, offering his services, without charge, to the volunteer forces of that state. However, the governor of Pennsylvania turned him away with the explanation that only residents of the state could command its forces. The Utica *Morning Herald* admitted that its favorite son "was anxious to get an opportunity to repel by acts the imputations cast on his courage." Finally, a few weeks later Christian tried to obtain a commission in the U.S. Colored troops but was again rejected. He eventually returned to Utica to live out his life in personal disgrace. Later, the public and his wartime comrades seemed to have forgiven him and he participated in many veterans' functions. He never overcame the personal anguish and humiliation resulting from his actions at Second Bull Run and Antietam. Gradually, he began to slip into insanity, walking the streets in a wide-eyed stupor or breaking into maniacal laughter. Unable to return to his job as a civil engineer to provide for his family, in 1886, at the age of fifty-one, he was committed to the state insane asylum in Utica and died the very next year as a helpless invalid.[67]

Following Antietam, the 26th New York went into what the officers and men thought would be winter quarters. William Bowen wrote home that "The army is lying still now around here. The rebels lay on the other side of the river and our men on this side. Neither one seems to want to try their fighting qualities."[68]

FREDERICKSBURG

The weather in Maryland was mild throughout October, almost like an Upstate New York Indian summer with warm days and cold nights. November brought the first snow storm, and thereafter snow and rain turned the roads into oceans of mud that made the movement of supply wagons difficult at best. Nevertheless, the new Union commanding general, Ambrose P. Burnside, was busy preparing a campaign to take Richmond. His plan was to move his army to the northern bank of the Rappahannock River across from the city of Fredericksburg, construct pontoon bridges across the water, then march his men south of the river to attack Lee's Southern army. Unfortunately for his plan, the pontoons were late arriving, thus providing Lee with an opportunity to move his army into a commanding position on the heights above Fredericksburg.

On December 9, Burnside issued orders to the Army of the Potomac requiring all units to be ready to move on the morning of December 11. Troops were to be issued three days cooked rations, forty rounds of ammunition in cartridge boxes, and twenty rounds in their pockets. In addition, ammunition wagons and artillery batteries would be supplied with three days' forage. The army was to cross the Rappahannock River at Fredericksburg on five pontoon bridges built by the engineers. Burnside hoped to complete the crossing on Thursday, December 11, at daybreak.

In the wake of Col. Christian's resignation, Lt. Col. Richardson was promoted to colonel, Major Jennings moved up to major, and Capt. Ezra Wetmore became the new major. The 26th New York, led by Lt. Col. Gilbert S. Jennings in the absence of Col. Richardson who was at home on sick leave, broke camp at

Major Ezra Wetmore
(USAMHI)

Lt. Hugh Lenard
(Donald Wisnoski)

5:00 AM on December 11, marching overland in the cold winter morning toward the Rappahannock as part of Lyle's 2nd Brigade, in Brig. Gen. John Gibbon's 2nd Division, of Maj. Gen. John Reynolds' First Corps, part of the Left Grand Division under Maj. Gen. William B. Franklin. The men arrived on the riverbank about one and one-half miles below Fredericksburg on schedule at 7:30 AM only to find that the two pontoon bridges for their crossing were not yet completed. The Confederates attempted to delay construction with heavy rifle and artillery fire directed against the engineers building the bridge; but, rebel fire was soon silenced by Union artillery and sharpshooters. Thereafter rebels offered only a feeble effort to prevent completion of the bridges, the first of which was finished about 9:00 AM and the second about 11:00 AM. Meanwhile, the two other Grand Divisions of the army crossed the river further north and advanced directly on Fredericksburg.

All afternoon the New Yorkers remained in formation awaiting the word to advance across the river to meet the enemy. Finally, at 4:00 PM, Gen. Charles Devens' brigade, consisting of men from New York, Massachusetts, and Rhode Island, received orders to cross. The 26th New York and 97th New York were ordered to provide cover for the troops as they crossed. It was said that the men crossed with great enthusiasm and very little opposition. By 1:00 PM the whole of the Left Grand Division was over. Gen. Franklin reported that they crossed in excellent order without the slightest confusion or delay. By 4:00 PM all units were across and in position, the 26th New York being placed in line to hold the Bowling Green Road. Lt. Col. Jennings sent out pickets, then the men settled in for the night. William Bowen reported laying on the wet cold ground, pulling his blanket over his head, and trying to get what sleep he could, awaiting the dawn.[69]

About 7:00 AM on the next day the regiment received orders to form into line of battle. In a continuing winter fog, the 26th advanced. Brigaded with it were the 12th Massachusetts, 90th Pennsylvania, and 136th Pennsylvania. The 12th Massachusetts was on the right of the 26th, with the 90th Pennsylvania on their left and the 136th Pennsylvania on the extreme left of the brigade. The regiments quickly advanced across the Bowling Green Road and into a cornfield between the Union line and a wooded area to its front. As they entered the field they were ordered to lie down and await further orders. They lay in this field all morning under a brisk fire of shot and shell from all sides. As they lay there awaiting further orders the 26th lost one man killed and six wounded, including Lt. Col. Jennings who suffered a broken leg when struck by a bullet. Major Wetmore assumed command. The 90th Pennsylvania, next to them in the field, suffered even more casualties with the loss of sixteen men including two orderlies who had their horses shot out from under them. Minutes turned into hours as the 26th remained in position in the field awaiting orders. "The warmth of our bodies drew the frost from the newly plowed ground," recalled Major Ezra Wetmore, "and the soil stuck to our clothes."[70]

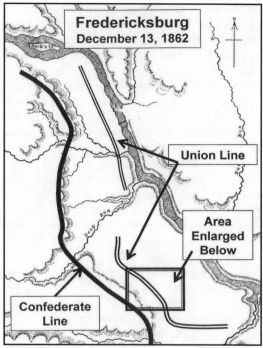

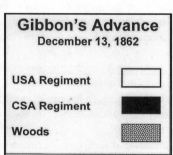

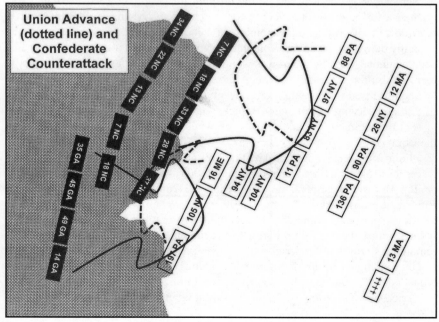

Finally, in the early afternoon the fog began to lift and at 1:00 PM orders arrived for 26th to advance. As the fog lifted the rebels could now see the entire Union force arrayed in battle order and they increased their fire. A massive artillery duel erupted until Union guns silenced the rebel artillery. Col. Lyle's brigade advanced out of the cornfield into a withering fire within fifty yards of the wood where Col. James Lane's North Carolinians held a strong defensive position. The 26th New York and 90th Pennsylvania remained in this exposed position for about a half-hour, returning fire as best they could until they had expended all of their ammunition. At this point, Col. Adrian Root's 1st Brigade was ordered to relieve the 26th, passing through the regiment's lines as it advanced. The 26th then received orders to pull back to a ditch about 100 yards to the rear where the men went about collecting what ammunition they could find from the cartridge boxes of their fallen comrades. But, before they could collect any great amount of ammunition they received orders to face about again, fix bayonets, and, along with the 96th Pennsylvania, charge the rebels in the woods.[71]

Quickly ordering his men to fix bayonets and dress their lines, Major Wetmore began the advance only to have troops retreating from the front come running through his lines, much as they had done at Second Bull Run. As the regiment advanced, rebel fire took a particularly heavy toll on the color guard. One of those caught in the maelstrom of hostile fire was 24-year-old Corp. Martin Schubert, a native of Germany who served in Company E. Wounded at Antietam on September 17, he was sent to the hospital for treatment, recovered, and was granted a furlough to return home for further recovery. Instead, he insisted on returning to the regiment. Rejoining at Brooks Station on December 10, he valiantly defended the colors, voluntarily carrying them after the color bearer had been wounded, until Schubert was wounded again in the left side, a ball he would carry in him for the rest of his life. Although he could no longer carry the colors, he again refused to leave the field. Twenty-year-old Pvt. Joseph Keene, a native of England serving in Company B, picked up the fallen banner, rushing forward to lead the regiment's charge. Both men would receive the Medal of Honor for their bravery.[72]

Following the action that day, the 26th remained in position until Monday, December 15, when orders arrived about 10:00 PM to re-cross the Rappahannock, ending Burnside's brief campaign. When the 26th New York mustered in at Elmira it consisted of about 1,000 men. When it went into battle at Fredericksburg only some 280 remained. Of that number, only 110 made it safely back across the pontoon bridges. The regiment had lost about 61 percent of its remaining strength at Fredericksburg, leaving it with only about 10 percent of its original strength. Its Fredericksburg casualties included 51 killed or mortally wounded, 108 wounded who recovered, and 11 missing. Among those who fell at Fredericksburg was its twenty-year-old adjutant, William Kirkland Bacon.

Wounded at Second Bull Run, he was wounded again in the thigh at Fredericksburg. The regimental surgeon amputated his leg, but he succumbed nonetheless a few days later.[73]

The Utica papers printed extensive casualty lists for the local regiments, with the 26th listing 29 men killed and 121 wounded. On December 20 the *Utica Morning Herald* printed a letter dated December 13 from Chaplain Bristol to his family:

> Our Regiment has covered itself with honor. Every man has fought like a veteran. Nearly all our officers are wounded; but I have heard of none as yet have been killed. I am surrounded with suffering men. The scene is terrible. ... I have visited such of our men as I could find.
>
> Two great battles have really been fought today, and at the same time—one in the rear of Fredericksburg—the other to the left or below, so that our line of battle could not have been less than five miles in length. I stood upon an eminence which overlooked nearly the whole line. It was a fearful but grand sight. I never wish to look upon the like again. But I cannot describe the scene now. We are surrounded by hundreds of wounded men who are suffering, many of them with intense pain. They have paid a high price for the integrity of our government. Our surgeons are doing everything that can be done for the sufferers. Their officers are with great tenderness and cheerfulness. It is now past midnight and I am sitting on the ground by campfire writing by its uncertain light. I have given my blankets and overcoat to keep the sufferers warm and am keeping watch and ward with the sufferers.[74]

A few days later another anonymous letter writer asserted informed readers that the "noble 26th did its duty. It stood like a wall of iron under the most murderous fire that ever fell upon brave men."[75] As the news of the casualties sunk in, and word of Burnside's retreat back across the Rappahannock arrived, many began to reflect the criticism of the Union command leveled in the *Clinton Courier*. Burnside, the newspaper opined, was no different than his predecessors. "Disguise it as we may," the *Courier* reported, "there is no use of denying the fact that in the recent battles at Fredericksburg we have been badly beaten. We confess that we can see no great strategy to it. But the people demand action, and that repeated vigorous and deadly blows be aimed at the Heart of the rebellion."[76]

FROM THE "MUD MARCH" TO THE MUSTER OUT

Following the Battle of Fredericksburg, Burnside attempted to turn his defeat into victory by marching his army west along the Rappahannock with the idea of crossing upstream to outflank the strong Confederate position at Fredericksburg.

It appeared to be a good plan when the men marched out of camp on a bright, clear January day with flags flying and bands playing. Spirits were quickly dampened after dark when it began to rain, continuing on through the night. The men tried to warm themselves around smoky fires made with wet wood. By morning they awoke to more rain that had turned the roads into a miserable mess of mud. Francis Carran of the 121st New York Volunteers described the situation in a letter to his mother in Cedar Lake: "Many a shivering frame crawled out from beneath their wet blankets and frail cloth tents the next morning but that same moistness and dreariness still existed all around."[77] Horses, wagons, artillery, and men all became stuck in a sea of deep sticky mud.

Burnside stubbornly ordered the army to continue its struggles through the mud, but by the end of the second day he realized the hopelessness of it all and reluctantly called the operation off. The 26th New York turned about, retracing its path through mile after mile of exhausting mud. Casualties were few, but morale plummeted. Carran wrote to his mother that "It has been something over a week since I have written a letter home and during that period has transpired the winter campaign No. 2. Although followed by defeat, yet it is freighted with no important result to the Union army. There is a good reason for this failure. And it was fittingly explained by the rebels when they exhibited from across the river a large door upon which was the inscription "Burnside Stuck in the Mud."[78]

The 26th New York slowly returned to its camp near Belle Plain where it spent considerable time cleaning the mud from its uniforms, guns, and equipment. Following this second fiasco, Maj. Gen. Joseph Hooker replaced Burnside as commander of the Army of the Potomac, while Gens. Franklin and Sumner were also replaced. The men of the 26th spent the next several weeks counting the days until their enlistments expired in May. On March 14, William Bowen wrote home that "There is some talk of taking our regiment to our state to give us our discharge. Well if I live I shall be home on the first of May and I shall be allright if I can find a place to work but I think it will be too late to find a place for this summer if you hear of any place let me know so I may know if there is any sight for me."[79] On April 3, Bowen wrote that "we expect to move in a few days towards Washington and then for home we have only twenty three days more to serve in the service and then I expect to come home to see how it looks."[80]

As the men of the 26th New York awaited their discharge, other regiments began leaving for home with the expiration of their service. Eventually their time came. Boarding a train for home, on May 11 they arrived back in Elmira where their arduous adventure had begun two years previously. From there they continued on by train to Canandaigua, then east to Utica at the same time the 14th New York was heading west from Albany for the same destination. On May 20, within minutes of each other, survivors of the two regiments arrived at Bagg's Square Station. Thousands of friends and family were on hand to welcome them home.

Before the soldiers could be released to the crowd ceremonies had to be conducted, with speeches delivered by local politicians and by the colonels of each regiment. A parade then formed on lower Genesee Street headed by the Utica Cavalry Company, the 45th Militia Regiment, various fraternal orders, and the Utica Fire Department. The 26th and 14th Regiments proudly followed, marching up Genesee Street to rousing cheers and applause. Adjutant Bacon's riderless horse led the 26th along with the torn and tattered regimental colors. Decorated with arches constructed of evergreens, Genesee Street was lined with various choirs singing "Home Sweet Home," "Hail Columbia," and the "Star Spangled Banner." The parade ended at Chancellor Square where local ladies had set up tables laden with all the homemade foods the men had missed so much during the last two years.[81]

Before they could be mustered out the men would have to wait several days until all the proper military paperwork could be completed. In the meantime, the 26th was quartered at the court house with its meals served at the nearby armory. On May 28th the regiment was finally mustered out, company by company.[82] The men were free to return to their homes to try to pick up their lives where they left off. Some had had enough of fighting, while others, anxious to continue the fight, would reenlist with other regiments. Regardless, all were welcomed home as heroes to be remembered with holiday parades, statutes on the village green, a cannon in the park, or carrying on their spirit through the Grand Army of the Republic, their new veterans organization. They had become "the greatest generation" of the nineteenth century.

---

[1]*Clinton Courier,* April 18, 1861, quote from April 25, 1861.

[2]*Clinton Courier,* April 25, 1861, quote from April 28, 1861.

[3]*Observer Dispatch*, October 22, 2000.

[4]Frederick Phisterer, *New York in the War of the Rebellion* (Albany: J. B. Lyon Company, 1912, 3rd edition); *The Union Army: a History of Military Affairs in the Loyal States, 1861-65—Records of the Regiments in the Union Army—Cyclopedia of Battles—Memoirs of Commanders and Soldiers* (Madison, WI: Federal Pub. Co., 1908), Vol. II.

[5]*Fourth Annual Report of the Bureau of Military Statistics* (Albany: Bureau of Military Statistics, 1865).

[6]*Utica Daily Observer*, April 27, 1861.

[7]*Utica Daily Observer*, April 27, 1861.

[8]*Utica Daily Observer*, May 4, 1861.

[9]*Utica Daily Observer*, May 11, 1861, May 23, 1861; Clay W. Holmes, *The Elmira Prison Camp: A History of the Military Prison at Elmira, New York* (New York: G. P. Putnam and Sons, 1912).

[10]*Utica Observer*, May 23, 1861.

[11]*Utica Observer*, May 11, 1861.

[12]*Clinton Courier*, June 13, 1861.

[13]*Clinton Courier*, December 10, 1861.

[14]*Utica Observer*, May 14, 1861.

[15]*Utica Daily Observer*, June, 1861, quoted in *Oniota*, November 1997, Vol. XXXI; John S. Applegate, *Reminiscences and Letters of George Arrowsmith of New Jersey Late Lieutenant-Colonel of the One Hundred and Fifty-Seventh Regiment New York State Volunteers* (Red Bank, NJ: J. H. Cook, 1893), 36.

[16]*Utica Morning Herald*, June 22, 1861.

[17]Applegate, *Reminiscences and Letters of George Arrowsmith*, 45.

[18]Paul Taylor, *Glory Was Not Their Companion: The Twenty-Sixth New York Volunteer Infantry in the Civil War* (Jefferson, NC: McFarland & Company, Inc., 2005), 12.

[19]*Utica Daily Observer*, August 12, 1861; Howard Thomas, *Boys in Blue from the Adirondack Foothills* (Prospect, NY: Prospect Books, 1960), 32-33; Taylor, *Glory Was Not Their Companion*, 22-23; *The Union Army*, Vol. II.

[20]*Third Annual Report of the Bureau of Military Statistics* (Albany: Bureau of Military Statistics, 1864).

[21]*The War of the Rebellion: a Compilation of the Official Records of the Union and Confederate Armies* (Washington, DC: U.S. Government Printing Office, 1880-1901), Series I, Volume 2, 751. Hereafter cited as *O.R.*

[22]Thomas, *Boys in Blue*, 27.

[23]Applegate, *Reminiscences and Letters of George Arrowsmith*, 54.

[24]Applegate, *Reminiscences and Letters of George Arrowsmith*, 59.

[25]Applegate, *Reminiscences and Letters of George Arrowsmith*, 102.

[26]*O.R.*, I, IV, 236.

[27]*O.R.*, IV, 236.

[28]*Clinton Courier*, January 2, 1862; William Bowen letter to parents, December 6, 1861.

[29]*Clinton Courier*, January 2, 1862.

[30]*Clinton Courier*, January 9, 1862.

[31]*Clinton Courier*, February 6, 1862.

[32]Applegate, *Reminiscences and Letters of George Arrowsmith*, 124.

[33]Records of Movements and Activities of Volunteer Union Organizations, Record Groups 94 and 407, Roll 117, 26th NYSV.

[34]*O.R.*, I, XII, Pt. III, 328; Bowen letter to parents June 14, 1862; Applegate, *Reminiscences and Letters of George Arrowsmith*, 139.

[35]Charles S. McClenthen, *Narrative of the Fall & Winter Campaign, by a Private Soldier of the 2nd Div., 1st Army Corps, Containing a Detailed Description of the "Battle of Fredericksburg," at the Portion of the Line Where the 2nd Div. Were Engaged, with Accurate Statements of the Loss in Killed, Wounded and Missing, in Each Regiment* (Syracuse: Masters & Lee, 1863); Taylor, *Glory Was Not Their Companion*, 53.

[36]McClenthen, *Narrative of the Fall & Winter Campaign*, 10.

[37]McClenthen, *Narrative of the Fall & Winter Campaign*, 7.

[38]McClenthen, *Narrative of the Fall & Winter Campaign*, 7.

[39]McClenthen, *Narrative of the Fall & Winter Campaign*, 11, 14.

[40]McClenthen, *Narrative of the Fall & Winter Campaign,* 14.

[41]Taylor, *Glory Was Not Their Companion,* 62-63.

[42]*O.R.,* Series I, Vol. XII, Part II, 389.

[43]William Johnson Bacon, *Memorial of William Kirkland Bacon, late Adjutant of the Twenty-sixth Regiment of New York State Volunteers, by His Father* (Utica: Roberts, 1863).

[44]Taylor, *Glory Was Not Their Companion,* 65.

[45]McClenthen letter, September 6, 1862.

[46]McClenthen letter, September 6, 1862.

[47]Thomas, *Boys in Blue,* 81.

[48]Taylor, *Glory Was Not Their Companion,* 64.

[49]*Clinton Courier,* September 18, 1862; *O.R.,* Series I, Vol. XII, Part II, 389; Taylor, *Glory Was Not Their Companion,* 65.

[50]Bacon, *Memorial.*

[51]Bacon, *Memorial.*

[52]Richardson; *O.R.,* I, XII, Part II, Reports, 389.

[53]*O.R.,* I, XII, Part II, Reports, 390; Thomas, *Boys in Blue,* 81.

[54]*O.R.,* I, XII, Part II, Reports, 390.

[55]Taylor, *Glory Was Not Their Companion,* 67.

[56]McClenthen, *A Sketch of the Campaign in Virginia and Maryland from Cedar Mountain to Antietam* (Syracuse: Masters and Lee, 1862), 20; McClenthen letter, September 4, 1862.

[57]Taylor, *Glory Was Not Their Companion,* 75.

[58]*O.R.,* Series I, Volume 12, 263-264.

[59]Letter, William Bowen letter to parents, September 30, 1862.

[60]David V. Finnell, "The Sad Case of Colonel William Henry Christian, 26th New York Volunteer Infantry," *Civil War,* Vol. 12 (March 1988), 64; Taylor, *Glory Was Not Their Companion,* 80-81.

[61]W. H. Halstead letter, March 9, 1893, Antietam National Battlefield Park library.

[62]Finnell, "The Sad Case of Colonel William Henry Christian," 64; Taylor, *Glory Was Not Their Companion,* 80-81.

[63]Taylor, *Glory Was Not Their Companion,* 81.

[64]Taylor, *Glory Was Not Their Companion,* 81; William Bowen letter, September 30, 1862.

[65]*O.R.,* I, 12, 263.

[66]Utica *Daily Observer,* September 22 and October 2, 1862.

[67]William Härrer, *With Drum and Gun in '61, A Narrative of the Adventures of William Härrer of the Fourteenth New York State Volunteers in the War for the Union from 1861 to 1863* (Greenville, PA: Beaver Print Co., 1908); Finnell, "The Man Who 'Walked Spanish'," 60-65; Thomas, *Boys in Blue.*

[68]Bowen, letter, October 5, 1862.

[69]Taylor, *Glory Was Not Their Companion,* 94-95.

[70]Taylor, *Glory Was Not Their Companion,* 95, 97-98.

[71]Taylor, *Glory Was Not Their Companion,* 98-99.

[72]*The Story of American Heroism: Thrilling Narratives of Personal Adventures*

During the Great Civil War as Told by the Medal Winners and Roll of Honor Men (Springfield, OH: J. W. Jones, 1897), 208; Samuel Scoville, *Brave Deeds of Union Soldiers* (Philadelphia: G. W. Jacobs & Company, 1915), 365-66; Taylor, *Glory Was Not Their Companion*, 99; Thomas, *Boys in Blue*, 111.

[73]Taylor, *Glory Was Not Their Companion*, 101-02.

[74]*Utica Morning Herald*, December 20, 1862.

[75]*Utica Morning Herald*, December 26, 1862.

[76]*Clinton Courier*, December 18, 1862.

[77]Letter, Francis Caran to mother, January 29, 1863.

[78]Letter, Francis Caran to mother, January 29, 1863.

[79]Letter, William Bowen, March 14, 1863.

[80]Letter, William Bowen, April 3, 1863.

[81]Thomas, *Boys in Blue*, 140-41.

[82]*Clinton Courier*, May 28, 1863; *Utica Daily Observer*, May 21, 1863.

CHAPTER 6

"YOU STAND ALONE ... FIGHT LIKE HELL!"
THE 97TH NEW YORK AT GETTYSBURG

by

Cheryl A. Pula & Dennis Kininger

The Third Oneida County Regiment, known officially as the 97th New York State Volunteer Infantry, was raised from among citizens of Oneida, Herkimer and Lewis Counties, the majority of men from the northern towns and villages, though it did count among its number one company from the city of Utica. In July 1861, shortly after the Battle of Bull Run, President Abraham Lincoln called for volunteers for the Union cause, asking that New York respond with its fair share. New York's quota was 25,000 men, each to serve three years or for the duration of the war. A prominent 49-year-old, two-hundred-pound produce dealer from Boonville named Charles Wheelock was tapped on September 23, 1861, by Governor Edwin D. Morgan to raise a regiment from the Mohawk Valley.[1]

At the time, Boonville was the gateway to the Adirondack Mountains, the most populous village between Utica and Watertown. It was also the terminus of the Black River and Utica Railroad. The Black River Canal meandered through the town, used to transport lumber from the North Country and dairy products from Lewis County to places like Rome.[2] With the call for more volunteers for the war effort, Boonville became the recruiting and training center for a regiment composed primarily of men from the foothills of the Adirondack Mountains.[3]

Wheelock concentrated his recruitment drive in Oneida and Herkimer Counties, under the leadership of John Spofford of Dolgeville (then known as Brockett's Bridge) and J. P. Leslie of Little Falls. To encourage recruitment, Wheelock was empowered to offer prospective soldiers a bounty of two hundred dollars and land.[4] Enlistment of men began in September 1861, only five months after the war began.[5] They were to receive $13 a month in pay, plus a clothing allowance of $3.75.[6]

Wheelock chose a converted canal warehouse belonging to Peter Post as a site for a camp where the new regiment would organize. The location, called Camp Rathbone, was located in Boonville. While it did not yet have a designat-

Col. Charles Wheelock
(Boys in Blue)

Lt. Col. John Spofford
(Boys in Blue)

ed number, the new regiment did acquire two nicknames. One was the "Boonville Regiment," in honor of the area where it was raised. The other nickname was the "Conkling Rifles," after Roscoe Conkling, a prominent Republican Congressman and lawyer from the Utica area. It had also been suggested that it be called the "Black River Riflemen," but it was Conkling Rifles that stuck. When informed of the regiment's official nickname, Conkling wrote home from Washington, saying,

> The Colors you carry will never be disgraced; they will be borne forward by men, many of whom I have long known and respected as neighbors and friends, and though the regiment ... would have been an object of interest and pride with me, I shall now watch its career with double solicitude, its advancement with double pleasure.[7]

The residents of the area were very supportive of a new regiment. The region of the Mohawk Valley and the Adirondacks had played a major role in the Revolutionary War, and that conflict was not so very long in the past. There was still quite a great deal of patriotic zeal about the region, and this helped to aid in recruiting soldiers for what was then being called the Third Oneida County Regiment. Recruiting was not easy, as several other regiments were also being raised in the area, so the Third Oneida was in competition with recruiters from what would later become the 14th New York Volunteer Infantry (The First Oneida) and the 26th New York State Volunteer Infantry (The Second Oneida), as well as the 34th New York Volunteers, which was being raised in neighboring Herkimer County.[8]

By the beginning of September, the ranks included 700 men. Company A was comprised mostly of Boonville boys, under the command of Captain Samuel Ferguson, a canal man. Company B from Lewis County was led by Captain A. Dayan Parsons. Company C from Boonville was commanded by Captain Stephen Manchester and Lieutenant Louis H. Rowan, both from Boonville. Companies D and F were from Salisbury in Herkimer County, and were under the command of Captains Stephen Hutchinson and Rouse Egelston. Company I from Little Falls was commanded by Captain James Leslie. Company E from Prospect was under the leadership of Richard Jones, a local carriage maker. This particular company became known as the Welsh Company, since many of its members were Welsh immigrants or men of Welsh descent from Remsen, Trenton, Prospect and the Town of Russia. Company G from Herkimer County was led by Captain William Smith. Company H from Utica was also a truly ethnic organization, made up of German speaking immigrants. Most of those men hailed from Lowville, Boonville, Croghan, White Lake, Utica and Hawkinsville. The company was led by Captain Anthony Brendle of Utica. One of the Lieutenants was Louis Dallarmi, a native of Baden, Germany, who had served in the army of that country for sixteen years.[9] Company K from Rome was raised and led by Charles Northrup, who had worked at the Oneida Central Bank.[10] By the time the ranks were filled, the Third Oneida boasted men from 106 separate villages, towns, cities and hamlets.[11] One of its officers, Isaac Hall, wrote,

> The men … were enlisted principally from the farmers, mechanics and woodsmen of the State, and were of a rugged and hardy physique. Many … were familiar with the use of the rifle and accustomed to daily toil, and especially the labor in the open air which gives solidity to bone and muscle—an excellent preparation for soldier life. Some … had been hunters of wild game … in the forests of the Adirondacks, and many … were skilled in the use of various mechanical tools.[12]

Though the regiment trained in Boonville, the men complained about a lack of some of the essentials and necessities of army life. They were especially upset by the lack of suitable uniforms. Clothing wasn't the only thing they lacked. They also needed blankets. Their rescue came through the ladies of the region, who provided them with quilts, towels, pillows, socks, bandages and other items they required. Probably what they appreciated most arrived on Thanksgiving, when they received turkey and all the attendant fixings, such as cheese and apple pie.[13]

The regiment was officially formed on October 16, 1861. Its colors were provided to the 97th by the ladies of Boonville.[14] A few days before Christmas, December 19, 1861, they held a four day Ladies' Fair which raised over $230 to procure the flags.[15] The regiment formally received its colors in a ceremony held at the Hulbert Hotel in Boonville on December 23.[16] As part of the flag ceremony, many dignitaries were present, including Col. Wheelock and the Honorable

Band of the 97th New York
(Boys in Blue)

Richard Hulbert who graciously accepted the generous gift from the women of Boonville and made the main speech that day saying, "A more fitting testimonial could not have been selected by them. It is a most beautifully wrought Banner—the flag of our country—emblem of Liberty, under which our fathers fought and won the Glorious Heritage of Freedom and bequeathed it to us."[17]

Wheelock accepted the new battle flag with remarks full of evident emotion and conviction, "Ladies, I now thank you for your kind and generous efforts on behalf of our brave boys who leave all for their country, and to sustain the honor of those stars and stripes. And when we think of this precious gift it will make our hearts beat high and our arms strong to strike."[18]

Normally, a regiment would go through training near Washington, D.C., but because the war was pretty static in the east at the time, the men were allowed to train in Boonville. The regiment was beset with problems before it even left for active service. Since the soldiers were packed into tight quarters, an epidemic of measles killed three men and caused sixty others to become sick. Other diseases, such as typhoid, diphtheria and scarlet fever also flew through the ranks. The good people of Forestport, Boonville, Alder Creek and the surrounding area went to the aid of the troops, caring for the ill soldiers and supplying medicine.[19] There were sixty reported cases of measles resulting in three deaths. A nineteen-year old private from Company E, John Stowe, became the first casualty of the disease. On January 11, the regiment marched solemnly through the streets of Boonville to the depot with the colors draped in mourning and the fife and drums muffled as Stowe was taken to his final resting place in North Gage.[20]

It was not until February 18, 1862 that the newly designated 97th New York State Volunteer Infantry was formally entered into Federal service. The regiment was commanded by Charles Wheelock, a produce dealer who was now the colonel. His second-in-command was Lieutenant Colonel John Spofford and Charles Northrup became the major. The regimental adjutant was Charles Buck. John Pembrook Spofford was born on April 10, 1818, in Brockett's Bridge. Before his military service, he worked as a merchant, manufacturer and commercial agent.[21]

The 97th departed for Albany amid cheering crowds, in spite of the fact that prior to their leaving, they had gone on a final tear and broken into a local liquor store, bowling alley and billiard parlor, inflicting over $1,500 worth of damage.[22] Harvey Willard, the editor of the *Black River Herald*, would comment, "With these exceptions their deportment has been uniformly soldier-like and exemplary. Rarely have so many soldiers been quartered so long in one locality, and committed so few excesses. The origin of this wanton exhibition of lawlessness we have been wholly unable to ascertain."[23]

The 97th New York, all 918 men, paraded up the main street of Boonville at 8:00 AM, on March 12. They stopped before Hulbert's Hotel, where Hulbert made a speech and Lt. Col. Spofford was presented with an "elegant sword."[24] The scene of their parting was also duly recorded by Harvey Willard,

> The scene … became exceedingly interesting and touching. There was a simultaneous rush of parents, sisters, brothers, sweethearts, for the ranks as they slowly moved toward the waiting train. Many and hearty were the hand-shakings, the adieus, the God-bless-yous.… Many were the cheeks of brave men and loving women suffused with tears.… The … train … at length moved off, when cheer upon cheer arose for the gallant Colonel and his men until they disappeared in the distance.[25]

The 97th traveled to New York by train, passing through Utica, Little Falls and Albany. In the state capital, the men were visited by a paymaster and paid for the first time. Col. Wheelock had graciously loaned the new regiment thousands of dollars of his own money to keep the families of his men from want and some of his officers had helped as well. Once in New York, they were sent to Park Barracks where they received their weapons, .577 caliber Enfield rifles.[26] They did not stay in New York long, but departed on the same evening on a steamboat bound for Philadelphia, then Washington, D.C. The day after arriving in Washington, they arrived at Camp Corcoran outside of the city, across the Potomac River in Arlington, Virginia. The 97th was assigned to the Military District of Washington, along with several other regiments, including one incongruously called the 12th Virginia. While it would seem odd to have a regiment of

Virginians in the Federal army, the troops were from several counties in western Virginia that were loyal to the Union and chose to fight for the Federal cause.[27]

The first duty of the men of the 97th was to garrison Fort Corcoran, Fort Woodbury, Fort Bennette and Fort Haggerty. They were to carry out the patrol and guard duties necessary to the maintenance of these numerous fortifications by day and by night.[28]

The 97th remained outside of Washington receiving further military instruction until April. A month later, the regiment was sent to Catlett's Station, and became part of a brigade commanded by Brig. Gen. Abram Duryee of the Department of the Rappahannock under Gen. Nathaniel Banks. They had been assigned to Banks as part of a movement to trap Confederate Gen. Thomas Jonathan "Stonewall" Jackson, who had been harassing and evading Federal troops all throughout the Shenandoah Valley in Virginia. For several ensuing weeks, the 97th and the rest of the regiments involved in the chase of Jackson were kept busy literally racing up and down the valley, trying to catch the wily rebel. Unfortunately for the Federals, Jackson managed to elude them and beat them in several battles in the Valley, in what would become Jackson's famous Valley Campaign. Eventually, Jackson forced Banks and his men from the Shenandoah, and the 97th found itself back at Catlett's Station, where it remained until the end of June.

In a case of mistaken identity, a reporter for the *Utica Evening Telegraph* traveling with the 26th New York Volunteer Infantry (the Second Oneida), claimed the 97th had left Catlett's Station on the run, burning tents and destroying property without ever seeing a rebel. "This is not a very good beginning for Col. Wheelock and his men," he reported.[29] He is thought to have confused the 97th with the 104th New York, which had done that very thing earlier at Thoroughfare Gap. The reporter corrected himself a week later with an account of Wheelock and his men retreating to Manassas Junction stating they had not destroyed their tents.

During that time, Wheelock become ill and doctors ordered him off the field for treatment, but he refused, opting to remain with his regiment. The men had a great deal of affection for their Colonel by this time, and one soldier wrote home,

> To form an adequate idea of the affection for him, you ought to visit us; he is to us Colonel and father. He looks after our every want with the same care that he would were we his own children. There is no department he does not visit; and correct all and every fault ... he settled any little disputes or differences that may exist, with his characteristic impartiality; ... he possesses all those qualities which make him the really good and great man he is.[30]

Supplies began to run low, and like many regiments, the 97th was forced to forage. According to Isaac Hall, "The 97th was destitute of provisions, but a plentiful supply of green corn was found, which with meat obtained by foraging supplied present wants. Forage from well-filled barns was obtained, and lovers of the weed did not fail to appropriate from tobacco-houses along the route a plentiful supply of that luxury."[31]

On July 28, 1862, the men of the 97th had their first taste of battle at Cedar Mountain. The 97th and the 26th New York were now part of Major Gen. J. B. Ricketts' Division of General Irvin McDowell's Army of the Rappahannock. As Gen. George McClellan continued to procrastinate and overestimate the size of the Confederate forces facing him, the 97th marched to Waterloo and Warrenton when McClellan began moving his troops out of Harrison's Landing. The men knew a fight was coming as more and more loaded trains came into Warrenton.

Rickett's Division finally saw action on August 9. The Army of Virginia had been gathering nearby. Banks had been ordered to stop Stonewall Jackson with an inadequate force and was getting beaten. General John Pope ordered Rickett's Division to rescue Banks.

On the way, the men of the 97th saw ambulances full of wounded, stragglers covered with bandages and blood, smoke and dirt. It was a difficult sight for men who hadn't been in a real battle yet.[32] The men of the 97th would spend the night being shelled while Rickett's artillery returned fire. Lt. Col. Spofford, commanding the 97th at the time, kept his untried men focused by standing as the shells flew and they were lying on the ground.[33] Of the cannonading, Lieutenant Isaac Hall would write, "the sublime spectacle of the cannonade in the evening, the sudden and almost painful stillness which followed, the bright moonlight of the solemn night and the stern expectation of battle on the morrow, all left a deep impression on the memory of those who witnessed and participated in these scenes, which can never be effaced."[34]

By August 29, the regiment marched passed Manassas Junction, their destination Sudley Church on the Warrenton Turnpike, where they would remain in reserve. That morning, Federal forces under Pope had run into twenty thousand rebels under Stonewall Jackson, who held their line even though they were outnumbered. Pope sent his Federals into battle with no good order, and soon they were being flanked by thirty thousand Confederates under General James Longstreet. Being in reserve, the 97th remained near the battlefield, but did not take part in the fight.[35] They did see the results of that battle, though, when they witnessed more Union casualties streaming to the rear with bandaged legs and arms, covered from head to foot with dirt and smudges of smoke.[36]

The next day, August 30, the regiment took up a position between Sudley Church and Groveton. Late in the day, Longstreet finally attacked, hitting the Union left flank. The rebels beat back the Federals until they got to the position occupied by the 97th, which was located in a wooded area. When the 97th first caught sight of the rebels, they were only two hundred yards away. As soon as they appeared, Lt. Col. Spofford ordered the troops to open fire. The unexpected fire from the Oneida County men caused the Confederates to hesitate, but only

Frank Faville
(History of the Ninety-Seventh)

Capt. Isaac Hall
(Boys in Blue)

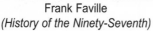

for a moment before their attack continued on at the double quick. Isaac Hall thought that this continuance of the attack was caused because the rebel officer in charge of the Confederate advance had determined the 97th was composed of raw troops who had not seen combat before. Said Hall,

> Their commanding officer, at a glance had probably taken in the situation, and noticed that our line was composed of raw troops.... As the Confederates advanced, fragments of their men struck by solid shot and shell from our guns on the hill, could be seen flying to their rear and they left a trail of dead and wounded, but kept on closing up their ranks ... an overwhelming Confederate force ... attacked our brigade, taking the regiments fronting the south in flank. The brigade now understood that the enemy...was upon them, and made a deter- mined resistance, fighting gallantly. The Confederate line was checked, and rapid firing on both sides began. But the troops which had passed our front were soon bearing down upon our left and rear, when the order came to fall back in the direction of Bull Run Creek; and this order came none too soon.[37]

The 97th lost two officers, Lieutenant Dwight S. Faville of Company D and Captain Richard Jones.[38] It was reported that the 97th had seven men killed, forty-two wounded and sixty-one missing.

In a letter home, Lt. Isaac Hall would write of the 97th's part in the battle, the marches, the skirmishes and the Confederate attack. He wrote with a great deal of respect for the Confederates. As they were fired upon by the Union bat- teries, "The same, steady onward step was kept up, though I could see many stag- ger to the rear, and fall to rise no more.... Though they were enemies I could not but admire their discipline and courage."[39] While Col. Wheelock was away on sick leave and missed by his men, Lt. Col. Spofford was praised for his actions while in command during the battle. Spofford became noted for his indifference to danger and his ability to keep a cool head while being fired upon. Spofford excelled at keeping his men eager to fight and pleasing their colonel while defending their Union and the flag entrusted to them by the women of Boonville.

Following Second Bull Run, the 97th was involved in the short-lived Battle of Chantilly on September 1. Confederate Gen. Robert E. Lee was pushing his forces to the Little River Turnpike and was heading to Pope's rear, in the direction of Fairfax Court House. A portion of Gen. James Ewell Brown (J.E.B.) Stuart's cavalry and some artillery had advanced to within a mile of Fairfax, where they shelled a train of wagons and ambulances but did no material injury to anyone.[40]

McDowell received an order from Pope to take his division to Fairfax Court House, assume command of the two brigades there and occupy Germantown to cover the Turnpike from there to Alexandria. Stonewall Jackson was reportedly advancing on Fairfax with twenty thousand men. McDowell wanted to obey the order as soon as possible, so the men of the 97th and the other regiments were on the move once again. Still part of Duryea's Brigade, McDowell marched the 97th at the head of the column on the Fairfax Road at a quick step for several miles. They reached the Little River Turnpike, when a halt was ordered and a skirmish line was advanced under the command of Captain Egleston. The men were deployed to the left of the turnpike. Soon after, the enemy opened up from the opposite bluffs and shelling began, exploding in the woods to the rear.

The Battle of Chantilly had begun with an "unabating roar of artillery and rattle of infantry."[41] During the fighting, a loud thunderstorm added to the overall din and chaos of battle. Chantilly was a short and decisive conflict, but with considerable losses on both sides despite its short duration and small amount of numbers actually engaged in the fighting. The men of the 97th would pass a most uncomfortable and dreary night, without shelter or the chance to build fires. By morning, the skirmish line was advanced a mile to the front but no enemy could be found. The men were able to build fires to roast corn and joke about their situation from the night before. The army was marched back to the defenses of Washington. According to Isaac Hall, the 97th arrived late in the evening of September 2, "with wasted numbers but unabated courage, repulsed but not broken in spirit; and although saddened by the loss of many brave comrades left unburied on the field, still hopeful in the final issue of events."[42]

In compliance with orders, the Corps was brought to Halls and Upton's Hills, in front of Washington and the campaign ended. Over the course of the short campaign, the men made forced marches with barely any rest and often marched through the night without food and still fought well despite their fatigue. Due to the movements of the enemy, even the generals were forced to do without as they became separated from their supplies. Despite many hardships, the men performed with gallantry, wanting to do their best for their country.

The 97th, in camp only a few days, received marching orders. At the time, both commanding officers, Wheelock and Spofford, were on sick leave, so command of the regiment devolved to Major Northrup. Wheelock and Spofford weren't the only ones sick. Many of the men were also, and when the regiment marched, it took them all day and well into the evening to finally catch up once the 97th went into camp again. The troops entered Maryland, a border state, and gratefully received food and drink from local citizens. The men marched accompanied by cheers as they headed toward the South Mountain range.

On September 2, 1862, General George Brinton McClellan, "Little Mac," was placed in command of the Army of Virginia, which would once again become the Army of the Potomac, for the defense of Washington. By September 7, Pope was relieved of command at his own request, and was transferred to the Northwest department.[43] McClellan began a project to reorganize the army and raise the spirits of the men who hadn't yet had time to rest and recover from the recent grueling campaign.

Facing no opposition, Lee had devised a plan to invade the north through western Maryland and Pennsylvania. As news of his movements spread, great consternation arose in the North, causing speedy preparations to repel such a formidable invasion. A mere four days after their arrival in Washington, the 97th, along with the 14th, 26th, 34th and 121st New York regiments were ordered to begin marching north through Maryland. Two roads crossed the South Mountains, at Turner's Gap and another at Crampton's Gap. The 97th was sent to Turner's Gap on September 14. Along with the 47th Pennsylvania Infantry, known as the Bucktails, the Oneida County men charged the Confederates holding the Gap and took the ground.[44]

Isaac Hall described the battle:

> Sunday near sunset found us at the base of South Mountain.... Though tired and worn by our long day's march under a burning sun, our brigade did not hesitate to follow their General (Duryee) ... heeding not bullets which were raining thick and fast down the mountain slope. We were coming into line when the General met us, and giving one tremendous shout we drove the rebels before us.... Many were taken prisoner separately, and squads skulked behind ledges of rocks and trees, choosing the lesser of two evils, to be bayoneted or taken prisoners. It was trying after a hard day's march to charge up a mountain, but it was animating to see the "gray devils" run...They attempted to rally, but a few rounds from us and a sudden charge, satisfied them that we still had them in remembrance, and we were not again molested. The prisoners taken said we had made an Alabama Brigade run which had never run before.... Major Northrup was in command of the regiment, and displayed much spirit and courage during the engagement ... he was conspicuous for his bravery, having his clothes pierced with bullets, but escaping uninjured.[45]

Lee had been moving his army north with the idea of invading Federal territory and bringing the war home to the Union. He devised a battle plan, Special Order 191, and wrote several copies which were to be delivered to his commanders. But on the way, a copy of the plan was found by a Federal patrol. The battle plan had been wrapped around several cigars which had been intended as a gift for the officer receiving the plans. The plan was turned over to McClellan, who rejoiced in the fact that he now knew Lee's entire strategy. Unfortunately for the Federals, the General failed to act upon this information for over eighteen hours, which allowed Lee to get his Army into position outside the town of Sharpsburg, Maryland, near a stream called Antietam Creek.

On September 17, the 97th found itself in a dense grove of trees near Sharpsburg known locally as the East Woods. McClellan's artillery began firing on the Confederates gathered on a rise near the Dunkard Church and in Miller's cornfield to the north of the church where the Hagerstown Road approached Sharpsburg. Observing the effect of the shelling, General Joseph Hooker reported, "Every stalk of corn in the northern and greater part of the field was cut as closely as could have been done with a knife, and the slain lay in rows precisely as they had stood in their ranks."[46]

Hooker ordered an attack, and two Oneida County regiments, the 97th and the 26th, began to advance across the cornfield. The Confederates had been hunched down on the Miller farm that had been shelled by Union artillery. By the time the Oneida County men advanced, the field was littered with dead rebels and blood stained corn stalks. In the dawn light, they tripped over bodies and torn corn, and the further they went, the more opposition they encountered from the Confederates. The noise from muskets and cannon soon became so intense, that even officers shouting orders could not be heard. Regiments became hopelessly separated. The battle swayed back and forth through the corn. It was during the 97th's advance that Lieutenant Louis Dallarmi was killed by enemy artillery. Isaac Hall later wrote,

> While we were halted, Lieut. Dallarmi was standing ... to the rear and left of me, in command of the next division, and I saw him when he fell. Hearing the noise of a shell as it passed me, I turned my head, and as I did so, the Lieut. fell to the ground. The shell having burst over our regiment ... he was killed by a passing fragment.... He was a brave and accomplished officer, and much respected by his men and the regiment.[47]

The 97th halted its advance just at the final row of corn, and encountered rebels dug in behind a rail fence. The Oneida County men began a steady fire into the Confederate ranks, loading and firing with determination. After several moments, they had to stop firing, as the smoke had begun to clear, revealing there was not a living rebel anywhere in front of them. The entire enemy had fled in the face of the New Yorker's fire. The lull did not last long, as the rebels sent more troops to face the Oneida County men, who by that time had not only sustained many casualties, but were in a very perilous location. Said Isaac Hall,

> ...a fresh brigade of rebels supplied the places of the first. Our boys, what were left of them, for we had been terribly thinned out, poured into these rebel columns as they marched up...this unequal contest could not be sustained without certain annihilation of our little band and Capt. Egelston looked to the right and left to see how we were supported. To his astonishment he saw no one on the left of his company, and going to the right, he found that his little band, consisting of parts of company A and B ... a small remnant of company F and D, were all that remained of our brigade. Over half of the last named company were killed and wounded....[48]

Considering its situation, the 97th withdrew, and the regiment managed to do so in an orderly manner while under shot and shell. The regiment retreated behind an artillery battery, and supported the artillery for the remainder of the battle after sustaining numerous casualties. Ricketts' Division had been in the battle in the cornfield only forty minutes but it seemed like a lifetime. The 97th reportedly went into the fight with two hundred and three men. Of that number, ninety-five were killed and wounded. Isaac Hall reported that his company contained twenty-nine officers and men, and fifteen of that number were killed and wounded.

Lee's first attempt at invading the North was thwarted. The Union had 2,108 killed; 9,549 wounded and 753 missing. The Confederates had 1,800 missing; 2,700 killed and 9,024 wounded. The total loss for both armies was 25,934 men.[49] Antietam ended as a stalemate, the single bloodiest day of the war.

Only a little while after the battle at Antietam, McClellan was relieved of command of the Army of the Potomac, and was replaced by General Ambrose Burnside. By December, Lee had withdrawn back into Virginia, and had dug in on the high ground beyond the city of Fredericksburg on a ridge called Marye's Heights. Burnside decided to attack Lee, even though it was ill-advised. Division after division, wave after wave of Federal troops were slaughtered in a futile attempt to reach the rebel positions on the high ground. At one point, troops under General George Gordon Meade were sent against the Confederate positions. The 97th was counted among those troops. Part way across the open field separating them from the rebel positions, they were ordered to lay flat on the ground. Lying prone, the New Yorkers watched as Meade's troops attempted to reach a stone wall behind which the rebels hid, but they were cut down. The 97th remained in its position on the field, even though half of the men had no ammunition.[50]

A common observation among the men of the 97th was the stalwart courage of their commanding officers, Wheelock and Spofford. During the battle, Wheelock remained on foot, walking up and down the lines of his men, encouraging them, trying to keep their spirits up. By the end of the fight, he had four bullet holes in his trousers, three or four in the coat, and a dent caused by a shot that struck a bullet-proof vest he wore. As for Spofford, he continually exposed himself to enemy fire, and was the target of many rebel rifles, but came out of the battle totally unscathed.[51]

The Army of the Potomac attempted to move during January 1863, but literally became bogged down in what would forever after become known as Burnside's Mud March. The roads around Fredericksburg had been turned to mud by the winter rains. Burnside decided to try and move south toward Richmond, the rebel capital. But when the army moved, it became hopelessly bogged down in the muck, unable to move. The Confederates found the hapless state of the Federal Army quite amusing, and taunted Burnside's men with signs which read, "Burnside's Army, Stuck in the Mud." As soon as they were able to extricate themselves from the sucking ooze, the Federals returned to winter quarters to wait until the quagmires that were Virginia's roads dried out in the spring.

Burnside was replaced as commander of the Army by General Joseph "Fighting Joe" Hooker, who instituted many reforms, one of the most notable of which was to form the Army into Corps. Under this reorganization, the 97th became part of the Federal First Corps, commanded by Major General John Reynolds.[52]

Hooker planned to root Lee out of Fredericksburg by sending Reynolds and the Sixth Corps under Major General John Sedgwick across the Rappanhannock River to flank Lee. Several Corps crossed the river, and the leading Union forces reached a small crossroads called Chancellorsville, where Hooker planned to engage Lee. Lee had other ideas, and sent Stonewall Jackson on a flanking movement against the Federal right. Hooker believed the Confederates were leaving, but found out how badly he was in error when Jackson attacked on May 2, and routed the Union Eleventh Corps under General Oliver Otis Howard.

Reynolds, who had been ordered to Fredericksburg, now received a new set of instructions, telling him to proceed as quickly as possible to Chancellorsville. His corps, including the 97th, crossed U.S. Mine Ford across the Rappahannock and drove toward the battlefield. But the closer they came to Chancellorsville, the more they became entangled with the retreating elements of the Eleventh Corps. Reynolds's men continued to advance, and took up position on the extreme left of the Federal line. The 97th halted around midnight, and commenced building a breastwork, aided in their labors by Colonel Wheelock, who took off his coat and joined in the work. Once the breastwork was completed, they remained in their position, seeing no further action.

Unfortunately for the Confederacy, but luckily for the Union, during the battle at Chancellorsville, Lee lost his "right hand man" to friendly fire. Jackson was wounded by his own men and died nine days later.

After his success at Chancellorsville, which is considered his greatest victory, Lee went to Richmond to confer with Confederate President Jefferson Davis to discuss strategies for the future conduct of the war. Both men were concerned about the loss of Jackson and what effect that would have on their future strategies. They were also well aware of the fact that little by little, even with Lee's recent victory, rebel territory was slowly falling back into Union hands, especially in the west, where General Ulysses S. Grant was scoring major victories. He was currently laying siege to the important Confederate port of Vicksburg, Mississippi, and it appeared as though the city would not be able to hold out much longer. If it fell, it would mean the Federals would effectively control the entire length of the Mississippi River, thus cutting the Confederacy in half.

Lee proposed to Davis a second attempt at an invasion of the North, similar to what he had planned when he had been turned back at Antietam in September of the previous year. The Confederate cabinet was not at all convinced that such a plan would work, but did approve Lee's plan, though with reservations. There were several reasons why Lee wanted to attempt another incursion into the North. One of the reasons was Grant's siege of Vicksburg in the west. That port city had been besieged by Federal forces for several months, including naval and land forces. Gunboats had shelled the city, forcing civilians to live in caves. The port and its surroundings contained approximately 30,000 Southern troops, who were faced by almost 60,000 Federals. It was thought that Vicksburg could not hold out without reinforcements from Lee, but he was unwilling to send any troops west to the city. He felt that by invading the North, he could cause Grant to send some of his troops east to protect Philadelphia and Washington.[53]

Some members of the Confederate cabinet doubted there could be a positive outcome of an invasion of northern territory. They also believed Lee was willing to sacrifice other areas of the South to defend Virginia, which he considered his "country," to the detriment of other areas of the South. He refused to send troops to Vicksburg, saying it was too far away, yet had troops in his Army of Northern Virginia from as far afield as Georgia and Florida. Some rebel authorities saw Lee's invasion as a way to protect his home state, though Lee denied this was true.[54]

Another plus Lee had on his side was obviously his recent victory at Chancellorsville. By this time, he and many of his commanders and soldiers had been victorious so many times against the odds, that they began to see themselves as invincible. The morale of the rebels was sky high, in spite of the reservations of some of the higher commanders, such as Longstreet. Lee was convinced the best way to defeat the Federals was a policy of aggressiveness, while Longstreet believed a more defensive posture was the way to go. But Lee was flush with success, and had determined that aggression was best, and an invasion of the North was the quickest way to prevail.[55]

Another reason Lee pushed for a northern invasion was that he wanted a decisive victory over the Federals, a "knock out punch" as it were, that would push the Union troops out of Virginia. It was true that he had scored many victories in the war, but none of them had resulted in prying the Federals out of Lee's home state. He felt if he could score a major victory in the North, Federal troops would have to withdrawn from Virginia to counteract his movements.[56]

Another factor in the decision was that both armies mostly had been waging the war within a few miles of the Rappahannock River, neither side making too many inroads in either direction. Lee was also afraid that the stalemate with the two forces staring at each other across the river would give the North time to fully mobilize its industry to defeat the South, and he did not want this to happen. He proposed to break the stalemate along the Rappahannock by moving north.[57]

It was no secret that Lee's army was also suffering from lack of food. The Federal Army had occupied the Shenandoah Valley, the South's breadbasket, effectively cutting off the supply of its grain to Lee's army. Other supplies of grain and meat were cut off with the Federal occupation of Kentucky and Tennessee. Mississippi and Georgia had plentiful corn, but it could not be shipped because the rolling stock of the railroad was being used to transport arms instead. The Federal Navy was successfully blockading Southern ports, so nothing could come through to the Confederacy in that way. And the South's main source of food, everything from wheat, to meat, to salt, was unavailable because before the war, most of its supplies had come from the North. Lee proposed that when he moved North, he take with him a wagon train that he could fill with food and supplies that he could "liberate" from Union territory. Going hand in hand with a lack of food was a shortage of other supplies, such as guns, cannon, wagons, footwear and all manner of other things the Confederate Army needed and lacked. Prior to the war, the South had relied on the North to provide just about anything that it needed in the way of manufactured goods, but with the advent of the war, those things were no longer readily available. In prior battle victories, such as the Seven Days around Richmond, Lee's troops had been able to capture thousands of firearms and ordnance, plus clothing, shoes and other items. He believed that invading the North might result in a windfall of captured enemy supplies for his army.[58]

Lee also thought to appeal to the growing peace movement in the North. Many north of the Mason-Dixon Line were growing weary of a conflict that was costing two hundred lives a day. In many northern cities, groups of anti-war protestors, anti-abolitionists and others who were against the war were growing in number. Lee believed that by invading the North, he could cause more people to join these groups and perhaps force the Federal government to seek peace with the South.[59]

One of the final reasons Lee wanted to move North was that he hoped a major victory on Union soil would convince either the British or the French, or both, to come into the war on the side of the Confederacy as the French had done during the American Revolution. Both England and France imported large amounts of Southern cotton, and the Confederate government hoped their desire for the product plus a rebel victory might convince them to officially recognize and back the Confederate States. To date, the British as well as the French had not officially endorsed the rebels, even though both countries had supplied arms and other goods. So far, the two European nations had been content to wait and see what would happen.[60]

The Confederates believed that a successful invasion of the north might spark a revolution of sorts in the border states, especially Maryland, which would lead to a coalition of pro-Southern sympathizers in the region. This, in turn, might lead to a negotiated peace between North and South, with the terms of such peace dictated by President Jefferson Davis.[61]

By June 11, 1863, the 97th had moved to a camp at White Oak Church, Virginia. The regiment was by then part of General Henry Baxter's Brigade, John Robinson's Division of the First Army Corps under General Abner Doubleday. It received orders to break camp only to be told a short time later to stay where they were. On the following morning, they were again ordered to strike their tents, and this time the orders stood. That afternoon, the regiment began marching northward on the left flank of the Army of the Potomac. Over the next five days, the 97th would march sixty miles to stop outside of Leesburg, Virginia. It remained in camp there for a week, along a stream called Goose Creek.[62] On the march anew, the 97th crossed the Potomac River into Maryland at Edward's Ford on June 25. A day later, it crossed the Mason-Dixon Line into southern Pennsylvania.[63]

At about this time, Hooker, the commander of the Army of the Potomac, requested to be relieved on June 27. The resignation was prompted by two factors. First, Hooker had wanted to be direct and attack and seize the Confederate capital at Richmond, but President Lincoln would not approve of the plan. Instead, the President wanted Hooker to take the Army and pursue Lee to the north, while at the same time protecting Washington. Hooker was doing a creditable job of keeping Lee from nearing Washington, but Federal leaders wanted him to attack Lee and drive him from the North as soon as possible, which Hooker was unwilling to do.[64] Second, he became embroiled in a dispute with Washington over Federal forces that were protecting Harper's Ferry, West Virginia, and became so frustrated that he offered his resignation. It was readily accepted by Lincoln, who was quickly loosing confidence in his General. Hooker was replaced by General George Gordon Meade. The change of command occurred on June 28, and some troops found it a bit demoralizing to have their commander relieved of duty on the eve of what could shape up to be a very huge battle. Though Meade had little time to form an effective plan to counteract Lee, he immediately began moving the Federals northward to intercept Lee's army and to drive them back to the south, proving to already be more aggressive in his tactics than Hooker.

Meade planned to pursue Lee through Maryland and threaten the Confederate supply line which was stretching longer and longer the further away

Lee was from Virginia. If the Army of the Potomac could put enough pressure on Lee's supply line, the Confederate leader would be forced to fight. Meade intended to organize a fortified line near the Maryland/Pennsylvania border.

By June 28, Lee was moving north to enter into Pennsylvania, with the idea of marching on the state capital at Harrisburg, then turning south to threaten Philadelphia and eventually the Federal capital at Washington. According to Longstreet, Lee's army was "in a condition of strength and morale to undertake anything."[65] Lee wanted to crush the Army of the Potomac and proceed on to Baltimore, then to Washington, but quickly learned of Meade's plan and sent orders to his commanders to consolidate their forces near the town of Gettysburg in south central Pennsylvania.[66]

On June 30, the 97th arrived in Emmitsburg, Maryland, where it camped for the night along Marsh Run. The following morning, Wednesday, July 1, it received orders at about 6:30 AM to hurry to Gettysburg, which was ten miles away. They were cheered when they received news that McClellan was back in command of the Army, as he had been very popular among the men. Later, much to their considerable dismay, the rumor would prove to be untrue. As the regiment neared Gettysburg, they could hear the sound of cannon fire in the distance.[67] The Oneida County men were one of the first regiments to arrive in Gettysburg, going into position on a ridge that looked out over the small college town. The 97th stopped near the Lutheran Theological Seminary on Seminary Ridge, and became part of the Union reserve.[68]

The battle had begun several hours before, when Confederate forces under Generals Henry Heth and A.P. Hill, which were coming down the Chambersburg Pike to the northwest of the town, had run into dismounted Federal cavalry commanded by General John Buford. What began as a skirmish quickly turned into something larger, as units from both sides quickly began to converge on the area on the outskirts of town. Neither Lee nor Meade had wanted to get into a major battle in that particular area, but as was the case with many Civil War battles, it was where the two armies met, and the conflict quickly began to escalate.

The 97th had not been on Seminary Ridge long when it was ordered to establish a skirmish line in a field over the crest of the hill, accompanied by the 11th Pennsylvania Infantry. Captain Delos Hall of Company A took the men forward to a point near the Mummasburg Road.[69] They stopped near a house close to some woods. They had no sooner arrived when a Federal cavalryman let the troops know in no uncertain terms what was at stake in the battle. As he rode up and down the lines, he yelled, "There are no troops behind you! You stand alone, between the Rebel army and your homes! Fight like hell!"[70]

The two regiments cautiously advanced through the field filled with timothy toward a high wooden rail fence about two hundred yards away from the hill where they had begun. The men could easily see the Confederate flags across the way, which were thought to belong to General Edward O'Neal's brigade.[71] As the

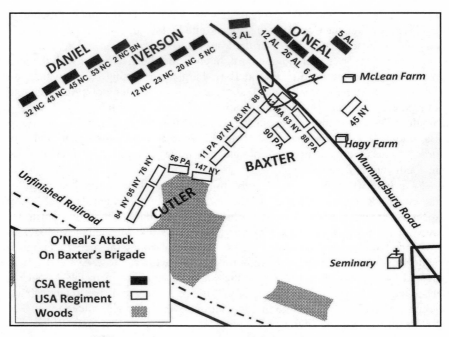

O'Neal's Attack
On Baxter's Brigade

CSA Regiment
USA Regiment
Woods

two Union regiments neared the fence, they engaged the forward enemy troops, driving them back. One man from the regiment was killed and several others wounded. As soon as they reached the fence, they were joined by the 12th Massachusetts on the right, and the three regiments changed direction, proceeding to a stone wall in their right front. Only a few moments later, the rebels came within range and a skirmish began.[72]

Said Isaac Hall,

> Not long after our second formation, in the rear of the wall, the enemy, who had been driven off … returned and occupied the first field south of the Mummasburg Road, and as skirmishers kept up a fire upon the right two regiments of our line till the approach of Iverson's brigade…. The 97th suffered from this Confederate skirmish line in the field and to the right, and covered itself as skirmishers as best it could … several men springing up…and firing as closely as possible whence the smoke from the Confederate fire arose. In this manner Reese Lloyd of Company A, was killed … and many others wounded by the enfilading fire of this line.[73]

When the fight wound down, many of the men laid on the ground behind the wall to get a rest. After that, nothing seemed to happen for several hours. But at 3:00 PM, their rest was interrupted by a volley of fire to the left, accompanied by the infamous "rebel yell." The 5th, 20th and 23rd North Carolina regiments of

Confederate Gen. Alfred Iverson's brigade threw themselves against the Union line at the stone wall and the 11th Pennsylvania in particular. The 97th responded by letting loose a withering fire into the advancing rebel line, both the front and the left flank, attempting to help the Pennsylvanians defend themselves. At the same time, the 12th Massachusetts on the rebel's right flank also opened fire, catching the Confederates in an enfilade fire. The initial Federal volley caused the rebels to hesitate, but they soon regrouped and came on again. The 97th poured in another volley, practically in the faces of the Confederates, and the gray line was devastated. The rebels who survived the Federal fire hid in a ravine only fifty yards away. The 97th, along with the 11th Pennsylvania and 12th Massachusetts had held the line, accounting for the deaths of over one hundred rebels, and the wounding of another two hundred.[74]

Discretion being the better part of valor as the saying goes, the men of the 97th soon saw white surrender flags being hoisted from the ravine where the rebels were hiding. Led by Lt. Col. Spofford on his horse, and Col. Wheelock on foot, the 97th advanced toward the ravine. Wheelock was not on his horse because Spofford had ordered the advance without the Colonel's knowledge or permission, but he did not rescind the order, and did not interfere while the 97th went forward.

The 11th Pennsylvania covered their movement. Spofford urged them on by saying, "Boys of the 97th. Let's go get them and capture them."[75] Though there was some firing here and there along their flank, the Oneida men reached the defile and found almost two hundred and fifteen Confederates who were prepared to surrender, and eventually the total was near four hundred. Company C's Sergeant Sylvester Riley of Osceola was the first member of the 97th to reach the rebels, and promptly grabbed the flag of the 20th North Carolina Infantry. One of the most heroic deeds one could accomplish during the war was to capture an enemy flag. He gave the captured colors to Lt. Ebenezar Harrington from Alder Creek.[76] The flag was then returned to the Federal lines along with the rebel prisoners. Taking the prisoners back to Federal lines was not easy, as they were harassed all the way back by Confederate fire. The rebels wounded not only some of the Federals, but many of their own also, obviously not showing much regard for who they shot and who they did not. Upon reaching the friendly lines, Harrington turned the captured colors over to Col. Wheelock. Not all of the rebel colors were captured, however. It was later revealed that two other Confederate regiments that had been taken prisoner had hidden their flags in the long grass of the field rather than surrender them to the Yankees.[77]

Not long afterward, another rebel line approached their position. Colonel Wheelock saw the Confederates coming, and ordered his men back over the stone wall. The 97th charged across the field, attacking the rebels who were members of two Confederate brigades belonging to Iverson and General Stephen Ramseur. The Oneida County regiment was again supported in its charge by the 11th

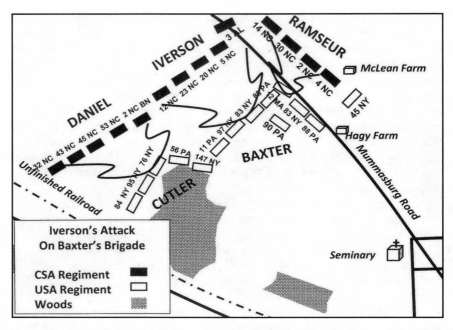

Iverson's Attack
On Baxter's Brigade

CSA Regiment
USA Regiment
Woods

Pennsylvania and the 12th Massachusetts. The rebel line broke, and the New Yorkers took eighty additional prisoners.[78]

But the triumph was short lived, as almost immediately another large Confederate force began to converge on the 97th supported by a rebel artillery battery. The new rebel attack placed the 97th in a tenuous position, threatening to catch it in flank and rear. Seeing the rebels approaching, Wheelock ordered the regiment to the rear so he could rally them and prepare them to meet the oncoming Confederates. One member of the 97th who did not seem to be either flustered or impressed by the rebel advance was the regiment's color bearer, Corporal James Brown of Leyden. As the regiment retreated, he stopped every few steps, turned, and waved the national colors in the face of the advancing Confederates. His actions, while unquestioningly brave, also proved to be highly fatal, as he was soon shot and killed.[79]

Company A did not notice the remainder of the regiment going to the rear to reorganize and rally. The captain of the company did not see the rest of the 97th, which had retired back beyond the crest of the hill. The confusion that reigned was the result of the company's captain not hearing the order to retreat. He did see some rebel prisoners who were about three hundred yards to the rear, and surmised that the 97th must also be in that direction. He ordered his men to double time toward the prisoners, thinking to rejoin the rest of the regiment. The mistake was soon uncovered, but when they turned around to go back to their original position, they found the Confederates already there, and again turned, heading back toward the town of Gettysburg itself. The company became lost during the retreat of the regiment back through town. The captain tried to make contact with the regiment, but only managed to find Chaplain Ferguson who informed him that the rest of the troops were seeking shelter to the rear of a ridge near town on which the Evergreen Cemetery was located. Appropriately, the hill was called Cemetery Hill.[80]

Said Isaac Hall of Company A's plight,

> Confederate batteries...opened upon the retreating forces of the First Division ... increasing their disorder, and fearfully cutting them. This precluded the possibility of reaching the 97th in that direction, and the squad sought safety in retreat. By dropping onto the ground, and springing up and running immediately after the discharge of the enemy's guns, and dropping again in time for another discharge, the captain and his men were enabled to reach the Emmitsburg road, where Chaplain Ferguson...said...the 97th had taken shelter in rear of Cemetery Ridge.[81]

By this time, rebel artillery batteries had attained the top of the hill where the 97th had been along Seminary Ridge, and was pouring grape and canister shot at the retreating Federals. The entire regiment's retreat was later reported in this way by Corporal John Manchester of Company A,

> When we were ordered to retreat...we were ordered to move back to Cemetery hill and not stampede. Our entire brigade would not have made a good-sized regiment. The situation was getting desperate. The fifth corps had gone in on our right. As soon as they were attacked, they broke and ran, and left us in a position to be surrounded and captured. It was necessary to get back to Cemetery hill to save ourselves. We moved back slowly to the Ladies' Seminary, making a short stand at intervals to hold the rebels at bay for a few moments. Just as a part of my regiment had left the cemetery grounds, the rebels on our left made a dash and surrounded about half the regiment.[82]

Manchester had made an error in that he stated the Fifth Corps had broken, when in reality it had been the Eleventh Corps. But the fact remained that so quick was the Confederate attack that seventy men from the 97th were taken prisoner after being surrounded.[83] Two of those taken captive were the regiment's commander, Colonel Wheelock and his second in command, Lt. Col. Spofford. Wheelock's capture became one of the many human interest stories connected with the battle.

The 97th was one of the last Federal regiments to retreat from the field. As they went back over the ridge, retreating toward the town, Wheelock and many of his regiment found they were fairly surrounded by rebels, and he concluded it was best to surrender rather than face possible annihilation. He took a white handkerchief from his pocket and stood on the steps of a local private school on

Seminary Ridge whose principal was a woman named Carrie Sheads. This was the Ladies' Seminary referred to previously by John Manchester. Wheelock waved the handkerchief, but it was evidently too small for the Confederates to see, as they kept pouring fire at the Federals. Wheelock asked Sheads for a larger cloth the rebels would be able to see, which she gave to him. He waved that, and the rebels ceased fire.

Exhausted from the day's battle, Wheelock and some of his men went down into the school's cellar to rest and await being taken off as prisoners. A Confederate officer, accompanied by several enlisted men, entered the school to take the Federals captive. As they went, they demanded the Federals turn over their sidearms and any weapons they might have. Wheelock did not relish the idea of surrendering his sword to the rebels, and attempted to break it, but it was too sturdy. The Confederates demanded that he hand it over to them. Wheelock responded that while there was still breath in his body, he would never hand his sword over to a "traitor." The rebel stated if Wheelock did not surrender his sword, he would be shot. The colonel stood at attention, tore open his uniform and told the Confederate to shoot him, but he would not give up his sword, further stating that he would defend it with his life.

Elias Sheads, Carrie's father, tried to mediate the situation by stepping in between the two and pleading with them not to be rash. The Confederate officer pushed Elias away, and repeated his demand for the sword, as well as his threat to kill Wheelock if he did not comply. Carrie then came forward and pleaded with the rebel not to shoot Wheelock, who was unarmed and totally defenseless. She argued that she had seen enough blood spilled on that day, and did not wish to see any more. She then begged Wheelock to turn over his sword so he would not be killed. He replied, "This sword was given me by my friends for meritorious conduct, and I promised to guard it sacredly, and never surrender or disgrace it; and I never will while I live."[84]

Before anything else could happen, the Confederate officer's attention was drawn away from Wheelock by other prisoners. While he was preoccupied, Carrie took Wheelock's sword from his belt and hid it among the folds of her dress. When the rebel officer returned and again demanded the sword, Wheelock told him he was too late, that he had already given the sword to another officer, and now he was willing to surrender. For some reason, forgetting that Wheelock had vowed only a few moments before to die instead of surrendering his sword, the officer believed him and Wheelock was ordered to fall in with the remainder of the prisoners.

Spofford did not relinquish his sword either. He threw his in a nearby bush, but unfortunately, it was later found there by a Confederate soldier, who kept it. The prisoners were all taken to a holding area to await their fate. Others from the 97th who became prisoners were Captains Rouse Egelston and Henry Chamberlain, along with Lt. William Morrin. Lt. Rush Cady and eleven men had

A. B. Snow
(Boys in Blue)

W. B. Judd
(Donald Wisnoski)

been killed on the retreat.[85] Others managed to escape back through Gettysburg. Among that number were Sergeant Arch Snow and Lt. W. B. Judd. Judd said, "It was running the gauntlet in the strict sense of the word. The bullets were flying from each side a perfect shower. The air seemed so filled that it seemed almost impossible to breathe without inhaling them. Some one fell beside me almost every step. It was here that Serg. Fred. Munson fell mortally wounded, and Lieut. James Stiles was killed."[86]

The remainder of the regiment that was not taken prisoner retreated back toward town to an unfinished railroad cut, where they intended to stop and attempt to make a stand. The bullets flew thickly from both sides, and men fell continuously in the murderous fire. The rebels seemed to pour in an unending wave over the ridge toward the railroad cut, and knowing they would be overwhelmed if they stayed where they were, the men of the 97th retreated at a run back through Gettysburg itself, finally finding cover on a rise to the south of the town, Cemetery Hill.

Though they had retreated, the 97th had given as good as they received. The battle near Seminary Ridge had taken about four hours. In that time, they had lost one hundred and twenty-six men of the two hundred and sixty-eight who had begun the battle, including fourteen killed, thirty-two wounded and seventy-six missing or captured. While this was a high number, the rebels suffered even more. The Confederates who had attacked the 97th and its sister regiments lost almost eight hundred of their number.[87]

About 5:00 PM, what was left the 97th marched from Cemetery Hill to the left and formed along the Emmitsburg Road in front of Cemetery Ridge, parallel to the road itself, and went into position to fortify the Union line.[88] They stayed there for the night, and were relieved at 10:00 AM, July 2, by a brigade of troops of the Second Corps under General Alexander Webb. Due to the capture of all the senior officers, the 97th was now under the command of Captain Andrew Wood. By then the 97th was battered and bloody, and retired to the rear until 4:00 PM. It was then sent in support of an artillery battery of the Eleventh Corps, where several of the members of the 97th fell victim to rebel sharpshooters and Confederate artillery fire. It was during this time that Captain Wood was wounded, and the command of the regiment devolved to Captain D. E. Hall.[89]

As night fell, the 97th, along with the remainder of Robinson's Division, was sent behind the lines to support a division of General Daniel Sickles's Corps. On the following morning, July 3, the 97th supported some artillery batteries of the Eleventh Corps, but was then withdrawn about 9:00 A.M., and sent to support the heavily engaged Twelfth Corps. The 97th remained in support until 1:00 PM, when it was moved again, to the rear of Cemetery Hill. It was while they were stationed there that they heard the incredible cannonading that marked the beginning of what would be known forever after as Pickett's Charge. The 97th found itself being hit by many of the shells dropping among the Federal troops.[90] Said Isaac Hall,

> … the cannonading began, the incessant whiz, the loud reports of bursting shells and crash of solid shot from more than a hundred of the enemy's guns and the deafening roar of as many of our own—which shook the earth—in close proximity, could not be considered at all soothing to the … men who had left nearly a half of their comrades on the battle grounds of the two preceding days…. When foliage and the very limbs of trees…came crashing to the ground … a look of inquiry towards their officers ran along these meager lines. Such men … could not break and run; their discipline and moral force chained them more firmly than could fetters of steel, to the ground. But no column could long exist uncovered amid this desolating storm, and the order came quick and sharp to move to the right … in the rear of a stone wall, it was halted and ordered to lie down.[91]

The movement might have helped to get the 97th out from under the rebel fire, but the men then found themselves in the direct glare of the summer sun, and some of them almost succumbed to heat stroke.

Lee thought to break the Union position at its center on Cemetery Ridge and roll up the Federal line, win the battle, and perhaps the war itself. He had attempted to flank the Federals the day before, by sending troops to attack both the northern and southern ends of the Union lines. But the Confederate attacks had been repulsed at pitched battles to the north at Culp's Hill and to the south at Little Round Top. Lee's frontal assault on the Union line involved divisions under General Isaac Trimble, General James Johnston Pettigrew and General George

Pickett. Attacking the Federal line with almost 15,000 troops, the Confederates failed to break the Union defense of Cemetery Ridge. The rebels were repelled with the loss of almost half their numbers.

While the 97th was in reserve, its members did see and hear the tragic results of the ill advised Confederate charge. During the rebel action, they were on the left flank in support of the Second Corps. From there, the soldiers listened for either the rebel yell, to tell them the Confederates had been victorious in their charge, or cheers from the boys in blue which would mean the charge had been unsuccessful. The suspense was finally broken when they heard a huge cheer arise from the Union line along Cemetery Ridge.

They were in position to the southwest of Gettysburg along with Joseph Hayes's artillery. They saw the mangled bodies of the Confederate dead littering the field all the way from their starting point across a field a mile and a half away to the base of a stone wall that marked the Federal positions on Cemetery Ridge. The wounded cried pitifully.

Isaac Hall later wrote, "The havoc upon the field in our front was appalling; the dead lay at intervals upon one another, torn and mangled; and were strewn over the field in every conceivable condition. From among the slain rose the wounded, who struggled to reach our line; some in their vain endeavor, fell to rise no more; others who could not rise cried for help and for water."[92]

On July 4, Independence Day, the 97th was not out of danger yet. In the morning, Confederate artillery lobbed shells into the Union lines, which fell in the soft ground to the regiment's left. Some of the shots hit a nearby pile of wooden rails, showering the 90th Pennsylvania with splinters, but no one in the 97th was injured. The men were also in range of some Confederate sharpshooters who remained in the nearby houses on the outskirts of Gettysburg, but no casualties were inflicted. After a few hours, the fire from the rebel artillery and sharpshooters died down and ceased all together.

The battle of Gettysburg was effectively over. It was the largest and bloodiest battle ever fought in the western hemisphere. In just three days, over fifty thousand casualties had been sustained. Of that total, seven thousand had died.[93] Lee began to withdraw his Army back toward the South and across the Potomac before the Federals could do him more damage or cut off his retreat. Two New York regiments were among those trailing Lee, the 97th and the 121st from Herkimer County. Neither regiment engaged the Confederates as they retreated.

Back home in the Adirondack foothills, July 4 was observed quietly even though the citizens of Oneida County had received the news of the tremendous Federal victory at Gettysburg. It was at the same time that they received the first reports of the casualties suffered by the local regiments in the battle, including the lists of killed, wounded and missing.

It proved to be an even worse weekend for the Confederacy, as on July 4, the same day that Lee began his retreat from Gettysburg, the Mississippi port of

Vicksburg fell to Ulysses S. Grant. The Confederacy was now effectively cut in two. Due to the date of the fall of the city, Independence Day would not be celebrated in Vicksburg for another 81 years, until after the Allied landings in Normandy, France, on June 6, 1944.

The Federals followed the rebels until they crossed the Potomac back into Virginia on July 13. The following morning, the errant Colonel Wheelock finally managed to rejoin the 97th. He had escaped from the Confederates while en route to prison in Richmond. He affected his freedom by rolling down a briar covered hill. It must have been a sight to see, as Wheelock as a large man, weighing in at two hundred pounds.[94] He was nearly recaptured by rebel pickets, who fired upon him, but he eluded them. He trudged through the mountains for two days, surrounded by rebels, living on berries and water. It rained constantly, soaking him. At one point he even fell over a small ledge. Three days after escaping, he happened upon a house belonging to a Union family. He had some money on him, so he gave it to the husband of the family, who bought some food and Wheelock stayed with them several days. He eventually made his way back to Union lines after being on his own for nine days.[95]

Wheelock later related his experiences in a letter,

> After passing picket lines and being fired on, I narrowly missed being recaptured, but succeeded in getting into the mountains, I traveled two days…The rebels were on each side of me, and I had no chance but to travel one way, while they were getting away as fast as possible the other…I can assure you my reflections were not very pleasant, two days and two nights without food or water, except berries, and water from the heavens, which was plenty, as it rained constantly. While making my escape … I fell down a ledge of rocks, about eight feet, and perhaps that saved me … as I was contented to remain there through the night for the reason that I could not well help myself. I am yet sore from the effects of that fall. I killed a rattle snake which I dislike almost as bad as I do a rebel…. On the third day I ventured down the mountain…found a good Union man and boy. Giving him money … he got provisions … to last his family and myself while I remained with him, which was not a very small amount … for I had been fasting for some nine days…. I shall always remember that family with kindness.[96]

Lt. Col. Spofford was not lucky enough to affect an escape, and ended up in the notorious Libby Prison in Richmond, for Federal officers who had become prisoners. His experiences were related in a letter he sent to Jean Stebbins, the editor of the *Herkimer County Journal* that was received in December of that year.

> I send you this little insight in regard to our manner of living in and around Richmond…. In … Libby are nine hundred officers; across the street is another "hotel" and eighteen hundred of our men; three rods from that is another twelve hundred more; still beyond that are others of like description, prisons for our

men. Castle Thunder is on the opposite side, containing about fifteen hundred, chiefly political prisoners and deserters.... In this building we occupy six rooms ... one hundred and fifty prisoners to each room. We sleep ... and sit on the floor, except when we have received boxes and barrels to make temporary seats. We now have two blankets each ... furnished by the U.S. Sanitary Commission and ... the Rebs.... For rations we get about twelve ounces of corn bread...two thirds of a gill of rice, no meat...in lieu thereof they give us one or two sweet potatoes.... Most of the officers have received boxes from home and manage to get along. But with our men it is very different ... many of whom are without coats, shirts, shoes, stockings, blankets or even shelter ... and hundreds of them die from starvation and exposure.[97]

Spofford went on to relate that officers were allowed to purchase rations and extra items, but the rebels offered them at highly inflated prices. Sugar went anywhere from $8 to $10 a pound; butter $9 or $10 a pound, and so on.

Wheelock received accolades for his handling of the regiment during the action at Gettysburg. In a report to the headquarters of the Second Division on July 18, General Robinson stated, "The instances of distinguished gallantry are too numerous to be embodied in this report.... As, however, they came under my personal observation, I cheerfully indorse the remarks of General Baxter in commendation of Colonel Coulter, 11th Pennsylvania; Colonel Wheelock, 97th New York."[98]

On July 21, 1863, Wheelock wrote a letter, describing the 97th's actions at Gettysburg:

I will not undertake to give you the details of the battle of Gettysburg, but will say that it was considered by all the hardest and most hotly contested battle yet fought in this war. The whole salvation of the Rebels seemed to depend on their success; and it also seemed that every Union soldier for himself was determined to win the victory or die. The Ninety-seventh made the first charge of the first day's fight, and captured more prisoners than we had men; also a flag of the Twentieth North Carolina Regiment ... we were put into the fight as soon as we arrived on the field, without waiting for our forces to come up, while the enemy were ready and waiting to receive us. We were engaged for four hours, and every round of ammunition was expended, and when surrounded on all sides, we yielded the ground. The Ninety-seventh had lost 2 officers killed, 7 wounded, and 6 taken prisoners. About 16 privates were killed, 40 wounded, 60 prisoners, besides many missing, whom I fear are killed. We have only a remnant of what left Boonville. We only numbered at this time as fit for duty, 150 men.[99]

In 1863, the United States celebrated its first official Thanksgiving Day on November 26. But for the men of the 97th, it would not be a holiday. Early in the morning, they left their bivouac, and headed for Mine Run, Virginia, along with the 152nd New York. The movement was part of a plan Meade had to try and attack the rebel capital at Richmond before winter. He felt that a quick attack on Lee's forces at Mine Run would result in the Army of the Potomac being able to get between Lee's forces and Richmond, giving Lee no chance to consolidate his scattered forces. Neither the 97th nor the 152nd got very far. Just after stepping off, the heavens opened up and the rains came, turning the roads into veritable quagmires. Roads were soon blocked by mired wagons and other vehicles. The 97th managed to get across the quickly flowing Rapidan River, but the 152nd was ordered back to its starting position.[100]

Not being totally blind, Lee noted the Federal movements, and shifted his forces to counter the movement. By the 27th, most of General Jubal Early's troops were in position to offer some resistance to Meade's move. Though the rebels were vastly outnumbered, they hoped to at least slow down the Federal advance. The 97th, which had been camped at Culpeper Ford, moved out onto the Orange Plank Road and marched around the Wilderness, toward Meade's objective, which was Orange Court House. When the lead Federal elements reached Locust Grove, they were attacked by Early's forces. This momentarily halted the Federal advance, and cost five hundred casualties. Early retreated to Mine Run, while the Federals camped at Locust Grove.[101]

The next morning, it rained anew and the Federal advance slowed when it encountered rebel breastworks near Mine Run. Meade called a halt to the advance, and the regiments camped for the night in bone chilling cold. The next day was no better. The cold continued, and the two sides stayed in place, glaring at each other. The standoff continued for several more days as Meade decided what to do. He had thought to try a headlong frontal assault on the Confederate fortifications, but General Gouverneur Warren refused to send his men across an open field to attack, deeming it nothing short of suicidal. Eventually, Meade was convinced and called off the attack. On December 1, he ordered a withdrawal.

The 97th was astounded when Wheelock was sent to Elmira, New York, to take charge of conscripts. In actuality, he had been relieved of duty for submitting fraudulent vouchers. The regiment was shocked into disbelief, because Wheelock had a sterling reputation for honesty. Upon investigation, it was found that two years before, in 1861, Wheelock had submitted a travel voucher in the amount of $10.46, but the total was changed by another officer. Once it was found it had not been the Colonel who had changed the voucher, he was reinstated and returned to the 97th on December 6.[102]

The regiment's respect and trust in Wheelock proved not to be misplaced. At Christmas, they found out what a truly honorable and wonderful man he was. Packages from home had arrived for the men in time for the holiday, and were distributed to whom they had been addressed. Only one package remained undelivered, and it had been sent to a man who had died a few days before. The dead soldier had left behind a family which was now destitute, as he had been the sole provider. Wheelock opened the package and found it contained a homemade fruitcake, a pair of suspenders, a skein of thread and a package of needles. The evening the package had arrived, the Colonel could not sleep, thinking about the man's family back in Upstate New York. The following morning, he drew the men around him, and told them the story of the man's family, and informed them they were going to have an auction. He cut the fruitcake into forty pieces, and announced he would auction them off for fifty cents each, but he would buy a piece himself for a dollar. The remaining pieces sold out quickly. He then offered the suspenders and received a bid of fifty cents, which he deemed totally insulting. He called for bidding, and they eventually sold for five dollars. A soldier who purchased them told the Colonel to auction them again, as he already had a pair of suspenders, and they eventually sold for nineteen dollars. The thread sold for three dollars, and the needles for a dollar each. By the time Wheelock's auction was complete, he had raised a total of $79.50. Generous to a fault, Wheelock chipped in enough of his own money to make an even $100 for the deceased soldier's family.[103]

By February 1864, some men of the 97th whose years of service were up, reenlisted for an additional three years. As an incentive to stay, they were promised a thirty-day furlough and a $400 bounty. The 97th had the distinction of being the only Oneida County regiment to serve in every year of the war, and under every commander of the Army of the Potomac. In an address to the Utica papers in 1898, A. B. Snow would later remark of the 97th, that "In length of service, list of battles, roll of dead, it stands at the head of Oneida County regiments."[104]

By spring of 1864, General Ulysses S. Grant had become commander of all Union armies in the field. The first time he and Lee would do battle with each other would be in May in an area of Virginia known as The Wilderness. A large region of dense undergrowth, masses of vegetation and forests, it was not a place conducive for battle. On May 5, the 97th found itself in line next to another Oneida County regiment, the 146th (Fifth Oneida). As the 97th advanced into The Wilderness, it sustained sixty casualties, both killed and wounded, including its color bearer, who was wounded. The staff on which the colors flew was shattered. The regiment had to spend the night in the dark woods, trying to get sleep while the wounded were evacuated around them.

Wheelock was nearly killed while in The Wilderness. On May 4, the day before the battle, he had been the victim of an accidental shooting, which resulted in his sustaining a foot injury. During the battle, the heat was so intense that he came down with exhaustion and sunstroke. He fell on the battlefield and was alone, in dire peril, unable to move to save himself. A member of the 97th, one Thomas Burke of Harrisburgh who was a first lieutenant, rescued the colonel. Under rebel fire, Burke went back alone at the risk of his own life, and carried the stricken Wheelock from the field, saving him from almost certain death. For his unselfish actions, Burke became the only member of the 97th to be awarded the

James McGurren
(Donald Wisnoski)

William Bartlett
(Donald Wisnoski)

Medal of Honor.[105] His citation for the decoration read, "At the risk of his own life, he went back while the rebels were still firing, and finding Colonel Wheelock unable to move, alone and unaided, carried him off the field of battle."[106] The 97th did lose some good men in the Wilderness, even though Wheelock was lucky enough not to be counted among them. Lost was one of the heroes of Gettysburg, Sergeant Sylvester Riley, who had captured the flag of the 20th North Carolina.

Grant's objective was ultimately to take the Confederate capital at Richmond, but had suffered setbacks at the Wilderness and Cold Harbor in May and June 1864. He moved the Army around Lee's right flank with the idea of advancing toward Petersburg, a major railroad and supply hub for Richmond. The 97th, along with the 146th (Fifth Oneida), were marched across the Peninsula and transported down the York River. By June, they were camped outside of Petersburg, part of the Union force laying siege to the city.

The year 1864 saw not only the siege of Petersburg, but a presidential election campaign. The state of New York was an important factor in the election, and the soldiers would be able to use a new invention called the absentee ballot to vote while in the field. This would be extremely important in New York, as many men of voting age were off fighting in the Union cause. The biggest question being asked in both local and national newspapers was whether or not the New Yorkers would vote for Lincoln, the incumbent, or go with the Democratic candidate, George McClellan, who at one time had been their beloved commanding general. In that capacity, the men held a great deal of respect for him. But as the election neared, it became evident that respect did not necessarily hold true in politics. Captain Oscar Hulser of the Second Artillery summed up the feelings of most of the soldiers in the field when he wrote, "Gen. McClellan was once held in high esteem by the soldiers in general, but since he set his traps in company with disloyal Democrats, the soldiers have repudiated him. And in the coming election Little Mac will be seen crawling out of the small end of the horn."[107]

Another anonymous writer said, "It may be you think the rebs are not Little Mac's friends, but they are.... They say they whipped Mac once and can do it ... again. They hurrah for him every time we talk about him, and they say they are going to vote for him.... All the rebs are holding out for is the coming elections in the North. If Mac is elected they are sure of independence. In his election their only hope rests."[108]

The split over politics was very evident among the officer corps of the 97th. Wheelock was an ardent Republican and supported Lincoln. Captain Isaac Hall, who would later write the regimental history of the 97th, was just as staunchly Democratic. Hall wanted to return home to vote for McClellan, but the request was denied, and he blamed Wheelock.[109]

While outside of Petersburg, the 97th took part in a raid along the Weldon Railroad, a vital supply line that entered the city from the south. For almost a year, the rail line had been the subject of attacks from Union forces. Wheelock led a brigade along the east side of the rail line towards Petersburg, and during a sharp encounter, four of the 97th's officers were captured by the rebels. The next day, a major battle for possession of the railroad took place. During the fracas, Wheelock noticed a gap form between his brigade and the Ninth Corps. He sent a message to General Samuel Crawford, but Crawford ignored it, so Wheelock sent a written note. Though some sharpshooters were sent to fill the gap, the Confederates broke through anyway. Captain Joseph Smith, who had been sent to Crawford by Wheelock, was on his way back to report to the Colonel when he was taken prisoner, and his horse taken away. Smith was sent to the rear, but found himself no longer within rebel lines, but back with the 97th. He told Wheelock where to send his men to get them away from sure capture by the rebels. The Colonel followed his instructions, and his men did not become prisoners.[110]

In January 1865, Lt. Col. Spofford, who had been a prisoner of the rebels since his capture during the battle of Gettysburg, returned to the regiment. His escape was a story for the ages. While in Libby Prison, he had busied himself making match boxes and watch charms of bone, which he carved with a knife he had smuggled into the prison in a box of food from home. In February 1864, he and approximately one hundred other prisoners decided they'd had enough of Libby, and formulated a plan to tunnel their way out. They worked at night, and dug a tunnel well outside the perimeter of the prison walls. On February 9, they crawled through the tunnel, and disguised as citizens of Richmond, made their way through the Confederate capital. Following the tracks of the York Railroad, they were halfway to freedom between the Confederate and Union lines when they were discovered and returned to Libby.

The recaptured officers stayed in the prison until May, when they were transported by rail from Dansville to Macon, Georgia and Fort Oglethorpe. When he arrived, Spofford was informed that he and forty-nine other Federal officers had been chosen by the rebels to be sent to Charleston, South Carolina, to be placed under fire of Federal artillery batteries which were shelling the city's defenses. He and the other doomed officers were kept in houses along the Charleston waterfront, thinking that any day could be their last, when they found out two months later, in July, that they were to be exchanged. They were turned over to the Union Navy, and by the end of August Spofford was back home in Dolgeville, where he received a hero's welcome.[111]

Wheelock was not so lucky. After the Weldon Railroad raid, it was noted by many in the regiment that the Colonel seemed to be continually tired and exhausted. When he had visited Boonville on a prior occasion, friends of his had attempted to talk him out of returning to the regiment, but Wheelock insisted that he was in it for the duration. Even so, he had remarked to a friend that his health was not good, and he probably would not return home from the war. While on a trip to Washington, he contracted typhoid fever and subsequently died.

A service was held, and his body was placed on a gun carriage and escorted to the train depot by an honor guard from the 97th. One of the visitors who viewed his remains in Washington was Carrie Sheads of Gettysburg, the lady who had hidden his sword so it would not be taken by the rebels. Wheelock's funeral was conducted from the Presbyterian Church in Boonville on January 26, and pall bearers were officers from the 14th (First Oneida) and 26th (Second Oneida) regiments. Two hundred members of the 45th Militia took the train from Utica to Boonville to attend, and marched in the parade to the cemetery along with Cataract Fire Company No. 1 of Boonville, veterans of the 97th, and the Masons. A riderless horse was led in the parade by Corporal Alfred Morling, a disabled veteran of the 97th.

Spofford then became the colonel of the 97th. After the episode along the Weldon Railroad, the 97th was sent along with several other regiments toward Dinwiddie Courthouse. While making the move, the rebels attacked the Second Corps, and the 97th dug in and repelled a Confederate attack. They then marched throughout the night over frozen roads, and ran into heavy enemy opposition near Hatcher's Run. It was during this phase of the battle that an amusing incident occurred. The 97th, along with the 16th Maine Infantry, charged what appeared to be a sizeable fort. Both regiments wanted to be the first to enter the fort and place their colors on the ramparts. When they arrived, they discovered the fort was actually a huge pile of sawdust. Thus the Battle of Fort Sawdust was over.[112] However amusing that might have been, the 97th was now in a precarious position, and was running low on ammunition. Indeed, many men were out of ammo. They had to retreat until they came upon an ammunition wagon and replenished their supply. They returned to the fight, which soon wound down and they made camp. The weather was freezing the next morning, and the men could not handle their weapons easily, and were forced to repulse several rebel attacks with freezing cold hands.

During the action, Spofford thought he detected a sniper in a tree nearby and grabbed a pistol and got off a few shots. When there was no returning fire, he assumed he must have dispatched the rebel, but the Confederate had just been playing "dead." He took a shot at the Colonel, and the bullet hit Spofford in the chest, ripping through his overcoat, uniform and two shirts, causing a nasty bruise to the Colonel, but no further damage. Again he had cheated death.[113] By the time the action at Hatcher's Run was over, only a dozen or so men still remained from the 97th.

The 97th marched out on what would prove to be the last campaign of the war in March 1865. On the 31st, Federal cavalry under General Philip Sheridan began an advance toward Five Forks, a vital crossroads. They were attacked by elements of rebel cavalry with supporting infantry, and were pushed back. The Fifth Corps, of which the 97th was part, attacked, but it proved futile, and they were driven off. The next morning, April 1, Sheridan reorganized his men for an attack on a position held by Gen. George Pickett. The Federal attack took place in the late afternoon, and the Fifth Corps, including the 97th, crushed the Confederate left flank. After rolling up the rebel line, the 97th crossed White Oak Road, flanked Pickett's forces, and routed a Confederate force at Gilliam Field. Pickett's men skedaddled back toward Petersburg and its defenses. The Federals had won the day.[114]

Only a week later, General Ulysses S. Grant accepted the surrender of Robert E. Lee's Army of Northern Virginia. For the 97th New York, the worst of the conflict was over. The 97th returned to Utica, via Syracuse, on August 1, 1865, and received a welcome home complete with refreshments in Chancellor Square. The regiment, now numbering a meager 270 men, was welcomed home by Brigadier General Rufus Daggett of the 117th New York (Fourth Oneida), then was escorted in a parade to the homecoming festivities by the Utica Fire Department and veterans of the other four Oneida County regiments, the 14th (First Oneida), 26th (Second Oneida), 117th (Fourth Oneida) and 146th (Fifth Oneida), all of which had returned to the city before them.[115] The parade made its way through the city from the railroad station to Genesee Street, and on to Fayette, Varick, Columbia and other avenues to Chancellor Square.[116] Addresses were given by several local luminaries, including Reverend Dr. S. Hanson Coxe, who stood in for the absent Roscoe Conkling. Of the regiment, Coxe said,

> To you we owe it … comrades in arms, that we are citizens to-day of the freest, and … the strongest nation on the globe.… Your splendid achievements

from Cedar Mountain, through so many battles ... till your eyes caught the light of the white flag of Lee's surrender ... are known and read and gloried by all. Your heroic endurance and self-sacrifice—your hardships, toils and trials, are they not written in our hearts; and in the book of God's remembrance, for your everlasting reward? You have borne the flag of our country triumphantly, and in the name of Oneida, in the name of Washington, in the name of GOD I thank you! We knew that it would be so, when we bade you a sorrowing farewell, and committed that sacred ensign to your hands; we knew that its bright stars would glow amid thunderbolts and its stripes amid streams of fire.[117]

Col. Spofford then rose to a thunderous ovation, to thank Coxe for his remarks. He spoke for the men of the 97th and his remarks were reported in the *Utica Herald,*

Col. Spofford ... regretted that the force of circumstance compelled his men to appear without arms and equipments. His soldiers, he said if not handsome were much better than they appeared.... Hard fought battles ... had worn their clothing. He closed by saying the "our late Colonel Brevet Brig. Gen. Wheelock, when he raised his regiment did not fill it with holiday, Fourth of July soldiers but with men who were expected to receive hard knocks, and the tattered remains of 2,200 men ... before you show how faithfully they have fulfilled their mission. Their hearts are right. We believe you ... are satisfied with our conduct on the bloody field. Permit me, on behalf of my officers and men to return to you our sincere thanks."[118]

Even though it was the third regiment raised in the area, it was the last to return home. The regiment ultimately had a distinguished and honored career by participating in more engagements than any other regiment which left Oneida County to serve in the Civil War. The 97th Regiment had taken part in the following engagements: Cedar Mountain, Rappahannock Station, Thoroughfare Gap, Second Bull Run, Chantilly, South Mountain, Antietam, First Fredericksburg, Second Fredericksburg, Chancellorsville, Gettysburg, Mine Run, Raccoon Ford, Wilderness, Laurel Hill, Spotsylvania Court House, North Anna River, Totopotomoy, Bethesda Church, White Oak Swamp, Petersburg, Weldon Railroad, Hicksford, Hatcher's Run, Quaker Road, Five Forks and Appomattox Court House, for a total of twenty-eight engagements. It had suffered the following casualties: seven officers and ninety-seven enlisted killed in action; five officers and seventy-three enlisted died later of wounds; one officer and one hundred fifty-six enlisted died of disease and other causes; for a total 339.[119] The 97th New York State Volunteer Infantry (Third Oneida) was officially mustered out of Federal service on August 5, 1865.

But that was not the end of the saga of the 97th New York. Lt. Col. Spofford's sword that he had thrown into a bush at Gettysburg, which was discovered and confiscated by a rebel soldier, was returned by the same Confederate thirty years later, a gift from one old veteran to another.

[1]T. Wood Clarke, *Utica for a Century and a Half* (Utica, NY: Widtman Press, 1952), 54; Frederick Phisterer, *New York in the War of the Rebellion* (Albany: J. B. Lyon Company, 1912).

[2]Howard Thomas, *Boys in Blue From the Adirondack Foothills* (Prospect, NY: Prospect Books, 1960), 45.

[3]Thomas, *Boys in Blue*, 46.

[4]David P. Krutz, *Distant Drums: Herkimer County in the War of the Rebellion* (Utica, NY: North Country Books, 1997), 14.

[5]New Century Club, *Outline History of Utica and Vicinity* (Utica, NY: L.C. Child and Son, 1900), 24.

[6]Thomas, *Boys in Blue*, 46.

[7]Thomas, *Boys in Blue*, 52.

[8]Thomas, *Boys in Blue*, 47.

[9]Thomas, *Boys in Blue*, 48; Phisterer, *New York*.

[10]Thomas, *Boys in Blue*, 49; Phisterer, *New York*.

[11]Thomas, *Boys in Blue*, 49.

[12]Thomas, *Boys in Blue*, 49.

[13]Thomas, *Boys in Blue*, 51.

[14]New Century Club, *Outline History*, 28.

[15]Krutz, *Distant Drums*, 15.

[16]Thomas, *Boys in Blue*, 52.

[17]Isaac Hall, *History of the Ninety-Seventh Regiment New York Volunteers ("Conkling Rifles") in the War for the Union* (Utica, NY: L.C. Childs & Son, 1890), 14.

[18]Hall, *History*, 16.

[19]Krutz, *Distant Drums*, 15.

[20]Thomas, *Boys in Blue*, 53.

[21]Ethan F. Bishop. *The Gettysburg Battlefield: The Union Regimental Commanders, a Guide to the Battlefield Sites of the Union Regimental Commanders Who were Casualties* (Westminster, MD: Heritage Books, 2008), 39.

[22]Thomas, *Boys in Blue*, 53.

[23]Thomas, *Boys in Blue*, 53.

[24]Thomas, *Boys in Blue*, 54.

[25]Thomas, *Boys in Blue*, 54.

[26]Krutz, *Distant Drums*, 29.

[27]Krutz, *Distant Drums*, 29.

[28]Hall, *History*, 27.

[29]Thomas, *Boys in Blue*, 63.

[30]Thomas, *Boys in Blue*, 64.

[31]Krutz, *Distant Drums*, 54.

[32]Thomas, *Boys in Blue*, 76.

[33]Hall, *History*, 53.

[34]Hall, *History*, 55.

[35]Krutz, *Distant Drums*, 54.

[36]Thomas, *Boys in Blue*, 76.

[37]Krutz, *Distant Drums*, 56.

[38]Thomas, *Boys in Blue*, 79.

[39]Thomas, *Boys in Blue*, 81.

[40]Hall, *History*, 77.

[41]Hall, *History*, 78.

[42]Hall, *History*, 79.

[43]Hall, *History*, 81.

[44]Thomas, *Boys in Blue*, 97.

[45]Thomas, *Boys in Blue*, 98-99.

[46]Thomas, *Boys in Blue*, 100.

[47]Thomas, *Boys in Blue*, 101.

[48]Thomas, *Boys in Blue*, 102.

[49]Thomas, *Boys in Blue*, 106.

[50]Thomas, *Boys in Blue*, 110-11; *O.R.*, Series I, Vol. XXI, 506.

[51]Thomas, *Boys in Blue*, 114.

[52]Thomas, *Boys in Blue*, 132.

[53]Thomas R. Flagel, *The History Buff's Guide to Gettysburg* (Nashville, TN: Cumberland House, 2006), 30-31.

[54]Flagel, *Guide to Gettysburg*, 29-30.

[55]Flagel, *Guide to Gettysburg*, 32-33.

[56]Flagel, *Guide to Gettysburg*, 33.

[57]Flagel, *Guide to Gettysburg*, 34-35.

[58]Flagel, *Guide to Gettysburg*, 35-37.

[59]Flagel, *Guide to Gettysburg*, 37-38.

[60]Flagel, *Guide to Gettysburg*, 39-40.

[61]New York Monuments Commission for the Battlefields of Gettysburg and Chattanooga, *Final Report of the Battlefield of Gettysburg, Volume II* (Albany, NY: J.B. Lyon Company, 1900), 746.

[62]Krutz, *Distant Drums*, 137.

[63]Krutz, *Distant Drums*, 138.

[64]Krutz, *Distant Drums*, 138.

[65]New York Monuments Commission, *Final Report, Volume II*, 746.

[66]Krutz, *Distant Drums*, 138.

[67]Krutz, *Distant Drums*, 139.

[68]Krutz, *Distant Drums*, 139.

[69]Thomas, *Boys in Blue*, 148.

[70]New York Monuments Commission, *Final Report, Volume II*, 747.

[71]Hall, *History*, 135; *O.R.*, Series I, Vol. XXVII, Part 1, 309.

[72]Krutz, *Distant Drums*, 140; *O.R.*, Series I, Vol. XXVII, Part 1, 309.

[73]Hall, *History*, 137.

[74]Krutz, *Distant Drums*, 140; *O.R.*, Series I, Vol. XXVII, Part 1, 292, 307, 310.

[75]Thomas, *Boys in Blue*, 149.

[76]Thomas, *Boys in Blue*, 149; *O.R.*, Series I, Vol. XXVII. Part 1, 249, 292, 307, 310.

[77]Hall, *History,* 136.

[78]Krutz, *Distant Drums*, 140; *O.R.*, Series I, Vol. XXVII, Part 1, 310.

[79]Thomas, *Boys in Blue*, 149.

[80]Thomas, *Boys in Blue,* 150; *O.R.*, Series I, Vol. XXVII, Part 1, 310.

[81]Hall, *History,* 141.

[82]Thomas, *Boys in Blue*, 150.

[83]Krutz, *Distant Drums* 142.

[84]*Gettysburg Daily,* "Christmas Decorations on the Carrie Sheads House," website, http://www. gettysburgdaily.com., 17.

[85]Thomas, *Boys in Blue*, 151.

[86]Thomas, *Boys in Blue*, 151.

[87]Krutz, *Distant Drums*, 142-43.

[88]Hall, *History,* 142; *O.R.*, Series I, Vol. XXVII, Part 1, 307.

[89]Hall, *History,* 143; *O.R.*, Series I, Vol. XXVII, Part 1, 307.

[90]*O.R.*, Series I, Vol. XXVII, Part 1, 307.

[91]Hall, *History,* 144.

[92]Hall, *History,* 145-46.

[93]Krutz, *Distant Drums*, 144.

[94]Krutz, *Distant Drums,* 148.

[95]Krutz, *Distant Drums*, 148.

[95]Thomas, *Boys in Blue*, 171-72.

[97]Thomas, *Boys in Blue*, 176-77.

[98]Thomas, *History,* 151.

[99]New York Monuments Committee, *Final Report, Volume II*, 746-47.

[100]Krutz, *Distant Drums,* 183.

[101]Krutz, *Distant Drums,* 184.

[102]Thomas, *Boys in Blue*, 172.

[103]Thomas, *Boys in Blue*, 174-76.

[104]New Century Club, *Outline History of Utica and Vicinity,* 27.

[105]Thomas, *Boys in Blue,* 189.

[106]United States Army Center of Military History, *Medal of Honor Recipients. Civil War (A-L)*, http://www.history.army.mil/html/moh/civwaral.html, 2009.

[107]Thomas, *Boys in Blue*, 238.

[108]Thomas, *Boys in Blue*, 238.

[109]Thomas, *Boys in Blue*, 238.

[110]*O.R.*, Series I, Vol. XLII, Part 1, 509-11.

[111]Thomas, *Boys in Blue*, 260-61.

[112]Thomas, *Boys in Blue*, 264; *O.R.*, Series I, Vol. XLVI, Part 1, 890.

[113]Thomas, *Boys in Blue*, 265.

[114]*O.R.*, Series I, Vol. XLVI, Part 1, 890.

[115]New Century Club, *Outline History of Utica and Vicinity*, 26.

[116]Hall, *History*, 277.

[117]Hall, *History*, 277-78.

[118]Krutz, *Distant Drums*, 351.

[119]Frederick Phisterer, *New York in the War of the Rebellion, 1861-1865* (Albany: J.B. Lyon Company, 1912), Vol. 4, 3111.

CHAPTER 7

"ONLY HONORABLE MARKS"
THE 117TH NEW YORK AT FORT FISHER

by

James S. Pula

By the summer of 1862 the reality of war had come home to the Upper Mohawk Valley. Long lists of casualties published in local newspapers provided terse notice of friends, neighbors and relatives wounded, dismembered or killed on bloody battlefields the like of which Americans had never before seen in their entire history. Worse still, the terrible suffering had not led to the swift victory over the secessionists people eagerly anticipated only a year before. The First Battle of Bull Run resulted in a shocking defeat for the Federal forces, leading to the realization that the war would not be over in ninety days, or even by Christmas. The horrible killing fields at Shiloh brought new horrors in the spring of 1862, followed by a series of Union defeats in the Shenandoah Valley and the spectacular failure of Gen. George B. McClellan's much heralded Peninsula Campaign. By mid-summer, it was clear to most that the North was losing the war, and losing badly.

Amid this discouraging backdrop, President Abraham Lincoln issued a call on July 1, 1862, for 300,000 more volunteers to fill the vacancies created by the killed, the wounded, and those whose original one-year enlistments were expiring. The following day, New York Governor Edwin D. Morgan called upon New Yorkers "to meet the demands of the government. The period has come when all must aid. New York has not thus far stood back. Ready, and more than willing, she has met every summons to duty. Let not her history be falsified, nor her position lowered."[1]

To answer the call, on July 5 the New York State Adjutant General's office issued a notice to each senatorial district in the state, calling upon local communities to raise the necessary regiments. In the Nineteenth District, the Hon. Horatio Seymour established a recruiting committee of prominent local citizens. On July 14, the committee met for the first time in Bagg's Hotel in Utica. One of its first actions was to recommend William R. Pease as colonel of the new regi-

Col. William R. Pease
(Oneida County Historical Society)

ment, an appointment he officially received on July 19, 1862. Born in Utica, Pease was an excellent choice, having graduated from the United States Military Academy and being on active duty in Utica as Mustering and Disbursing Officer for Central New York at the time of his appointment.[2]

Despite the sobering casualty lists and mounting losses that appeared daily in local newspapers, Oneida County responded to the nation's call with the same dedication it had in the confident early days of 1861. Volunteers came forward from the machine shops of Rome, the iron forges of Washingtonville, and the textile factories of New York Mills. Farmers left their families in Westmoreland, Bridgewater, Deerfield, and Floyd. The Welsh settlements in Remsen and Steuben responded, as did the French Canadians in Forestport and the Irish in Utica. Men came forward from Hamilton College in Clinton, from the law firm of Stevens & Stone in Camden, and from the general store in Knoxboro. By ones and twos, dozens and scores, they arrived at Rome to begin their introduction to military service.[3] In Rome, the new recruits met at Camp Huntington where they mustered in for three years service with the 117th New York Volunteer Infantry between August 8 and August 16. Normally additional training would have been expected, but the nation needed men. Trained or not, the regiment was ordered to Washington. When it left by train on August 22, some of the new soldiers had been in the army less than two weeks.[4] So quickly did the regiment depart that its colors were not yet ready when it boarded the train for the front. Instead of the formal ceremony many regiments remembered with fondness years later, the ladies of Utica had to mail the new flag to the unit once it was in Washington. They wrote:

> The ladies of Utica, desirous of evincing their interest in the great work you have undertaken and their faith in you, the sons of Oneida, have prepared this banner with its motto chosen from your national anthem, which they hope will be satisfactory to you all, reminding you at once of the high responsibility which we devolve upon you, the chosen defenders of our liberty and happiness of the dear ones you have left behind, whose honor is inseparably bound up with your own, and above all, of your duty towards and your dependence on that higher power without whose aiding hand none can prosper.
>
> This is no time for words and we have but few to give you. Go forward with a will, bearing bravely on the glorious banner which is the ensign of all we hold

most dear. Come back when your work is done, and well done, bringing this same emblem, torn and defaced it may be, but bearing only honorable marks which shall add a glow of thankfulness and pride to the heart of every maiden, wife and mother whose hopes rest so fondly upon each of you; or, come not back to us again forever. Sorrow we can bear; disgrace, never. But this is a word which, in connection with you of the One Hundred and Seventeenth, we need not use. Oneida has not known its meaning and we feel assured that it is not at your hands she will be taught to.

Take therefore, our banner and with it receive our prayers for your safety, your happiness, your glory and above all, for the safety of the land which you go forth to defend and redeem.

Unlike the other infantry regiments from Oneida County, the "Fourth Oneida" was not ordered to duty with the Army of the Potomac. Instead, perhaps because of the minimal training it had received, the regiment was assigned to the defenses of Washington where it manned fortifications and trained until January 1863.[5] During the long weeks that fall, while the Union army fought some of the costliest battles of the war at Second Bull Run, Antietam and Fredericksburg, the 117th New York was broken into smaller detachments to man various fortifications leading into the nation's capitol. Anxious for something other than continuous drilling and digging fortifications, the men began to show their frustration. "Our Regiment is all split to pieces and some think that it never will get together again," James M. Hewitt of Marshall wrote to his brother George. "There is a report that we will be shoved into old Regiments; if we are it will be one damned shame. But it is all humbug down here anyway. As for news, you can find out more at home than I can down here."[6]

Frustrated with the repetitive boredom of garrison duty, the men were generally pleased with the arrival of Special Orders No. 57 dated April 14, 1863, assigning the 117th New York to the Seventh Corps in the Department of Virginia.[7] Soon after arriving at Norfolk, the regiment received further orders to march to Suffolk, Virginia, a key strategic point near the mouth of the James River, to participate in a Federal movement toward Richmond. Before the offensive could be launched, however, a large Confederate force under Gen. James Longstreet arrived causing cancellation of the Federal plan. With this, the command settled down to intermittent patrols, reconnaissance operations, and skirmishing in support for Stevens' Battery on Calhoun Point along the James River. On the opposite bank, rebels constructed their own battery to fire on Union shipping, while Confederate sharpshooters attempted where possible to harass any Union sailors and soldiers careless enough to expose themselves within their range. To counter this, Col. Pease had his men dig rifle pits and open "a brisk fire" to suppress the rebels.[8]

From Suffolk, orders arrived transferring the 117th New York to the Tenth Corps on Folly Island, South Carolina, where it took part in the sieges of Forts Wagner and Gregg on Morris Island in an attempt to capture the port city of

Charleston that the fortifications guarded. En route, the ocean voyage caused great seasickness, while once ashore one soldier recalled: "Ague, fever, and bowel affections, in a few days unfitted one hundred for duty. To these diseases, a little later, scurvy was superadded."[9]

In April 1864, the 117th New York found itself transferred once again to Virginia to join Gen. Benjamin Butler's Army of the James operating against Richmond and Petersburg. Assigned to man the siege lines at Bermuda Hundred on the approaches to these two cities, the regiment lost two enlisted men killed and one mortally wounded in skirmishing over the next few days. It then took part in the

Col. Alvin White
(Oneida County Historical Society)

Battle of Drewry's Bluff on May 14-16, an attempt by Butler to break the Confederate defensive works along the James River on the outskirts of Richmond. The initial Federal assault by the Eighteenth Corps made progress, but was finally halted, pushed back by a rebel counterattack.[10]

The 117th came up as reinforcements, went quickly into line, and was almost immediately attacked by superior numbers of the enemy. In its first real full-scale battle, the regiment came immediately under rebel musket fire that ripped through its ranks. Color Sergeant William E. Pease of Utica was severely wounded while waving the colors defiantly at the enemy. Others fell wounded, but new volunteers came forward to keep the colors aloft. Despite mounting losses, including the wounding of its commanding officer, Col. Alvin White, whose predecessor had been promoted to higher command, the regiment stemmed the retreat and held its ground until ordered off the field. Although behaving with great gallantry, the regiment's combat baptism was costly—20 killed, 62 wounded, and 7 missing.[11]

On May 30 the regiment sped rapidly north by forced march to cooperate with Gen. Ulysses S. Grant's assault on the Confederates north of the Chickahominy River. The 117th next found itself holding a portion of the Federal front line exposed to the deadly missiles of Confederate sharpshooters slicing into them from trees and hills to their front and flank.[12] "A head or hand could not be exposed above our fortified line, without drawing the musket shot or minnie," reported Surgeon James A. Mowris. "A man sitting a few steps from the entrenchments, sheltered as he supposed, in earnest or mirthful conversation, would sud-

George B. Fairhead
*(Oneida County Historical
Society)*

denly cease speaking, his comrades, on looking round, would be shocked at the sight of his prostrate corpse."[13] For several days the regiment held its ground under constant threat of death or painful wounding, but its fate could have been much worse. It remained in reserve during the ill-advised and disastrous frontal assault on the Confederate lines on June 3, an attack that saw the Federals lose thousands of their comrades in only fifteen minutes of concentrated fury. It was the only assault Gen. Grant ever admitted he regretted making. Although it did not participate in the disastrous assault, the 117th New York still lost nine men killed and mortally wounded.[14]

Several days after its failure at Cold Harbor, the Union army was on the move again, pushing further south. Alternately manning the siege lines at Bermuda Hundred and Petersburg during the next few weeks, the regiment also participated in Grant's attempt to capture Fort Harrison losing several men in the process. George B. Fairhead, a teacher from New York Mills in Company D, described in his diary how the Confederates attacked the regiment's picket line, only to be driven off by a counterattack that left several wounded rebels lying between the hostile lines. "Three lay between our & the reb lines all day," he wrote. "Our men carried them water although one of them was nearer the Reb line than ours. After dark he crawled into our lines. Farther on the left of the line a reb officer was very officially and magnanimously inviting our men to desert, saying we wont hurt you. This officer felt a sharp, severe pain in his breast, & dropped instantly. A 'Yank' had sent a piece of lead through him. A poor remuneration for his generosity."[15]

Capt. William J. Hunt, Company F, 117th New York, led 100 skirmishers from the regiment in advance of a major attack on the Petersburg Heights on June 15. Taking advantage of Confederate preoccupation with the main assault wave, Hunt led his men into a gap between two rebel batteries, formed into line and opened fire into the rear of Battery 5. Struck unexpectedly from behind, the defenders threw down their arms while their officer tendered his sword to Hunt. In this amazing coup, Capt. Hunt's small command captured four artillery pieces, 211 prisoners (including a lieutenant colonel, two majors, four captains, and nine lieutenants), and the battle flag of the 26th Virginia Infantry.[16]

On September 29, 1864, Grant once again tested the Confederate lines at Chaffin's Farm. Assigned to the attacking force, the 117th New York was ordered to cross three-quarters of a mile of open ground to assault Ft. Gilmer. Knowing well what lay before them, the men ate a hasty breakfast, their minds no doubt on the task before them, then filed quickly into line to form for the attack.[17] Moving forward as part of the reserve, they marched through a woods where artillery shells shredded the tree limbs above their heads. Moving into the clear, they passed dead and wounded black soldiers lying about the ground, casualties from an earlier attack on the rebel rifle pits. As they formed line of battle perpendicular to the road, artillery began to find the range. Several men fell dead or wounded. "The Rebs had a battery of two guns a short distance in our front, which were sending canister among us," explained George Fairhead. Then

Capt. William J. Hunt
(Oneida County Historical Society)

the commands rang out. "Attention!" "Fix bayonets!" "Forward!" The lines moved forward at a steady pace, Confederate artillery now joined by musket fire to blanket the field with deadly missiles.[18] "As the lines went forward," Mowris reported, "the severity of the fire increased." Shells burst just over the heads of the advancing men, "while grape and canister were used with frightful effect. Soon a withering musketry was superadded. ... The storm of every known missile of warfare was most effective. Men fell on every hand. ... Still they moved on. The carnage was awful."[19]

"Charge!" The command screamed above the din of battle. "In an instant every man was up," George Fairhead confided to his diary, "bayonets on, & going forward. The cannon in our front, a large Reb batt. away on our 'left,' dealt death into our advancing column. Still on we went. Bullets began to cut down many. The ground was newly ploughed, men got exhausted & had to lay down & rest before they reached the position of the two guns. During this rest the Johnnies 'limbered up' and dusted, before this was done our men had breathed a little & were only up in time to give the 'dusting' Graybacks a few shots. This position gained we came to a Halt."[20]

In the chaos of battle, the color bearer carrying the state flag was wounded, falling to the ground unnoticed with the flag beside him. Passing nearby, John D. Ernst, a shoemaker from Paris, spied the colors lying on the ground. Lunging for them, he grabbed the flagstaff as the Union assault finally stalled and all around him men recoiled in retreat. Amid the confusion, Ernst carried off his regiment's colors, saving them from the dishonor of imminent capture. For his heroism, he

G. W. Roys
(Donald Wisnoski)

was promoted to color sergeant.[21]

The horrible process was soon repeated at Fair Oaks where Butler received orders to make a diversion to support Grant's assault at Hatcher's Run on October 27-28. As its part in the engagement, the 117th New York formed line of battle along the Darbytown Road. The assault is vividly described by George Fairhead in his diary entry for October 27:

> In this order we advanced toward a reb work, shot and shell began to fly as usual. Onward we crowded, some were falling. After getting about 1/2 mile through the woods the column laid down and took a little rest. The command "forward" was again given. I raised up and repeated the word and was just urging the men up and forward when a bullet went "thug" through the side of my neck. It knocked me down. In a moment I was conscious of the locality of my injury. Finding the carotid artery was not severed I was aware that I should not bleed to Death. I laid here a little while to allow the bullets to slack a little when I worked my way to the rear. Reaching the Doctor I had him examine the wound. He had no time to dress it. I tied my kerchief around it and getting into an ambulance was carried to the flying Hospl. Many horrid wounds were being dressed. Doctor Carpenter dressed mine, and then assigned me to a bunk which was occupied in part by an adjt. who had a bullet wound through the leg just above the knee (flesh wound). He moaned considerable through the night.[22]

"BUTLER'S FOLLY"

By the fall of 1864 the war had finally taken a decided turn in favor of the Union. After a long and arduous campaign, forces under Gen. William Tecumseh Sherman captured the key commercial and transportation center of Atlanta, destroying a significant portion of the remaining Southern industrial system. From there, Sherman drove his army east toward Savannah, destroying railroads, manufacturing centers, warehouses, and anything else that might be of aid to the Confederacy in its attempt to prolong the rebellion. At the same time, Union forces in Virginia under Gen. Ulysses S. Grant waged a very stubborn and bloody fight against Robert E. Lee's Army of Northern Virginia, finally succeeding in pinning the largest remaining Confederate army into the earthworks surrounding

Richmond and Petersburg. Unable to execute the maneuvers at which he excelled, Lee's smaller army, though still defiant, was seemingly pinned in an endless siege that negated any remaining striking power it might yet hold. As December dawned, Sherman stood poised to invest Savannah, while Grant relentlessly expanded his lines to cut off the remaining railroads supplying Lee's army.

Once Sherman succeeded in taking Savannah, which he eventually accomplished on Christmas Day, he then had the option to move north, striking at any remaining rebel opposition while at the same time destroying remaining Southern industrial or transportation facilities. He might even continue north through the Carolinas, eventually linking up with Grant's forces in Virginia to administer the *coup-de-grace* to Lee. Such a movement north through the Carolinas would be reminiscent of Lord Cornwallis's march in 1781 that eventually ended in disaster at Yorktown. While the British plan held high hopes, Cornwallis's Achilles heel was the need to re-supply his army with provisions and ammunition. Expecting the British navy to bring these to him in the sheltered waters off the York Peninsula, his plan was foiled when the French navy defeated their British rivals, denying Cornwallis the needed re-supply and pinning him hopelessly at Yorktown with no avenue of escape.

While a movement north by Sherman held much promise, it also held the same hidden danger Cornwallis faced more than four score years before. Once he moved north, should Sherman face unexpectedly significant Confederate resistance, or a scorched earth policy that denied him resupply, he would be in a dire predicament if he could not be reinforced or re-supplied along the coast by the Union navy. For this reason, Federal planners focused their eyes and attention on Wilmington, North Carolina. The only significant seaport still in Confederate hands following the capture of Mobile, Alabama, in August 1864, Wilmington was the last safe haven for blockade runners attempting to bring goods into the Confederacy. Regarded as "the last gateway between the Confederate States and the outside world," the port was only 570 miles from Nassau in the Bahamas and 674 miles from Bermuda, both thriving centers of smuggling activity into the Confederacy. As a sign of its importance, the Wilmington & Weldon Railroad running from the port into Virginia served as one of the major supply lines for Lee's army, while the port itself was guarded by what was then considered "the most powerful seacoast fortification in the Confederacy."[23]

As early as August 30, 1864, Secretary of the Navy Gideon Welles confided to his diary: "Something must be done to close the entrance to the Cape Fear River. ... Could we seize the forts at the entrance of the Cape Fear and close the illicit traffic, it would be almost as important as the capture of Richmond on the fate of the Rebels, and an important step in that direction." On September 15 he returned to the subject: "The importance of closing Wilmington and cutting off Rebel communication is paramount to all other questions—more important, practically, than the capture of Richmond."[24]

The Lincoln administration agreed, assigning Adm. David Dixon Porter to command the naval forces involved in the planned operation. To lead the ground attack Gen. Grant selected Maj. Gen. Godfrey Weitzel, chief engineer of the Army of the James. Weitzel, however, came under the authority of Maj. Gen. Benjamin F. Butler, commander of the Department of Virginia and North Carolina, who decided to accompany the expedition.[25]

Born in New Hampshire in 1818, Butler graduated from Colby College in Maine, was admitted to the bar in 1840, and built an impressive criminal practice in Lowell and Boston. Elected to the Massachusetts legislature as a Democrat, he supported the nomination of Jefferson Davis for president at the Charleston convention in 1859, then backed the outspoken States' Rights advocate John C. Breckinridge when he was eventually nominated. Nevertheless, when Southerners fired on Ft. Sumter he immediately took up arms as brigadier general of Massachusetts militia and personally led the 8th Massachusetts to Washington to protect the capitol. The first major general appointed by Lincoln, he led a successful amphibious landing at Hatteras Inlet in August 1861, commanded the troops who occupied New Orleans after its surrender to Admiral David G. Farragut, then served as military governor in the Pelican state, earning the enmity of Southerners for his strict administration and liberal lining of his own pockets. Appointed to command of the Army of the James in 1863, his career took a turn for the worse when he allowed his forces to be bottled up by a numerically inferior Confederate force.[26] The assault on Fort Fisher would be his opportunity to revive his flagging career.

Butler's plan was both unorthodox and bold. He proposed loading the USS Louisiana with tons of explosives, making it into a floating bomb that could be sailed toward Fort Fisher where it would be detonated, destroying everything within hundreds of yards. In the ensuing destruction and confusion, Federal forces could easily rush in and capture the remains of the great fortress. Lincoln was not impressed, but Assistant Secretary of the Navy Gustavus Fox was taken with the idea and approved it.[27]

To make the assault, Butler selected 6,500 infantry from the 3rd Division, Twenty-fifth Corps under Gen. Charles J. Paine and the 2nd Division, Twenty-fourth Corps under Gen. Adelbert Ames, supported by two artillery batteries. The 1st Brigade of Ames division, led by Brig. Gen. Newton M. Curtis, included the 3rd, 112th, 117th, and 142nd New York Volunteer Infantry Regiments.[28]

The troops broke camp on December 8, marching down the James River to Fortress Monroe where they boarded transports for the journey south. Hermon Clarke, a general store clerk from Waterville serving in Company D, wrote to his father that the regiment was roused very early, leaving Fortress Monroe on the transport Weybosset at 3:00 a.m., December 13, steering first for Mathias Point and then on to Cape Henry. The transports arrived off Wilmington on the 14th, to be joined by Porter's fleet of 64 warships on the 18th.[29]

As the ships moved into position off the coast on December 19 the weather turned threatening, blowing into a full gale by the next day. With the increasing wind, the roiling waves dramatically increased the rolling and pitching of the *Weybosset,* causing the soldiers to become hopelessly seasick. To pass the time, impromptu groups debated the issues of the day, while others sang songs in hopes of taking their minds off their plight. When the winds increased even more, terror magnified the effects of the dreadfully ill stomachs.[30] Since the storm made any landing on the hostile shore impossible, the transports received orders to sail for Morehead City, North Carolina, to replenish supplies and ride out the tempest. With over 500 desperately ill men on board for nearly two weeks, Clarke expressed the desire of many when he wrote: "we are in hopes to get ashore here to give the men an opportunity to clean up a little. We have been on board since the 8th—over 500 men; you can judge of our condition."[31]

When the storm finally abated, the transports left Morehead City on December 24, headed back to Wilmington. Although it was Christmas Eve, the men now had more on their minds than the holidays. Clarke reported the news to the folks back home in a letter to his father: "To our Brigade is given the work of assaulting Fort Fisher when we get to it. Most officers think [the assault] will be a failure unless the Navy does better than usual, for charging works is a played-out idea for our Brigade."[32] Veterans that they now were, the men realized all too well the casualties they could expect to take in a headlong charge on entrenched enemy works. The thought was enough to dampen any holiday spirit they may have felt.

Their collective mood did not improve when they awoke the next morning to find themselves within sight of their destination. Considered to be the "largest and most powerful earthen fort in the Confederacy," Fort Fisher was the most significant of "an elaborate defensive network of riverside batteries and fortifications that guarded the approaches" to Wilmington.[33] Gen. Braxton Bragg commanded Confederate forces in the region, but the two officers most immediately responsible for the defense of Fort Fisher were Major General W. H. C. Whiting, who was largely responsible for the development of the fortifications, and Col. William Lamb commanding Fort Fisher itself. Upon his arrival, Lamb later wrote, "I immediately set to work, and with 500 colored laborers, assisted by the garrison, constructed the largest earthwork in the Southern Confederacy, of heavy timbers covered by sand from 15 to 20 feet deep and sodded with turf."[34] By the time Lamb was finished, the fortifications were indeed impressive. The land approaches from the north were covered by twenty heavy guns, two mortars, and four pieces of light artillery, all protected by embrasures and fronted by abatis, ditches, rifle pits and land mines. The seaward face of the fortification boasted twenty-four heavy guns including one 170-pound Blakely rifled gun and one 130-pound Armstrong rifled gun. Battery Buchanan at the south end of the peninsula's point held another four heavy guns. This side, too, was well protected with embrasures and other obstacles similar to those facing north.[35]

Lamb's work, aided by Whiting, progressed as fast as resources would allow. The fall of Fort Fisher, they realized, would be a disaster. As Lamb explained: "The position commanded the last gateway between the Confederate States and the outside world. Its capture, with the resulting loss of all the Cape Fear River defenses, and of Wilmington, the great importing depot of the South, effectually ended all blockade-running. General Lee sent me word that Fort Fisher must be held, or he could not sustain his army."[36] General Lee also sent troops. By December 25 the garrison included five companies of the 36th North Carolina Artillery and two companies of the 10th North Carolina Artillery, along with a few sailors, marines, and junior reserves, a total of 1,431 men. On December 20 Lee dispatched by rail Maj. Gen. Robert F. Hoke's division of 6,155 combat-hardened veterans from his own army to assist in the defense of Wilmington.[37]

Assaulting a formidable fortress would not be easy, especially one protected on three sides by water with only a thin, sandy beach facing the open sea where the federal invasion force lay. Nevertheless, Butler put his plan in motion on the evening of December 23 when the *Louisiana*, loaded with 215 tons of explosives, was set adrift on the incoming tide. At 1:40 a.m. on the morning of Christmas Eve a tremendous flash lit the night followed almost immediately with the crashing sound and concussion of an enormous explosion. The huge pyrotechnic display awoke everyone for miles around, but exploded too far from the fort to do much damage other than rearranging some of the sand. Thereafter, soldiers on both sides found "Butler's Folly" a source of many creative jokes.[38] Unfazed by the failure of his secret weapon, Butler ordered the operation to proceed.

All Christmas Eve and into Christmas morning Porter's warships bombard-ed the works, expending some 20,000 rounds of ammunition, but the earth and log construction of the fort kept damage to a minimum, while the garrison, hiding in bombproof dugouts, suffered only twenty-three wounded. As the bombard-ment continued, Brig. Gen. William W. Kirkland's Confederate brigade of 1,300 men arrived at the base of the peninsula to support the garrison. Hoke's entire division was not far behind.[39]

About noon on Christmas Day the order came to begin disembarking the troops about three miles north of Fort Fisher. Curtis's brigade had the honor of being first ashore, the 142nd New York leading, followed by the 117th. Over the side of the ship the troops carefully climbed, down into the whaleboats that would row them ashore. One false move might land them in the water where the weight of their equipment would quickly pull them underwater to their deaths. "We watched anxiously," wrote Edward King Wightman, a soldier in the 3rd New York aboard the transport *Weybosset*. "Before they touched shore, the men were over the sides of the boats waist deep in water and were actually deploying, skirmishing and advancing at a double quick ere they had reached dry land. A rousing cheer—a stentorian Christmas cheer—went up from the whole fleet."[40]

Capt. Almond R. Stevens	Capt. John T. Thomas
(Oneida County Historical Society)	*(Oneida County Historical Society)*

Once ashore, Gen. Curtis arrayed his brigade across the peninsula facing toward Fort Fisher, detaching the 117th New York, now under Col. Rufus Daggett, to protect the brigade's rear. "I ordered the One hundred and seventeenth New York Volunteers to proceed toward the Wilmington road and hold it against any re-enforcements that might be sent against me from the city," explained Curtis in his official report of the action.[41] In response, Daggett led the regiment across the peninsula, turned north, and sent out companies B and H under the command of Capt. Almond R. Stevens. Moving cautiously forward, Stevens's men captured two abandoned Confederate artillery pieces. Stevens then sent out skirmishers under Capt. John T. Thomas, a stone cutter from Trenton, to search the area ahead and give warning in the event the enemy approached in force.[42]

Warily, Capt. Thomas edged forward until suddenly the brush parted and he stood face-to-face with Confederate Major John M. Reece of the 8th North Carolina Reserves. Thinking quickly, Thomas, though alone at the time, announced to the equally startled major that the rebel was surrounded by Union forces and might as well surrender. The major agreed. Thomas brought him back to Stevens, then the two of them reported with their prisoner to Col. Daggett. During the trip back to the Union lines, Major Reece revealed that he commanded more than 200 troops only a short distance away. When he heard this, Daggett suggested they surrender, repeating Thomas's earlier claim that the Confederates were hopelessly surrounded by the Federal army. Reece responded that he believed his men would surrender, suggesting that an officer and some men accompany him back to his lines. Daggett, of course, was immediately suspicious of a trap.[43]

"Are you a Mason?" inquired the rebel major.

"No, but he is," replied Daggett, pointing at Capt. Stevens.

Reece swore to Stevens that he meant no trick or subterfuge, whereupon Stevens, satisfied that the Masonic bond between the two men would ensure his safety, volunteered to accompany the Confederate alone back to his lines. The two men had gone about 200 yards beyond the 117th's picket line when the distinct sound of rifles being cocked reached their ears.

"What does that mean?" Stevens nervously inquired.

"The boys are preparing to fire on us," the major calmly replied, "wait a moment." With that he stepped forward, gave the countersign, then said "Don't fire, boys."

"No major, we won't," came the response from an unseen rebel.

"Come on, Captain," Reece said, turning to Stevens as he moved toward his men, "it's all right." Then turning back to the men beginning to crowd about him, Reece said matter-of-factly, "Well, boys, I've surrendered."

"Not by a damn sight," replied Lt. F. M. Hamlin stepping from the startled group.

"Yes! Yes! I have," the major affirmed. "We are surrounded and can't get away."

"Yes," confirmed Stevens stepping from behind the rebel major. "We have got you boys, you may as well give it up."

"Be you a Yankee officer?" a startled Southerner asked in disbelief.

"Yes," Stevens replied.

" Well, by God!"[44]

Stevens ordered the Confederates to follow him and soon several other men from the 117th, sent out by Daggett to see what had become of Stevens, arrived. Together, the small band moved the mass of prisoners into the federal lines. A few, led by the disgruntled Lt. Hamlin, melted into the dusk, but when the count was made Stevens learned that he had captured a major, a captain, five lieutenants, and 230 enlisted men from the 8th North Carolina Reserves. In addition, the Oneida County boys also captured a Confederate courier carrying important dispatches that they turned over to Gen. Curtis's staff.[45]

Despite Stevens's amazing accomplishment, there was little time to bask in the glory of the moment. While the prisoners were being marched into captivity, Curtis's main force pushed skirmishers to within 75 yards of Fort Fisher's outer works. One enterprising officer from the 142nd New York was actually able to sneak forward onto a rampart and make off with a rebel signal flag as a trophy. But at the same time, news arrived that Hoke's Confederate division was within five miles of the Union positions. Although Curtis, convinced he could quickly force his way into the rebel works, wanted to attack immediately, Gen. Weitzel vetoed the idea, believing the attack would be too costly and that any delay would subject the Federals to an attack by superior numbers of Hoke's infantry approaching from their rear. Instead of the anticipated assault on Fort Fisher, Butler ordered a retreat to the beach for re-embarkation.[46]

The order to retreat presented two major problems for Col. Daggett and the 117th New York. First, there were nearly as many captives as there were captors. It was not possible for Daggett's men to spare enough men to both guard the prisoners and carry the captured weapons back to the beach while still maintaining an effective rear guard to protect their withdrawal. This problem was solved by trusting the rebels to carry their own weapons along with them. Potentially dangerous though it was, the strategy worked. Not a single Confederate took advantage of the situation to either escape or cause mischief.[47]

The second problem was the withdrawal itself. For some reason Curtis received the order after the other troops had already withdrawn, leaving the boys from Oneida County in a very exposed position. Although Curtis was able to get some men out to the ships, darkness and an increasingly violent surf made it impossible to extract them all. "We succeeded, however, in getting nearly all the prisoners and about a quarter of the Brigade shipped when several boats were lost and it [the operation] was given up for the night," reported Waterville's Hermon Clarke. Some 600 men, including the entire 117th New York, were stranded on the beach with more than 6,000 angry Confederates moving toward them. There were no entrenching tools, no tents or other shelter, and the cold December night was accompanied by an even colder rain that beat down on the men without mercy. Surrounded by the enemy, only the forbidding guns of the fleet at their back prevented the Confederates from launching what would surely have been a murderous attack on their exposed position. Cold, wet, miserable, they spent Christmas night huddling on the beach praying for morning to come. When it did, they found the waves still too violent for the small whaleboats to approach the shore. Clarke reported that all they could manage was that "a line was got ashore and they sent us some bread, meat, coffee, and a barrel of whiskey." All day they waited anxiously, all night they waited cold and wet to the skin.[48]

Finally, on the 27th, after two days and nights on the beach, the surf finally calmed enough for an attempted rescue. Even so, the boats could not make it all the way to shore for fear of being damaged or marooned themselves. Instead, the exhausted men had to wade out into the icy surf up to their armpits to clamor aboard the rescue boats. Clarke described the scene: "Four lines were got ashore and surfboats put each of them to work. The work of embarking 1000 men commenced. I wish you could have seen it. The boats can't come down to the beach; they halt where water is about 4 feet deep when the surf is out and when the surf comes in it will [be] from 6 to 10 [feet] deep. The men wade out to the boat and climb in. When the surf comes they catch the line and hang on. For 2 1/2 hours I stood in water from my knees to my neck, putting men and equipment into boats. At 11 o'clock we were all on board ship and had orders to proceed to Deep Bottom and occupy our old camp."[49] Miraculously, no one was lost.

When the transports finally anchored again off Fort Monroe, Clarke summed up the campaign for the folks back home: "Well, the expedition is pronounced a failure and who it will be laid to I don't know. Butler will lay it to someone. ... I suppose our running under that Fort and bringing away their prisoners was the cunning thing of the war. It was a kind of Ethan Allen trick."[50]

Butler, who hoped to use the campaign to rejuvenate his career, failed miserably. Weitzel, a generally competent officer, suffered somewhat from his association with Butler, but managed to retain a command in the army. Grant, furious over the failure, insisted upon another attempt because he badly wanted Wilmington as a base of supply and succor for Sherman's planned movement north beginning in January. To accomplish this he shipped Butler off north to "await orders," replacing him with Gen. Alfred H. Terry.[51]

"A SAVAGE HAND-TO-HAND CONFLICT"

Born in Hartford, Connecticut, in 1827, Alfred Howe Terry gained admittance to the bar in 1849, serving as clerk of the New Haven County superior court from 1854-60. A militia officer, he served at First Bull Run as colonel of the 2nd Connecticut, then recruited the 7th Connecticut which he led during the capture of Port Royal, South Carolina, in November 1861, and in the siege of Fort Pulaski, Georgia, in April 1862. Appointed brigadier general in the same month, he joined the Army of the James in command of the Tenth Corps that autumn.[52] For the renewed effort at Fort Fisher, Terry would command an expanded force consisting of Col. Joseph C. Abbot's 2nd Brigade, 1st Division, Twenty-fourth Corps, Brig. Gen. Adelbert Ames 2nd Division, Twenty-fourth Corps, and Gen. Charles J. Paine's 3rd Division, Twenty-fifth Corps, supported by four guns of the 16th New York Independent Battery, six guns of Battery E, 3rd U.S. Artillery, and three companies of siege artillery with twenty-four guns and twenty small mortars. Labeled "Terry's Provisional Corps," the entire force numbered some 10,000 men.[53]

Although the Federal force would be slightly larger than the previous effort in December, the Confederates, too, would be better prepared. In addition to the veterans of Gen. Robert F. Hoke's division from Lee's Army of Northern Virginia poised to support the fort and oppose any landing of Federal troops, Gen. Whiting and Col. Lamb had some 2,500 men within the garrison itself. These included two companies of the 10th North Carolina (1st Artillery); ten companies of the 36th North Carolina (2nd Artillery); Battery D, 1st North Carolina Artillery Battalion; Battery C, 3rd North Carolina Artillery Battalion; Battery D, 13th North Carolina Artillery Battalion; four companies of the 40th North Carolina; and about fifty sailors and marines of the Confederate navy. When the federal landing eventually took place, Hoke sent veteran infantry from the 11th, 21st and 25th South Carolina of Gen. Johnson Hagood's Brigade as reinforcements.[54] It was a strong force, sufficient to man the fort's batteries and ramparts against the Union forces arrayed against it.

Returning from its ordeal at Fort Fisher, the 117th New York reached Aikin's Landing on the James River on the evening of December 30. Back in camp, the soldiers enjoyed muted New Year's celebrations, but had little time to rest from the recent campaign before orders arrived on January 2 requiring them to prepare to march once again. The very next day the men formed into lines, then marched to Bermuda Hundred where they boarded transport ships on the evening of January 4. On the 6th the fleet began leaving Hampton Roads for the open sea, heading south. This time, however, the seas were calmer and the 117th felt much more comfortable aboard what Surgeon Mowris described as "the splendid and capacious ocean steamer *Atlantic*."[55]

The transports began arriving off Fort Fisher on January 8, but Porter's flotilla was delayed by bad weather until the 12th. When it arrived, it brought 58 vessels mounting 627 guns that opened a thunderous bombardment on the Confederate works around midnight the same day. About 7:30 a.m., elements of the fleet began shelling an area about five miles north of the fort in preparation for a landing. As the troops began loading into the small boats for the journey to shore, Mowris watched the frigate *Brooklyn* move in close to shore, "firing directly onto the proposed landing area like an enraged lion."[56]

A heavy surf bounced the boats as the sailors struggled to row them ashore heavy with the weight of the soldiers and their equipment. "The rolicking white-capped breakers did not suffer many to gain *terra firma* without an involuntary bath," noted Mowris, "but on the beach a nicely tempered air, and a genial sunshine, awaited to dry, cheer and comfort." As soon as the troops gained the shore, Capt. David Magill from New York Mills and Lt. John H. Fairbanks, a cordwainer from Rome, deployed a skirmish line from the 117th to protect the rest of the units as they landed. When sufficient troops had landed, Lieut. Col. Francis X. Myer of Utica led the 117th forward, moving across the peninsula to a position behind the Flag Pond Battery where it began digging entrenchments to protect the force from any Confederate attack by Hoke's division in their rear. By the end of the day, some 9,600 troops were ashore, a force Confederate Gen. Hoke judged to be too large and well entrenched to successfully attack. Fort Fisher had very quickly been cut off from its supporting force.[57]

About 11:00 p.m., Lt. Col. Meyer received orders from Gen. Terry to move south toward Fort Fisher. Myer led the weary men south to a position near the Half Moon Battery where they once again went to work digging entrenchments before camping for the night.[58] While the 117th dug fortifications, the 142nd New York pushed forward as far as the outworks to Fort Fisher where the men began digging rifle pits, the skirmishers advancing to within about 150 yards of the fort. When dawn came, the rebels opened fire on the skirmish line, but the 142nd held its position until nightfall, even enlarging the rifle pits somewhat.[59] At 10:00 p.m., orders arrived for the troops to form ranks. Gen. Curtis led his men forward to a position in rear of the advanced rifle pits, forming with the 117th New York on the right, followed to the left by the 3rd New York, the 142nd New York, and 112th New York.[60]

While the troops tried to sleep, their arms at their sides, Gen. Terry reviewed with his officers the assault plan for the following day. The plan contained two basic elements. The first prong of the attack was to be an assault by sailors and marines along the Atlantic shore against the Northeast Bastion and the seaward side of the fortress. The second portion of the attack would be a charge against the landward fortifications by Ames's entire division, spearheaded by Curtis's brigade including the 117th New York.

Dawn on January 15 found Curtis's brigade dug into the sand facing the foreboding north wall of Fort Fisher. Before them was a formidable task. The Confederates had prepared their defenses well. Any attacking force from the half-mile-wide peninsula side of the fort would first face a series of buried torpedoes that could be detonated from within the fort. Next came a heavy line of sharpened logs, nine feet high, constructed completely across the peninsula. This log palisade was pierced at intervals with loopholes so enfilade fire could be trained on attackers. In the center was a redoubt built in front of a sally port from which two artillery pieces could be run out to fire directly into any attacking force. On the Confederate left, bordering the river, there was what the commander of the rebel defenses described as "a deep and muddy slough" designed to protect the land entrance by creating a muddy slime pit that would engulf any troops trying to cross. A wooden bridge crossed the slough leading to the land entrance to the fort. A field piece defended the entrance, with another off to the left set to enfilade the entrance way and three mortars in rear of the entrance so placed as to fire on any attacking force.[61] All of these obstacles needed to be negotiated under fire before any attacking force would even come close enough to assault the fort itself.

The walls of the fort raised twenty feet to the parapet, their slope inclined at forty-five degrees and the sides sodded with a slippery marsh grass to both secure the walls and make scaling them difficult. The parapet itself was some twenty-five feet thick, with twenty heavy guns on the land side mounted in individual emplacements with very heavy traverses at least twelve feet high protecting the sides of each gun from flanking fire should a breech in the walls be made at any location. The effect was to make the entire length of the landward fortification a series of small redoubts that would have to be taken one at a time to secure the entire fortress wall. All along the length was ample room for Confederate infantry to add their deadly missiles to the shells and canister spewed forth by the guns.[62] It was a menacing fortress, manned by experienced gunners and veteran infantry from the battlefields of northern Virginia. Fort Fisher would not be easy to take.

During the night, Adm. Porter's fleet opened fire on the rebel works trying to dismantle the defending artillery and shatter the will of the defenders. All day the fierce bombardment continued while the assault troops waited for the order to charge. "Men were cheerful, but not mirthful; serious but not solemn," wrote Mowris. "In every eye might be read, not fear, but volumes of thought, too deep for utterance. ... The demeanor, on the eve of battle of an intelligent soldiery, whose cause is that of God and humanity, I had observed before, but never when so apparent."[63] In Company E, George G. Spencer, a farmer from Rome, recalled that it was his nineteenth birthday. To a friend lying next to him he quipped that the attack would be "a great birthday excursion."[64] Lt. Frank H. Lay from Westmoreland surveyed the situation: "As I looked down the line I knew that very many of the brave boys who formed must fall. It was a most solemn moment. The very air seemed oppressive. A silence such as I never before witnessed seemed to rest on all, but it was not fear. Men were thinking of the loved ones far away."[65] Surgeon Mowris was also effected by the scene: "Not far in advance towered the frowning Fortress, within which were the desperate emissaries of red-handed treason, and, though none saw, all knew, that above, in imperial majesty, sat the Angel of Death. It was an awful moment, and, while with compressed lips our troops were breathing a silent petition for home and country, the signal was given."[66]

At 3:25 p.m. the order finally came. Along the beach, the column of 2,261 Federal sailors and marines burst forth across the sandy soil. Led by naval Capt. K. R. Reese, the men came under a heavy fire from both artillery and rifles that cut swiftly into their ranks. Staggering forward, they reached the defensive berm, and some pushed forward to the base of the parapet, but Confederate fire soon routed the survivors. It was all over in half an hour. Reese's men suffered over 300 casualties in their bloody repulse. It was now up to the infantry alone.[67]

On the land approaches to the fort, Gen. Ames arrayed his division of 4,200 men in three lines for the assault. First came Curtis's First Brigade with the 112th New York on the left, to the right of which came, in order, the 142nd New York, the 3rd New York, and the 117th New York. Behind, in a second line came Col. Galusha Pennypacker's Second Brigade arrayed, from left to right, with the 47th New York, 48th New York, 76th Pennsylvania, 97th Pennsylvania, and 203rd Pennsylvania. The Third Brigade under Col. Alonzo Alden comprised the third line with, again left to right, the 13th Indiana, 115th New York, 4th New Hampshire and 169th New York.[68]

About 3:00 p.m., Curtis received orders to move his men forward from their position about 300 yards from the fort to a position about 50 yards behind the forward rifle pits, placing them 225 yards from the fort, in position for the final advance. But the movement attracted the attention of the vigilant Confederate commander, Col. William Lamb, who opened fire with two Napoleons placed in the redoubt fronting the sally port and another located at the bridge over the slough. At the same time, he ordered sharpshooters into the gun emplacements to pick off the federal officers. Reaching its designated position, the 117th came under increasing artillery and rifle fire. Col. Henry C. Lockwood, aide-de-camp to Gen. Curtis, observed the scene, recalling that the men "threw themselves on the sand, and using their hands, tin cups, or anything else that would aid them in their work, threw up little trenches as soon as possible. In the meantime they hugged the sand and fired as best they could." Gen. Ames's recollection was similar: "The whole division was covered from the fire of the enemy, as far as possible, by the inequalities of the ground and slight pits formed by throwing up the sand." In Company I of the 117th New York, Charles Meeker, a farmer from Boonville, was killed instantly when struck in the head. He left a wife and a three-year-old daughter.[69]

While the men waited for the final order, Captain Albert G. Lawrence, aide-de-camp to Gen. Ames, made his way cautiously forward to ask Lt. Col. Francis X. Meyer if he could join the 117th in the charge. Permission granted, Lawrence took a position in the forward line, hugging low to the sand for protection. Soon, word came down the line that the charge would be made when Gen. Curtis waved his hat. The general would not issue the lengthy commands normally required to get the men moving, it would waste too much time and expose them for a longer period to the fire of the Confederate artillery. The men were cautioned not to yell as it would attract the attention of the enemy to the advance, and not to fire their weapons until they reached the fort. Stopping to fire and load would prolong their time in the killing zone before the fort's walls. Speed in reaching the fort would reduce the time they were in the artillery's zone of fire.[70]

Any chance for whatever surprise remained was lost when the ships offshore let loose with the prolonged screeching of their whistles as soon as the order to charge was given. Ashore, Curtis stood up to his full six-foot-six-inch height, waved his hat above his head and yelled in a loud voice "Forward!" The 117th rose quickly, the men loosing a spontaneous "Hurrah!" despite their earlier orders. "The hat is moved and we are off, every man running with all his might for the huge mound comprising the work," recounted Lt. Frank Lay. The rebels increased their fire with a vengeance. "The very air seems darkened with death dealing missiles," recalled Lt. Lay. "I could feel the wind of the balls as they flew past."[71]

At first, the attackers were lucky. When Col. Lamb ordered the firing of the buried torpedoes he found that the bombardment by the Federal fleet had cut the wires. The mines would be useless. Then, the first Confederate volley flew high, a misjudgment of the range no doubt, but soon canister fire began to take its toll in what Mowris described as a "storm of bullets and canister which strewed the interval with dead and wounded." As Lt. Lay ran through the soft sand, men to both sides of him were hit. "Major [Egbert] Bagg was shot on one side, and a pri-

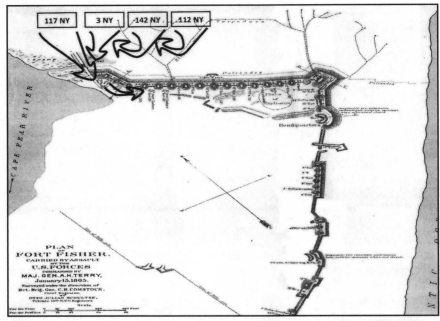

Map of Fort Fisher's northern face with the line of assault used by the 117th New York.
(Modified from the Official Records*)*

vate of my company on the other side of me." Soon Lt. Col. Meyer fell, grievously wounded, command of the regiment devolving on Capt. John T. Thomas. On they charged across the wide, sandy plain, friends and neighbors falling at every step.[72]

Elsewhere along the brigade's front, losses mounted from the fire sweeping the plain. Particularly deadly were the two Napoleons in the sally port redoubt, belching forth flurries of canister into the flanks of the attacking lines. Early in the fight, rebel fire killed Col. James F. Smith at the head of the 112th New York. The left of the advance soon went to ground under the torrent of rebel fire, the 112th and 142nd New York hugging the sand for whatever little cover they could find. "The whole line was invisible," remembered Chaplain William Hyde of the 112th, "the men having, like worms, worked themselves into the sand." Those who did not hug the ground pushed unconsciously to their right, away from the guns in the sally port redoubt, forming a disorganized mass of struggling men pushing in on the men of the 3rd New York to the left of the 117th.[73]

The 117th advanced along the Wilmington Road on the western side of the peninsula, holding position on the extreme right flank of the Union line. In front, a contingent of axemen rushed forward, their tools ready to go to work on the line

Lt. Col. Francis X. Meyer
(Oneida County Historical Society)

Lt. Frank Lay
(Oneida County Historical Society)

of pointed logs barring the way to the fort. Surgeon Mowris described the foreboding obstacle: The palisades "constituted a pretty substantial barrier, being a file or line of logs set upright, with the lower ends secured in horizontal sills or sleepers, covered with dirt, the upright pickets being in so close contact that a hand could not be inserted between them, and the upper extremities sharpened, and terminating 10 or 12 feet above the level of the ground."[74]

Under a withering fire, the axemen went to work, slowly creating, then enlarging holes in the palisade. First a few men struggled through, then larger groups rushed in as the holes widened. Ahead of them they faced an even more daunting task. To their right lay Shepherd's Battery armed with a 12-pounder Napoleon and a 3.2-inch Parrot rifle, both belching death into their flank. Manned by Capt. Kinchen Braddy and his 36th North Carolina, the battery posed a serious threat to the entire Union line, especially the nearest units, the 117th and 3rd New York.[75]

Major Egbert Bagg
(Oneida County Historical Society)

The approaches to Ft. Fisher
(Oneida County Historical Society)

View from inside Ft. Fisher of some of the area attacked by the 117th New York.
(Oneida County Historical Society)

Ahead of the attackers loomed the fort, its parapets now manned by Major James Reilly's 250 North Carolinians, reinforced by 350 South Carolinans from Gen. Johnson Hagood's veteran brigade. To the Confederate right, facing the 112th and 142nd New York, Col. Lamb led another 500 men.[76] Yet, before these could be confronted there remained another obstacle to overcome. Moving south along the Wilmington Road, the right flank of the 117th headed straight toward the wooden bridge into the fort's gate, only to find that the Confederates had removed its planking as a precaution against just such an attack. Instead, they found the same thing those who burst through the palisades found, the muddy, slippery slough between them and the fort's walls. One of the first to breach the palisade was Capt. Lawrence, General Ames's staff officer who volunteered to make the charge with the boys from Oneida County. No sooner did he step through the logs than a shell exploded close to him, shrapnel tearing off his left arm and burrowing into his throat.[77]

Into the boggy ooze the men charged, many being held fast by the suction of the clinging mud. They made easy targets for rebels atop the parapets or those firing through loopholes in the wooden gates barring the way into the fort. Raked from in front by canister and riflemen, their flank exposed to enfilade fire from the Parrot gun along the river bank to their right, some of the men sought what little cover they could find by hugging the bank of the slough or ducking under the remaining stringers of the now plankless bridge.[78]

As more men struggled through the palisades into the mire below the fort, Curtis knew he had to do something soon or the whole attack would bog down as surely as the men floundering to fight clear of the mud. "Forward!" the general yelled, moving for the base of the walls. "Forward!" echoed Capt. Thomas before a rebel bullet pierced his heart, killing him instantly. Into the leadership gap stepped New York Mills native Capt. David Magill. Jumping up, he yelled to the men and began scaling the wall toward Shepherd's Battery some twenty-three feet above. Sergeant Fred Boden, a butcher from Rome, lifted the national colors aloft and surged forward, then John B. Jones, a farmer from Sangerfield, followed with the state colors. In a massive surge, the regiment pushed its way forward to the base of the wall, then upward.[79]

Above them Capt. Braddy's North Carolinians could not depress their guns far enough to fire on the attackers scaling the walls, but they could fire their rifles down the slope, hurl grenades, and even rocks and other debris, whatever they could get their hands on to repel the bluecoats. Below, the rebel fire fell on the 117th, zipping through the air, ricocheting off of accoutrements, piercing uniforms and slashing into flesh. Men tumbled and fell, but others took their places, climbing, pushing, scrambling to the top.[80]

As the first attackers reached the parapet, Braddy fired a volley directly into them that sent the dead and wounded tumbling down the wall onto their comrades below. But others quickly followed. George Spencer, celebrating his nineteenth birthday, was one of the first to scale the battery. As he reached the top, a rebel projectile shattered his skull, killing him instantly. In the vanguard also were Gen. Curtis, Capt. Magill, Lt. Lay, Lt. Fairbanks, Sergt. Boden and Jones. A ferocious hand-to-hand struggle began as the two forces clashed for control of the parapet. Boden jammed his flagstaff into the sod atop the wall, but a Confederate bullet

Capt. David Magill   Perry B. Miller
(Donald Wisnoski)   (Oneida County Historical Society)

split the staff. He jammed the remaining staff into the dirt a second time, but again the hail of bullets cut it in two. Perry B. Miller, a merchant from Camden, stepped forward and held the two ends of the splintered flagstaff as Boden paused amid the carnage to tie them together. His task completed, he waved the banner high above the combatants, the first Union flag to reach the top of Fort Fisher's walls.[81]

John Jones followed Boden to the top with the state flag, repairing it under fire when it was shattered much as Boden had just done. Rifles flashed, bayonets slashed, and those who could not reload swung their muskets as clubs, lashing out against anyone they could not identify as a friend. Waiting below the parapet, Col. Lamb sent the 21st and 25th South Carolina clamoring up to join in the melee. "The Rebels attacked our men like savage dogs," exclaimed Edward D. Williams, a farmer from Whitestown. "Give and take was the watchword on both sides, face to face and gun to gun." Confederate Colonel Lamb agreed: "The contestants were savagely firing into each other's faces, and in some cases clubbing their guns, being too close to load and fire." Screams and groans alternated as men were shot, stabbed or clubbed to death. But slowly, almost imperceptibly at first, the 117th, now reinforced by the 3rd, pushed the rebels back off the parapet into the fort.[82] The vital foothold had been gained, but the battle was far from over. The huge traverses erected by the Confederates along the parapet as a protection from enfilade fire now proved to be every bit as strong defenses as the fort's walls themselves. Each one would have to be taken individually if the attackers were to be successful. Forward came Col. Pennypacker's Second

This drawing from *Frank Leslie's Illustrated Newspaper* shows the 117th New York assaulting Ft. Fisher and the planting of the regiment's colors atop the fort's walls.

Brigade to lend its weight to the renewed assault, only to suffer severely in the face of Confederate fire from the remaining guns and infantry. The colonels of the 48th New York and 76th Pennsylvania were both severely wounded, while the 203rd Pennsylvania had its colonel killed. Every man in the color guard of the 47th New York was either killed or wounded.[83]

While Pennypacker's men struggled forward, Curtis, with his New York regiments, moved left attacking the first two traverses. Confederate Colonel Lamb led another counterattack as the fighting again surged along the bloody parapet. Back with the reserves, Surgeon Mowris looked toward the violent show atop the walls in awe: "All along on the crest of the parapet, as far to the left as our line extended, might be seen the desperate contest. The national colors and the insurgent rag, were seen simultaneously and then alternately, on the same traverse. Hand to hand, foot to foot, the combatants fought. Inch by inch, did our brave boys press back that serrated line of gray."[84]

With the situation deteriorating, Gen. Whiting led the next Confederate counterattack in person, but was quickly felled with two severe wounds in the thigh. His men carried him away to the hospital. Col. Lamb led yet another counterattack with survivors from some of the North Carolina artillery units and South Carolina infantry, but this too met with stiff resistance Lamb described as "a savage hand-to-hand conflict." Still the 117th not only held its own, but led the Union assaults on first one and then another Confederate traverse. In one, Corp. Elbridge S. Foskett, a mechanic from Camden, seized a rebel flag from the hands of a Confederate, winning a prized trophy for his regiment.[85]

"It was a soldier's fight at that point, for there could be no organization," recalled Col. Lamb, "the officers of both forces were loading and firing with their men. If there has ever been a longer or more stubborn hand-to-hand encounter, I have failed to meet with it in history." His men slowly being dislodged from one traverse after another, Lamb brought 100 men from the south wall of the fort to reinforce those on the north, ordering a bayonet charge to clear the nearest traverse. He explained: "[I] sprang upon the breastwork, waved my sword, and, as I gave the command ... fell on my knees, a rifle-ball having entered my left hip."[86] Lamb was carried away to the hospital, command devolving on Major James Reilly who ordered yet another counterattack, only to see two-thirds of his men shot down and the rest retreat.[87]

Corp. Elbridge S. Foskett
(Oneida County Historical Society)

By about 4:45 p.m., after an hour and a quarter of vicious fighting, the Federals had succeeded in capturing seven traverses, but the troops were exhausted and ammunition was running low. Curtis sent a corporal back to Gen. Ames asking for additional reinforcements to press the attack, but Ames responded that it was late, dusk was rapidly approaching, and Curtis should dig in to hold what he had for the night. Incredulous, Curtis assumed Ames did not know the situation in the fort. He was certain that continued pressure would break the Confederate resistance. He sent an orderly back with another request for reinforcements. Ames repeated his order. A third request, again sent via the orderly, resulted in Ames sending back a shovel as if to emphasize his order to Curtis. Enraged at the insult, Curtis headed for the rear to rally men of his own command and confront Ames, leaving Capt. Magill in charge with orders to press the attack.[88]

Finding Ames, Curtis began arguing with him. During the confrontation, Curtis climbed atop a sand dune for a better view of the fort, but a Confederate shell exploded nearby seriously wounding him with two shell fragments in the head. Meanwhile, Capt. Magill pressed forward with what troops he could scrape together, capturing the eighth traverse. "The fight was no doubt the closest and longest of the war," concluded Hermon Clarke. "It was hand-to-hand for nearly six hours." Lt. Lay explained that "From three o'clock until nine at night the battle raged with a fury without precedent in the war. It was a hand to hand fight, from mound to mound went the colors of the 117th, in advance of everything else." Surgeon Mowris noted that "The sun sank slowly and lay on the western horizon—the rattle of musketry knew no abatement. Twilight came—but no lull

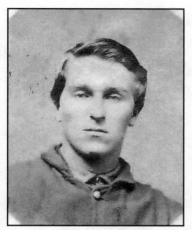

E. D. Williams
(Oneida County Historical Society)

in the storm of battle. At length darkness came—only to reveal more distinctly the lurid flash of battle, and to disclose perchance a glimpse of the pallid faces of the dead."[89]

With the last rays of the sun rapidly departing, and the smoke of battle obscuring vision even more, it was very difficult to determine the positions of the contending sides. Trying to support the infantry ashore, Adm. Porter's warships opened fire. By 8:00 p.m. most of the landward side of the fort had been cleared of rebels, but the fleet could not see where the battle lines were. Its shells dropped amid friend and foe alike. One exploded near Capt. Magill, mangling his leg so badly it would have to be amputated at the left thigh. The feisty captain stayed with his men until relief finally arrived. "It seemed too bad," commented Clarke, "after leading the Regt. so nearly through the fight to be so badly wounded by our own fire."[90]

Finally, mercifully, Battery Buchanan at the south end of the fort fell and the Confederates hoisted the white flag of surrender. Surgeon Mowris described the scene thusly: "Ten o'clock arrived—but with it no rest, except for him who had lain him down in his last sleep. From 3 till 10 1/2. more than 7 long hours of untold effort and agony—and there was a calm—a welcome stillness—a short suggestive interval of sound, and then—a cheer—O! such a cheer. It thrilled ones every nerve and reached the inmost soul, suffusing eyes unused to weep. Fort Fisher had fallen with her arms and garrison."[91] In the fort, the word to cease fire seemed almost unbelievable to Lt. Lay, now the senior officer present in the regiment. "My very heart went up in Thanksgiving. Never did I feel as I felt then. I cannot describe it, nor will I try. Men grasped each others hands and wept only as brave men can in the hour of victory. I was in command of the regiment and proceeded to get them together, which took me more than two hours. Capt. [William L.] Bartholomew came to my aid and after much labor we at last got them together, but alas! many had formed in line for the last time."[92]

In the morning, when dawn finally cast its rays upon the gruesome scene, it was time to take stock of what veterans called the "butcher's bill." Both the national and state flags the regiment carried into the battle were riddled with holes, the staffs broken, but carried still with honor. The Union Army suffered 955 casualties at Fort Fisher. Of those, the 117th New York lost fifteen killed, 76 wounded and 33 missing, an aggregate of 124 men, the highest toll of any regi-

Remnant of the regimental colors of the 117th New York returned to
Oneida County following the war with "Only Honorable Marks."
(Oneida County Historical Society)

ment in Ames's assault division. On January 29, 1865, Clarke wrote to his brother, telling him: "Our Regt. is getting small. We have now only 270 men for duty; last spring we reported 800. But what few we have left are pretty tough old veterans, I tell you."[93] Tough veterans they were. And at Fort Fisher the men from Oneida County had much of which to be proud. As Lt. Lay wrote, "The 117th was the first to gain the fort, and we have the credit for it. Our naval officers say that every private in our regiment should have a gold medal with Fort Fisher engraved on it.... Our regiment took more than twice its number in prisoners. We had taken 500 prisoners and 16 heavy guns."[94]

The successful assault on Fort Fisher effectively closed the port of Wilmington to Confederate blockade runners and led directly to the capture of the city itself on February 22. Once in Union hands, the port served as a vital supply base supporting the movement of General

William T. Sherman's army through the Carolinas in its successful campaign against Gen. Joseph E. Johnston's Confederate forces. Gen. Ulysses S. Grant, in his autobiography, stated that the capture of Fort Fisher was "one of the most important successes of the war." Rear Adm. David D. Porter asserted, "We had some very important naval victories during the war, but none so important as Fort Fisher." On the Confederate side, Vice President Alexander Stephens noted that "the fall of this fort was one of the greatest disasters which had befallen our Cause from the beginning of the war."[95] The men of the 117th New York Volunteer Infantry won for themselves both the honor and the satisfaction of knowing that their sacrifices contributed significantly to the final outcome of the war. They had done what the ladies of Utica had bid them in presenting the regiment with its colors—they would return the tattered remnant of their flags to Oneida County with "only honorable marks."

---

[1]J.A. Mowris, *A History of the One Hundred and Seventeenth Regiment, N. Y. Volunteers* (Hamilton, NY: Edmonston Publishing Company, Inc., 1996), 14-15.

[2]Frederick Phisterer, *New York in the War of the Rebellion 1861 to 1865* (Albany: J. B. Lyon Company, 1912), 3371; Mowris, 16-17.

[3]Phisterer, 3371.

[4]Phisterer, 3371; Frederick H. Dyer, *A Compendium of the War of the Rebellion* (New York: Thomas Yoseloff, 1959), 1450; Mowris, 17-18.

[5]Phisterer, 3371.

[6]Letter, James M. Hewitt to George Hewitt, September 3, 1862, in the possession of Jonathan D. Kettl, Sr.

[7]Phisterer, 3371; Dyer, 1450; Special Order No. 57, *War of the Rebellion: A Compilation of the Official Reports of the Union and Confederate Armies.* (Washington, DC: U.S. Government Printing Office, 1864-1927), Ser. I, Vol. XVIII, No. 26, 608 (hereafter cited as *O.R.*).

[8]Dyer, 1450; Mark M. Boatner, *The Civil War Dictionary* (New York: David McKay Company, Inc., 1959), 817; Mowris, 60; *O.R.*, Ser. I, Vol. XVIII, No. 26, 609.*O.R.*

[9]Phisterer, 3371; Dyer, 1450; Boatner, 301; Mowris, 77, quote from 81.

[10]Phisterer, 3372; Boatner, 247-249; Mowris, 105-106; Edward G. Longacre, *Army of Amateurs: General Benjamin Butler and the Army of the James, 1863-1865* (Mechanicsburg, PA: Stackpole Books, 1997), 96-98.

[11]Phisterer, 3372; Boatner, 247-249; Mowris, 105-106; Longacre, *Army of Amateurs*, 96-98; William F. Fox, *Regimental Losses in the American Civil War* (Dayton, OH: Morningside, 1974), 227; Rufus Daggett note, George Fairhead Papers, Oneida County Historical Society.

[12]Phisterer, 3371, Dyer, 1450.

[13]Longacre, *Army of Amateurs*, 121-123; quote from Mowris, 110.

[14]Dyer, 1451; Phisterer, 3372; Boatner, 162, 165; Longacre, *Army of Amateurs*, 121-123.

[15]*O.R.*, Ser. I, Vol. XL, Pt. 1, No. 80, 701; George Fairhead Diary, Aug. 24, 1864, Oneida County Historical Society.

[16]*O.R.*, Ser. I, Vol. LI, Pt. 1 [S# 107], 1247.

[17]*O.R.*, Ser. I, Vol. XLII, Pt. 1 [S# 87], 760-61.

[18]Fairhead Diary, September 29, 1864, Oneida County Historical Society.

[19]Mowris, 137.

[20]Fairhead Diary, September 29, 1864.

[21]Statement of John D. Ernst, Fairhead Papers, Oneida County Historical Society.

[22]Fairhead Diary, October 27, 1864.

[23]Robert U. Johnson and Clarence C. Buel, eds., *Battles and Leaders of the Civil War* (New York: Castle Books, 1956), IV, 642; Moore, i, 5.

[24]Mark A. Moore, *The Wilmington Campaign and the Battles for Fort Fisher* (Mason City, IA: Savas Publishing Company, 1999), iii, 14.

[25]Moore, 15.

[26]Ezra J. Warner, *Generals in Blue: Lives of the Union Commanders* (Baton Rouge: Louisiana State University Press, 1972), 60.

[27]Moore, 19.

[28]Boatner, 293; *O.R*, Ser. I, Vol. XLII, Pt. 1 [S# 87], 133.

[29]Boatner, 293; Howard Thomas, *Boys in Blue from the Adirondack Foothills* (Prospect, NY: Prospect Books, 1960), 247; Moore, 19; Harry F. Jackson & Thomas F. O'Donnell, eds., *Back Home in Oneida: Hermon Clarke and His Letters* (Syracuse; Syracuse University Press, 1965), 1, 5, and letter to father, December 21, 1864, 180; *O.R.*, Ser. I, Vol. XLII, Pt. 1 [S# 87], 980..

[30]Dyer, 1451; Boatner, 292-293; Longacre, 231, 247-258; Mowris, 148-49, 152; Moore, 19.

[31]Mowris, 150; Jackson & O'Donnell, 181; Thomas, 247; *O.R.*, Ser. I, Vol. XLII, Pt. 1 [S# 87], 980.

[32]Mowris, 151-52; Jackson & O'Donnell, 181; *O.R.*, Ser. I, Vol. XLII, Pt. 1 [S# 87], 980.

[33]Moore, iii.

[34]Moore, iii, 3, 13; William Lamb, "The Defense of Fort Fisher," in Robert U. Johnson and Clarence C. Buel, eds., *Battles and Leaders of the Civil War* (New York: Castle Books, 1956), IV, 642, 643; Hill, 273-74.

[35]Hill, 273-74.

[36]Lamb, 642.

[37]Moore, 19; Boatner, 293; Hill, 274; Douglas Southall Freeman, *Lees's Lieutenants* (New York: Charles Scribner's Sons, 1944), III, 617-18.

[38]Moore, 19.

[39]Moore, 20, 23; Hill, 274.

[40]Jackson & O'Donnell, 181; Boatner, 293; Moore, 23; Mowris, 153.

[41]*O.R.*, Ser. I, Vol. XLII, Pt. 1 [S# 87], 982.

[42]Thomas, 248; Mowris, 154.

[43]Thomas, 248; Mowris, 154; Rod Gragg, *Confederate Goliath: The Battle of Fort Fisher* (New York: HarperCollins Publishers, 1991), 90.

[44]Story and conversation reconstructed from Thomas, 248-49; Mowris, 154-55; Chris E. Fonvielle, *Last Rays of Departing Hope: The Wilmington Campaign* (Campbell, CA: Savas Publishing Company, 1999), 167; Gragg, 91.

[45]The figures used are those from the Gen. Curtis's official report of the incident printed in *O.R.*, Ser. I, Vol. XLII, Pt. 1 [S# 87], 982. Other sources vary, but regardless of the number the feat was one of the most unusual of the war. See also Mowris, 154, 157; Jackson & O'Donnell, 181; Fonvielle, 166; Longacre, 255.

[46]Mowris, 156; Boatner, 293; Moore, 25, 27; Lamb, 643; Jackson & O'Donnell, 182; *O.R.*, Ser. I, Vol. XLII, Pt. 1 [S# 87], 980, 982.

[47]Mowris, 156; Boatner, 293.

[48]Mowris, 157; Jackson & O'Donnell, 182; Moore, 25; Fonvielle, 169; *O.R.*, Ser. I, Vol. XLII, Pt. 1 [S# 87], 980, 982.

[49]Jackson & O'Donnell, 183; *O.R.*, Ser. I, Vol. XLII, Pt. 1 [S# 87], 980, 982.

[50]Jackson & O'Donnell, 183.

[52]Moore, 35.

[52]Warner, *Generals in Blue,* 497.

[53]Boatner, 293; *O.R.*, Ser. I, Vol. XLVI, Pt. 1 [S# 95], 403.

[54]Lamb, 647, 661; Boatner, 293; Hill, 276; Gragg, 150.

[55]*O.R.*, Ser. I, Vol. XLVI, Pt. 1 [S# 95], 415; Mowris, 148, 158, 160-161; Boatner, 293; Moore, 37; Thomas 250; Dyer, 1451; Longacre, 260-267.

[56]Boatner, 293; Moore, 37; Mowris, 148, 161.

[57]Mowris, 162, 164; *O.R.*, Ser. I, Vol. XLVI, Pt. 1 [S# 95], 418; Moore, 39.

[58]*O.R.*, Ser. I, Vol. XLVI, Pt. 1 [S# 95], 418; Jackson & O'Donnell, 185.

[59]*O.R.*, Ser. I, Vol. XLVI, Pt. 1 [S# 95], 418.

[60]*O.R.*, Ser. I, Vol. XLVI, Pt. 1 [S# 95], 418.

[61]Lamb, 643.

[62]Lamb, 643.

[63]Mowris, 166-167.

[64]Thomas, 251; Fonvielle, 273.

[65]Thomas, 251; Fonvielle, 273.

[66]Mowris, 168; Moore, 49.

[67]Lamb, 650; Boatner, 294.

[68]*O.R.*, Ser. I, Vol. XLVI, Pt. 1 [S# 95], 403-04.

[69]Boatner, 294; Thomas, 251; Lamb 649-50; Moore, 49; Blanche Ames, *Adelbert Ames: General, Senator, Governor, 1835-1933* (London: Macdonald, 1964), 190.

[70]Ames, *Adelbert Ames,* 190; Moore, 49; Thomas, 251.

[71]Gragg, 175-76; Thomas, 251; Moore, 49.

[72]Thomas, 251; Mowris, 168, 175; Lamb, 651; Fonvielle, 266.

[73]Moore, 50.

[74]Boatner, 294; Mowris, 168.

[75]Fonvielle, 263; Gragg, 174.

[76]Moore, 43; Lamb, 649.

[77]Fonvielle, 263; Fonvielle, 265; *O.R.*, Ser. I, Vol. XLVI, Pt. 1 [S# 95], 417.

[78]Moore, 50.

[79]Moore, 50; Jackson & O'Donnell, 185; Fonvielle, 266.

[80]Moore, 50; statement of Perry B. Miller, Fairhead Papers, Oneida County Historical Society.

[81]Fonvielle, 265, 273; Moore, 50; Thomas, 251; Gragg, 181; *O.R.*, Ser. I, Vol. XLVI, Pt. 1 [S# 95], 419; statement of Perry B. Miller, Fairhead Papers, Oneida County Historical Society.

[82]Lamb, 650-51; Fonvielle, 281.

[83]Moore, 51-52.

[84]Mowris, 169.

[85]Moore, 53; Lamb, 650.

[86]Lamb, 652.

[87]Moore, 55.

[88]Moore, 55-56; Gragg, 209-10.

[89]Moore, 55-56; Jackson & O'Donnell, 185; Thomas, 252.

[90]Lamb, 652-53; Jackson & O'Donnell, 185; Mowris, 175; Gragg, 211; Fonvielle, 288.

[91]Mowris, 169.

[92]Thomas, 252.

[93]Boatner, 294; O.R., Ser. I, Vol. XLII, Pt. 1 [S# 87], 133; Jackson & O'Donnell, 188; Fox, 456.

[94]Thomas, 251-52

[95]Moore, i.

CHAPTER 8

"FIELD OF FIRE"

THE 146TH NEW YORK IN THE WILDERNESS

by

Cheryl A. Pula

The 146th New York State Volunteer Infantry, which began its career as the Fifth Oneida County Regiment, was mustered into federal service on October 10, 1862, in Rome, New York. The regiment was formed under the authority of Henry S. Armstrong, who began recruiting for the unit in August of 1862. Major DeLancey Floyd Jones, an officer of the Eleventh United States Infantry, had been chosen as colonel of the regiment, but he could not accept the position. After much correspondence between Oneida County officials and the War Department, the command was offered to Colonel Kenner Garrard, a member of the regular army and at the time the Commandant of Cadets at the United States Military Academy at West Point. Garrard was not native to the Central New York area, but a southerner, having been born in Bourbon County, Kentucky, on September 30, 1827. He had attended West Point, graduating in the class of 1851. He became a cavalry officer prior to the outbreak of the Civil War. In April 1861, he was captured by Confederate forces in Texas, but was soon exchanged in one of the many prisoner exchanges that took place in the first half of the war. Known as a strict disciplinarian and able commander, he became the colonel of the newly formed 146th New York on August 27, 1862. The regiment quickly adopted his name into one of its nicknames, "Garrard's Tigers," but it was also known as the "Halleck Infantry," after General Henry Wager Halleck, a native of Westernville, a small village located just outside of Rome. At that time, Halleck was the Chief of Staff to President Abraham Lincoln.[1]

The regiment was composed of recruits from throughout Oneida County. Under the exacting eye of Colonel Garrard, they were initiated into the drill and discipline necessary to convert the civilians into a formidable military force at Camp Huntington in Rome. Marching orders arrived on October 8, 1862, ordering the regiment to report for duty in Washington, D.C. Officially mustered in two days later, it left for the seat of the war on October 11. Upon its arrival in

Col. Kenner Garrard
(USAMHI)

Lt. Col. David T. Jenkins
(USAMHI)

Washington, D.C., the regiment marched down Pennsylvania Avenue to Long Bridge, crossed the Potomac River into Virginia, and encamped at Arlington Heights. They arrived at Camp Seward at 3:30 PM, October 13. There, they received rations, outdated Austrian muskets were distributed, and each man received ten rounds of ammunition. More drill followed, until November 2 when Gen. Henry Halleck arrived to inspect the men and inform them that they had been assigned to the Third Brigade, Second Division, Fifth Corps, Army of the Potomac. The need for new manpower in the wake of heavy looses at Second Bull Run and Antietam required their presence in the field. Their days of relative leisure were over.[2]

Marching toward Centreville, the men passed through Fairfax Court House, experiencing the first campaign march of their careers, then on to their destination the next day. Reaching Bull Run, the men beheld the destruction, the scattered equipment and clothing, and the scarcely concealed bodies of dead comrades beneath a thin layer of soil under which they had been partially buried. The reality of war wrought a sobering affect on the troops. The continued march was much quieter and the regiment moved through Warrenton, joining the Army of the Potomac at Snicker's Gap, Virginia, on November 13.[3]

Brigaded along with two other Empire State regiments, the 5th New York, known as Duryea's Zouaves, and the 140th New York from Rochester and Monroe County, the men were no doubt pleased to find that the Fifth Corps was commanded by Utica's own Gen. Daniel Butterfield, while their brigade was commanded by another New Yorker, Gen. Gouverneur K. Warren. The Army of

Surgeon Thomas M. Flandrau
Breveted Lt. Col. for Meritorious Service
(Donald Wisnoski)

the Potomac was then commanded by Gen. Ambrose P. Burnside, who was about to begin a winter campaign in an attempt to redeem the federal losses of the summer and fall. Marching through falling rain as the days grew colder, men unaccustomed to the grueling marches fell out, while the rest slogged along, mile after mile, until they arrived a few miles from Fredericksburg, Virginia. Fortunately for the rookie regiment, it was held in reserve, the men watching with awe the spectacle of artillery bombardments and the gallant but futile attempts of line after line of blue-clad infantry as they launched doomed assaults against the impregnable Confederate positions on Marye's Heights.[4]

About 3:00 PM, the call to action came. The Fifth Corps received orders to cross the Rappahannock River to reinforce Union forces battling the Confederates. As the men formed, Lt. Col. David T. Jenkins rode along the line calling upon the men to behave with honor in their first engagement; they responded with cheers. Slowly they marched down the hill to the river, then across the narrow, undulating pontoon bridge. As they marched, they loaded and capped their weapons, then clamored up the southern bank of the river, marching swiftly through the town. Passing files of wounded heading to the rear, the regiment emerged from town and went into line of battle as the last rays of sun began to set in the west. With the onset of darkness, the suicidal assaults on Marye's Heights were halted. The 146th lay in the mud all night, listening to the groans and pitiful cries of the wounded left on the now-freezing field; but they had been spared the carnage. The next day, Gen. Burnside ordered a retreat. Retiring through town to re-cross the river the following morning, the regiment was subjected to scattered rebel artillery fire, with one shell severely wounding Private Chester Hall of Boonville. He died in a Washington hospital on December 30, the regiment's first combat fatality.[5]

Following Fredericksburg, the 146th was involved in Gen. Burnside's notorious "Mud March" of January 1863. Determined to strike another blow at the Confederates, Burnside decided to march the army west along the Rappahannock to cross one of the fords away from Fredericksburg, then turn south toward Richmond. However, he did not take into consideration the fact that the roads in

Fifes and Drums of the 146th New York.
(From Boys in Blue*)*

northern Virginia can become quagmires in the winter months, which is exactly what happened. The roads, such as they were, turned to mud, bogging down the entire Federal army. The men became so mired in the mud, even the Rebels got in on the "fun," taunting the boys in blue with homemade signs reading "Burnside's Army stuck in the mud," and other equally pithy sayings. The Union troops began to circulate stories that entire wagons and several mules had been swallowed up by the viscous goo, never to be seen again. Eventually, Burnside's troops extracted themselves from the mud, returning to their original positions outside of Fredericksburg to await the spring—and firmer roads.

Once the change of seasons brought better weather for campaigning, Garrard's Tigers moved out with the rest of the army, now under the command of Gen. Joseph Hooker, to begin a new season of campaigning. Hooker proposed a movement much like Burnside's aborted January march, planning to move about half of his army upstream, cross the Rappahannock behind the Confederate army at Fredericksburg, and crush the rebels between his force and the other half of his army. The campaign began on April 27 with the 146th New York marching slowly westward to Ely's Ford where they removed their clothes below the waist to wade across the cold waters to the south side of the Rapidan River, then marched south to United States Ford where they repeated the process crossing the Rappahannock. By May 1, 1863, Hooker's plan was unfolding exactly as he envisioned, with Gen. Robert E. Lee's Southern army caught between the two wings of the Army of the Potomac.[6]

About an hour before noon, Hooker ordered his force forward in an attempt to further pin the rebels in the closing pincer. Deployed along the road leading to Fredericksburg, the Fifth Oneida was on the far right of the brigade as it came under fire from rebel skirmishers, the bullets zipping through the air in a hitherto unfamiliar tune. One entered the breast of Sergt. William P. Burnham of Whitestown, killing him instantly. A sharp firefight broke out, with the regiment pushing forward to the top of a hill where Confederate artillery began to find the range while bullets still sought targets. As the flank regiment, six companies were ordered into the woods on the right to push back rebel sharpshooters. However, when Hooker ordered a general retreat to the previous line, companies A and G did not get the word. Surrounded by advancing Confederates, they attempted to fight their way out, but a good number were killed, wounded, or captured. Among them was Capt. Joseph H. Durkee of Company A who was seriously wounded and captured. The Confederates pursued, but were met with the concentrated fire of the brigade which hurled them back. The rebels regrouped and came on a second time, but again the Union line held with the 146th standing firm in its first major test against a Confederate assault. Again the rebels recoiled. The Union line held.[7]

On May 2, Stonewall Jackson's famous flank attack fell on the right of the Union line, driving it in and threatening Hooker's entire force. Along with the other units of the Fifth Corps, the 146th New York was rushed forward to help plug the breakthrough. Placed in reserve, the regiment remained in line the next two days, but took no further active part in the fighting except for occasional picket fire. On May 5, Hooker began a withdrawal to the north, back across the Rappahannock to the army's previous camps. The campaign, the regiment's first real test in combat, brought comments of approval for its conduct, but cost the regiment fifty casualties.[8]

Following the Chancellorsville campaign, Gen. Lee determined to move north into Maryland and Pennsylvania to take the war into Union territory. He had tried to invade the North once before, in September 1862, when he was turned back at the Battle of Antietam. Now he was attempting another invasion. About the same time, as the Confederate Army of Northern Virginia began its trek northward, the 146th New York underwent a radical change in appearance. It abandoned their traditional U.S. Army issue uniforms, converting to a *Zouave* unit on June 3, 1863. The 146th based its uniform on the *Tirailleurs Algerians*, the native Algerian troops of the French Army, also known as *Turcos*. It consisted of a sky blue tunic with gold trim, baggy blue pantaloons, white leggings, a red sash, and a soft red fez with a yellow tassel. There was also a white turban for ceremonial occasions. This made them feel special; they were one of the few volunteer regiments in the Union army that was allowed to become a *Zouave* outfit during the middle of the war. They were also unique from other *Zouave* units that had dark blue tunics with other color combinations. This served to further set them apart, giving them a heightened sense of their own unique identity.[9]

Shortly after the 146th received its new attire, Gen. Hooker received word that Lee's army was heading north, and the Army of the Potomac began the long trek to intercept it. The two armies met again on July 1, 1863, at the small rail-

Lt. James P. Pitcher
Wounded at Gettysburg
(Donald Wisnoski)

Lt. James E. Jenkins
Seriously Wounded at Gettysburg
(Donald Wisnoski)

road town of Gettysburg, Pennsylvania. A long and grueling march brought the Fifth Corps to Union Mills, Maryland, by the last day of June. As the First and Eleventh Corps battled superior Confederate forces on July 1, the 146th New York hurried north with the Fifth Corps to support their comrades-in-arms. The regiment arrived behind the Union position about 7:00 AM after an exhausting overnight march.[10]

About 4:00 PM on Thursday, July 2, the call came. Confederates of Gen. John Bell Hood's division were attempting to turn the Union left flank. The regiment moved forward at the double-quick, advancing toward the Peach Orchard where Confederate troops were in danger of breaking the Union line. En route, the regiment was intercepted by Gen. Warren with news that rebels were about to overrun a little rocky hill to the south called Little Round Top, held precariously by a single brigade of federal infantry and a battery of artillery. Its fall would endanger the entire Northern position. Climbing the steep hill while rebel infantry drove in the right flank of the Union brigade clinging uncertainly to the top, Garrard and his men arrived with little time to spare. As soon as he arrived, Gen. Stephen Weed, the brigade commander, was killed by a Confederate sharpshooter. As the senior officer present, Garrard took command of the brigade while Lt. Col. Jenkins assumed command of the regiment. Jenkins placed his men among the rocks just below the crest of the hill, ordering them to use loose stones to build a makeshift wall for defense. No sooner had the regiment arrived in position than

Confederate infantry made a determined attempt to carry the hill, but fire from the 146th and its sister regiments threw them back, saving the hill, and possibly the battle, for the Union. In this fight, Garrard's Tigers lost 28 casualties.[11]

Shortly after the Battle of Gettysburg, Col. Garrard gained promotion to brigadier general of volunteers, leaving the regiment on July 25, 1863.[12] David Jenkins assumed permanent command of the 146th New York. By January 1864, the 146th had been combined into a brigade with several other *Zouave* regiments including the 5th New York, 140th New York, and the 155th Pennsylvania, which from then on was known as the Fifth Corps' Zouave Brigade.[13]

In February 1864, President Abraham Lincoln decided the time had come for a change in the overall command of the Federal forces. He had tried several officers up to this point, but none had proven to be the man for the job, so he named Gen. Ulysses S. Grant to command all of the Union armies. Grant received the rank of lieutenant general, the first time it had been bestowed upon any soldier since George Washington in the Revolutionary War. Grant was a westerner, having been born in Ohio, and had lived in that state, Kentucky, and Illinois. A graduate of West Point, he had served in the Mexican-American War. After the end of that conflict, he saw tours of duty in the West at posts in California and the Washington Territory, including Forts Vancouver and Humboldt. Living in Galena, Illinois, at the beginning of the war, Grant was given a colonelcy of the 21st Illinois Infantry, and quickly rose in rank, soon becoming a brigadier general. His early service was in the western theater, highlighted by notable victories at Fort Henry, Fort Donelson, Shiloh, Chattanooga, Lookout Mountain, and Missionary Ridge in Tennessee. Perhaps Grant's most significant accomplishment was the capture of the strategic river port of Vicksburg, Mississippi, which gave the Federal army and navy control of the entire length of the Mississippi River. Very impressed with Grant's work, Lincoln decided he was exactly the type of leader the army needed. Grant had thought to make his headquarters in the west, but decided instead to place it with the Army of the Potomac, to be closer to Washington, D.C., and his lines of communication with President Lincoln.

Grant was received with some skepticism among the "easterners" in the Army of the Potomac. Many saw him as a western interloper who needed to prove himself. After all, fighting against Braxton Bragg in the west was a far cry from tangling with "Bobby" Lee and his Army of Northern Virginia. Grant devised a plan to cross the Rappahannock River, move quickly through the tangle of woods and underbrush known as the Wilderness, and force Lee's undermanned army out into the open fields north of the rebel capital at Richmond. Once in the open, Grant's superior numbers could overwhelm Lee, defeating his army and ending the war. The plan might have worked, but the Army of the Potomac moved too slowly and Lee was able to react before the Northerners cleared the Wilderness. Instead of a stand-up fight in the open fields, Grant and Lee would meet for the first time in May, 1864, in an overgrown and nearly impenetrable tangle of trees and underbrush in which the 146th would see its most difficult trial under fire, as well as its bravest moments.

Early May found the 146th New York camped near the Warrenton Railroad at the town of Warrenton Junction. On May 4, the Federal army was poised to engage the Confederate forces near the Orange Turnpike. Norton C. Shepard, a native of Turin and resident of Rome who was a corporal in Company B, remarked on the general chaos that reigned as the army broke camp, calling it a "vast, noisy mob." However, once the bugle call to "fall in" sounded, the men formed into orderly lines, shoulder to shoulder, ready to obey when they were given the order to march. Once the drums sounded, the regiment was a cohesive unit that stepped off on its journey to meet Lee's army.[14] Happy to be doing something after a long period of inactivity, the men marched all day in the direction of the Rapidan River. The Fifth and Sixth Corps crossed Germanna Ford, then pushed south into the wild undergrowth. Corp. Shepard found the term "wilderness" to be different than what he was accustomed to north of the Mason-Dixon line.

> I have been much in The North Woods and find a great contrast in the meaning of "wilderness" there and in the South. In the North a wilderness is a wood in a state of nature with great trees that have stood for ages, with other trees uprooted and fallen, with old logs lying prone upon the ground, with dry stubs and dead trees ready to fall at the first storm, so that the place is almost impossible to travel.... In the South ... most especially in Virginia ... the land has been cleared off and cultivated ... it has become worn out and had been abandoned as useless ... it grows up to pine and scrub oak to become a wilderness.... The trees are usually about six inches in diameter with branches growing thick from the ground to the top.[15]

The terrain and the forest made for slow going. Lee quickly determined Grant's plan, reacting to the threat by immediately dispatching two Confederate corps of over 39,000 troops to the area of the Wilderness. The broken terrain and underbrush was perfect for defense and would offset to a large extent Grant's numerical advantage. One of the corps sent to halt the Federals was Gen. Richard S. Ewell's Second Corps. Lee assigned Ewell to locate Grant's army, but not to engage it in a major battle until reinforcements could be brought up. These reinforcements were to be troops led by Lee's "Old War Horse," Gen. James Longstreet.

On May 4, Adjutant William Wright of Clayville submitted a report to army headquarters listing the strength of the 146th New York as 24 officers and 556 men present for duty.[16]

About 6:00 AM on May 5, Ewell's Corps located the Federal forces. The Confederates immediately began to spread out along both sides of the road, building hastily constructed breastworks overlooking a clearing known locally as

Saunders' Field. The position Ewell chose was a good one. The Confederates were on high ground overlooking the clearing, their line hidden among trees that would provide them with cover from the Federal troops. It was a strong defensive position, providing the rebels with excellent advantages, offering a clear view of anyone trying to cross Saunders' Field and an unobstructed field of fire. Ewell's troops were augmented by John M. Jones' Virginia brigade and Gen. Edward "Allegheny" Johnson's division. A brigade led by Gen. George "Maryland" Steuart arrived and dug into the woods to the left of Jones' position. Also in line were the Louisiana Tigers, commanded by General Leroy A. Stafford, and the remnants of the famous Stonewall Brigade led by General James A. Walker. By the time they were in place, the Confederates defending Saunders' Field would number about 10,000 men. There would be another 4,500 men in reserve behind the rebel lines, in the form of Gen. Jubal Early's division, plus artillery.[17]

One of the few open space in the Wilderness, the area leading up to Saunders' Field was covered with nearly impenetrable pine thickets and brush causing both sides problems moving men into position. To reach the Confederate positions, the Union troops would have to attack uphill across a totally open area with no cover. This provided the rebels with a perfect killing zone.[18] While the rebels hastily constructed their breastworks, advanced skirmishers from the Fifth Corps were making their way into the area under the command of Col. David T. Jenkins of the 146th New York. The pickets were surprised to see the Confederates, as the area had been patrolled by Union cavalry earlier and they had not reported seeing any rebel troops; yet, Jenkins could clearly see the Southerners building fortifications. Jenkins quickly sent word of the rebels back to Gen. Warren, reporting the location of the enemy. This intelligence proved to be the cause of the day's events. Warren forwarded Jenkins' report to Gen. George Gordon Meade, who in turn sent it on to Grant. It was the first intelligence Grant had of the position of the rebel forces.[19]

Grant was surprised to find Lee's men so close. Nevertheless, he quickly sent the following message to Meade: "If any opportunity presents itself for pitching into a part of Lee's Army, do so without time for disposition."[20] Meade did not believe the Confederate force his command was facing was one of any great size, so he saw no reason to change any of his orders for the day. He did, however, issue additional orders that he be kept apprised of the situation, should anything change or more exact intelligence be garnered.

Gen. Gouverneur K. Warren, now the commander of the Federal Fifth Corps, ordered Col. Jenkins to remain on the picket line, reinforcing him with two companies of men from the 146th New York. Warren also assigned Gen. Charles Griffin's First Division to engage the enemy, but Griffin had misgivings. While known to be an aggressive leader, Griffin lacked support on his flank; consequently, he believed such an assault could only be accomplished if other units bolstered his division. He surmised the strength of the force opposing him to be

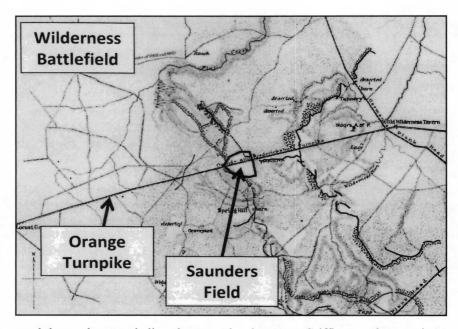

much larger than was believed at army headquarters. Griffin was also cognizant of the terrain his men would have to cross, and he was not happy about having to assault the enemy over those deadly, open spaces. The area in which Griffin and his division found themselves was not conducive to offensive warfare. Thick underbrush, prevalent throughout the area, hindered any type of organized advance. He asked Warren for more troops in support; however, his request was denied, leaving it up to his men to bring the fight to the enemy. With no alternative, Griffin planned his attack. The First Brigade of the Fifth Corps, commanded by Gen. Romeyn Ayres, would lead the attack.

Knowing that an attack was imminent, Col. Jenkins asked Gen. Ayres to allow him to return to his regiment to lead it into the coming battle. Ayres granted his request.[21] About noon, Griffin's division began its advance. As the men moved into the dense growth of trees, they were on the alert for the enemy. It was not easy going, as many units were forced to literally hack their way through the dense underbrush in the area. Regiments in line to either side of the 146th became disorganized struggling through the briars and dense underbrush, resorting to moving forward in single file rather than as a united front. Some regiments were separated from those on their flanks. Troops became confused about which direction to take. Often, the only guidance they had was the sound of other regiments snapping and crashing their way through the woods, or the sound of soldiers slogging their way through the bogs and swampy areas. Several regiments had already become detached from the main force. General disorganization reigned.[22]

Adding to the problem was the fact that the men heard the sporadic firing of Federal and Confederate pickets sniping at one another, knowing it meant a battle was imminent. This slowed the movement further as the troops advanced with care, knowing they could engage the rebels at any moment. After struggling through the woods for several minutes, the Federals halted to determine what to do next. Indeed, several Federal units, including Col. Jacob B. Sweitzer's brigade, had become completely lost in the dense tangle of trees and brush.[23] Oddly, very few commanders thought to use compasses to feel their way through the forest, but relied more on hearing and seeing what was going on around them. Because of the disarray, commanders also had a difficult time sending orders from one regiment to another. Often, the only knowledge one regiment had about the location of another regiment was when it appeared beside them in line.[24] The disorderly advance caused large gaps to appear in the Federal line. As a result, when the men eventually emerged from the woods, their officers had to organize them into some semblance of order.

Sometime between 10:00 AM and 11:00 AM the Federals reached the edge of Saunders' Field.[25] The small oasis amid the Wilderness was not very extensive, measuring approximately 800 yards by 400 yards. The Orange Turnpike crossed the clearing, as did a gully that ran under a small bridge. The regimental history of the 146th New York contains this description:

> It was a narrow, deserted clearing, oval in shape, extending about 800 yards both north and south and four hundred yards east and west, and lay between two irregular ridges in the forest. The turnpike crossed it a little diagonally just south of its center. The field sloped gently between its eastern and western sides, and in the middle was a gully through which had once run a small stream, but which now lay bare and dry. The clearing had evidently been planted with corn the season before, much of the stubble remained. At the north end ... there was an irregular intrusion of stunted pines and cedars, intermingled with bushes and vines of every description. Surrounded on every side by the somber forests, the clearing was the only open, sunny spot visible as far as the eye could see.[26]

The clearing posed a hazard for another reason. No one knew how many of the enemy were present on the opposite side. As the troops waited out of sight in the underbrush alongside the field, they could hear the firing in the distance growing in intensity as the battle expanded and more troops on both sides became involved. As they waited, the officers arranged the troops in two lines of battle. The 140th New York held the left position in the first line, its flank resting on the turnpike. To the right came the 2nd, 11th, 12th, 14th and 17th U.S. Regulars. The 146th New York found itself on the left of the second line, with their right extended by the 91st and 155th Pennsylvania.[27]

To some of the men, it seemed as though they were waiting to begin a "pleasure excursion," rather than a major battle. They passed the time chatting, swap-

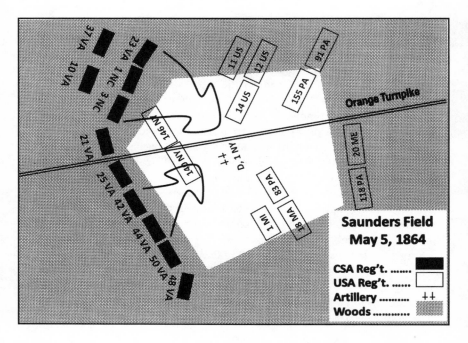

Saunders Field
May 5, 1864

CSA Reg't. .... ▄
USA Reg't. ...... ☐
Artillery .... ++
Woods .... ▒

ping stories, telling jokes, or playing games such as throwing dice.[28] After a short wait, however, notions of joviality were quickly dispelled when bullets from skirmishing in their front began to zip among them, cutting through the trees, clipping leaves, and severing branches which fell to the ground on top of the apprehensive troops. As unconcerned and casual as they might have seemed just a few moments before, the mood changed to apprehension as they realized what awaited them on the other side of the clearing. A member of the 140th New York said, "The men who for those few minutes lay there and faced the possibilities of tragedy then inevitable can never forget it. The suspense and dread and hope which possess men during such minutes cannot be adequately told in words."[29]

Meanwhile, Gen. Warren had been awaiting the arrival of support in the form of a division from the Sixth Corps. After a considerable interval, when the expected reinforcement did not appear, he finally decided to wait no longer. The attack would go ahead. The troops, who were growing increasingly anxious, were almost grateful when the order to advance arrived. Across the field from them, behind their newly erected breastworks, lay Brig. Gen. George H. Steuart's brigade including the 1st and 3rd North Carolina and the 10th, 23rd and 37th Virginia. To Steuart's left, prolonging his line, lay Brig. Gen. Leroy A. Stafford's brigade with the 1st, 2nd, 10th, 14th and 15th Louisiana. Between the two opposing forces lay the deceptively quiet open field that would soon witness the brutality of armed conflict. Into this serene scene the first Federal battle line emerged from the woods, their lines overlapped by the rebels so that the Union flanks lay unprotected, exposed to a possible Confederate flank attack. By hurrying into battle before the arrival of the Sixth Corps supports, Meade had thrown away numerical superiority, and exposed his assaulting troops to potential flanking fire.[30]

As the Federals began their advance across Saunders' Field, skirmishers rooted out some Confederates lurking in the gully that ran across the clearing. However, as the Federal battle line appeared, the Confederate positions erupted in an explosion of fire that swept across the field. On the Union right, the 2nd and 11th U.S. Regulars encountered difficulty struggling through the tangled underbrush along the edge of the field, gradually falling behind the 140th New York which advanced in the center of the field. At the same time, the New Yorkers bore slightly off to the left, following the course of the turnpike. The resulting gap allowed the Confederates to pour a withering fire into both flanks of the 140th New York and to bring the regulars to a virtual halt. Led by Col. George "Paddy" Ryan, the140th pushed to the left, where Confederate resistance seemed to be less concentrated than in the center, but soon found itself advancing alone upon the formidable rebel works.[31]

As the infantry assault ground slowly to a halt, a section of Battery D, 1st New York Light Artillery, under Lt. William H. Shelton, dashed forward along the Orange Turnpike, unlimbering on the flank of the 140th New York to add support to the beleaguered infantry. The two brass Napoleon smoothbores attempted to rake the Confederate line with canister, but found it difficult to fire on the rebels without also hitting friendly troops. Attempts to lend support sewed as much confusion in the attacking Union lines as they did within the Confederate defenders. Now thoroughly disorganized, survivors of the 140th clung desperately to their advanced position before the rebel breastworks.[32]

With his attack faltering, Gen. Ayres threw in his second line in an attempt to press home the assault. "Attention!" shouted Col. Jenkins to the 140th. "Take arms! Fix bayonets! Forward march!" The men rose to their feet, fixed their bayonets, and moved forward out of the woods into the edge of the field. "Forward, double-quick!" ordered Jenkins. The regiment rushed forward to be greeted by a hail of enemy fire. To their right, the two Pennsylvania regiments moved forward with them. As the regiments reached the gully bisecting the field, they were raked with two destructive volleys that cut through their ranks, while Shelton's guns continued to belch forth, as much a threat to their friends as the enemy. One soldier recalled "The rattle of musketry was interspersed with the cannon booming on the road, the fire from which obliqued across the front of the 146th. Some of us were so close that we could feel the strong wind of the discharges."[33]

"As we ran shouting across the field many of our brave comrades fell on the right and on the left," recalled Corp. Shepard. "It seemed almost impossible that any should escape the storm of leaden hail." As he ran forward, "a man who was directly in front of me halted suddenly. As I was about to say to him 'Go ahead,'

Capt. B. Franklin Wright
Wounded in the Wilderness
(Donald Wisnoski)

1st Lt. Joseph S. Lowery
Wounded at Cold Harbor
(Donald Wisnoski)

he fell to the ground in a heap—dead. I saw that he had been shot directly in the forehead."[34]

Hidden in the thick trees on the opposite side of the clearing, the Confederates had a clear view and unobstructed field of fire at the advancing Federals. The attackers found the Confederates hard to distinguish behind their breastwork hidden in the trees and shadows of the woods. "We had only smoke and evergreens to fire at," explained Corp. Shepard, "whereas we stood out in the plain sunlight, a good target for our foe." Casualties mounted dramatically. Looking across the field from his position in reserve, Lt. Holman Melcher of the 20th Maine "could see spurts of dust started up all over the field by the bullets of the enemy as they spattered like big drops of a coming shower.... But that was not the thing that troubled us. It was the dropping of our comrades from the charging line as they rushed across the fatal field with breasts bared to the terrible storm of leaden hail."[35] As one Confederate soldier stated later, the Union troops were "mowed down like grass before the sickle."[36]

But the worst was yet to come. To their right, the Regulars and the two Pennsylvania regiments floundered, their attack stalled. The result was that as the 146th New York advanced to support the 140th, grimly holding its advanced position, both flanks of the Oneida County regiment became exposed. The Confederates lost no time taking advantage of this opportunity.[37]

The leading companies made it into the fringe of the woods on the Confederate side of the field. "Closing with the enemy, we fought them fiercely

Corp. Norton D. Shepard
Wounded and Captured in the Wilderness
(Oneida County Historical Society)

Corp. George H. Palmer
Wounded in the Wilderness
(Oneida County Historical Society)

with bayonet, as well as Bullet," recalled Lt. William H. S. Sweet of Marcy, "men ran to and fro, firing, shouting, stabbing with bayonets, beating on his resources, grimly and desperately."[38] Faced with the murderous fire, officers quickly passed the word to lie down, an order that need not have been given as many men had already decided that was the wisest course of action. With no cover, there was no recourse but to hug the ground to keep from being shot. The men from both New York regiments returned fire as best they could, hampered by trying to reload their weapons while lying on the ground. Yet, even prone, the 146th and 140th managed to send unrelenting fire into the rebel lines, which caused several elements of the gray clad troops to fall back. What the Federals did not know was that the rebel retreat was planned. The Confederates withdrew slightly, making it appear as though they were retreating, when it was simply a plan to draw in the already battered Union regiments.[39]

As their comrades fell back to lure in the Yankees, other rebels moved quickly forward on the flanks of the now isolated New Yorkers. "We were not only flanked but doubly flanked," explained Lt. Sweet. "We were in a bag and the strings were tied. Those of our regiment who escaped were principally from the right, where the movement of the rebels seems to have been discovered in time to make escape possible."[40] Withering flanking fire swept through the regiment, spreading death everywhere. "The regiment melted away like snow," reported one soldier. "Men disappeared as if the earth had swallowed them."[41]

Lt. Col. Henry R. Curran
Killed in the Wilderness
(Donald Wisnoski)

Capt. James G. Grindlay
Senior Surviving Officer after the Wilderness
(Donald Wisnoski)

Confederate Capt. McHenry Howard looked out over the field as "a destructive fire was poured into them, so that it appeared to me the ground was more thickly strewn with their dead and wounded than I had ever seen."[42]

Corp. Shepard heard his captain order "Fall back!" as he was preparing to fire. "I had hardly straightened up when I received a bullet in my right shoulder.... I raised my gun to my shoulder, determined to give them one parting shot to remember me by. As I took aim I received a shot through my right elbow joint. The bullet broke the bone and shattered the joint. I never knew whether or not I fired. The gun dropped from my grasp and my arm hung loose and useless by my side." Turning to run for the rear, another bullet slammed into his side. When he rose again, he faced a rebel pointing a musket directly at him. Corp. Norton Shepard was a prisoner.[43]

In the color guard, Corp. George F. Williams, the color bearer, fell with three separate wounds. Another soldier picked up the fallen banner, only to be killed. Every member of the color guard was killed or wounded except for Corp. Conrad Neuschler who took up the colors and sprinted for the rear, intent on saving the regiment's honor. He made it as far as the gully where he was shot down, wounded. Sergt. J. Albert Jennison of Utica seized the colors just as the rebels closed in, calling on him to surrender. Jennison ignored them, running for the rear in a zigzag fashion as bullets zipped past him. He reached the woods unharmed. The regimental history reported "The flag, torn and soiled, was preserved for the regiment."[44] Jennison became an instant hero.

Saunders' Field as it looked shortly after the end of the war.
(Library of Congress)

———

Behind Jennison, Gen. Leroy Stafford's Confederates rushed to prevent any further escape. Outnumbered, outgunned, and outflanked, with no hope of victory, the New Yorkers faced two alternatives: stay and be killed or captured, or retreat. Most chose the latter, beginning a rather disjointed withdrawal back across the field. Col. Jenkins was seen leaning against his sword in front of the rebel works, wiping blood from his face. It was the last anyone would see of him. Lt. Col. Henry R. Curran, a former Hamilton College student, struggled through the underbrush in front of the Confederate breastworks. Looking about him, he shouted to Lt. Alonzo I. King of Whitestown, "This is awful!"

"Where are all our men?" King asked.

"Dead," Curran replied, a split second before a bullet tore through his head killing him instantly.[45]

King was shot through the right arm. Lt. William A. Walker was shot through the neck, forearm, and leg. Attempting to crawl to safety, he was captured by the Confederates. Lt. Peter D. Froeligh of New York City, captain of the regimental baseball team, was killed. A musket ball shattered Adjutant William Wright's elbow, requiring amputation. Capt. James Stewart of Clinton marveled in a letter to his wife that any survived: "How any of us escaped is to me a mystery. As regards myself, nothing short of Almighty interposition saved me. Men fell

Chauncey Smith
Colorbearer
(Oneida County Historical Society)

around me like autumn leaves."[46] Many men were hit as they retreated back across Saunders' Field, their bodies falling among the numerous corpses already there.[47]

Another member of the 146th taking part in the fight was the regimental chaplain, Edward P. Payson. Just before they stepped off from the woods to attack the Confederate positions, the men gave Payson their watches, rings, money, whatever was valuable to them. It was his job to take care of these items and return them to their owners after the fight. It was taken for granted that when the charge was made, the chaplain would remain behind. The men had not counted on the grit and loyalty of their chaplain. When they headed out into the deadly field, he did not stay behind. He went along, remaining several yards to the rear of the advancing line. His intention was to minister to the wounded and aid them in any way he could. He soon became so involved in this work that he forgot about his own safety, charging—along with the regiment's valuables, which he still carried—across the field when the 146th made its final assault on the rebels in the woods. He actually took part in the hand to hand fighting in the thicket, and when the regiment was forced to retreat, he went with them. Payson managed to minister to the wounded, make the charge, fight in the woods, and retreat without getting a scratch or losing a single item entrusted to him. He could have been severely reprimanded for this feat, but the officers of the regiment could not bring themselves to do it. All they could do was warn him not to do it again, a warning he accepted with a sheepish grin and a promise to be more prudent in the future.[48]

On their way back to Union lines, the 146th came upon the remnants of Shelton's section of Battery D. Both the wounded and unscathed sought refuge behind dead artillery horses that lay along the Orange Turnpike.[49] Those who could, helped the artillerymen battle the attacking rebels. Once again they found themselves engaged in hand-to-hand fighting with bayonets and whatever else they could locate. With Confederate reinforcements arriving, it soon became evident they could not hold out.[50] As he was being led away to captivity, Lt. Shelton later reported that he saw Confederate soldiers from the 6th Alabama "in butternut suits and slouch hats, shooting straggling and wounded Zouaves."[51] These could only be members of either the 146th or the 140th New York.

During the battle, wadding from the muskets and artillery pieces had fallen into the dry underbrush of Saunders' Field, causing it to begin to smolder. Now, as the Federals retreated, the smoldering erupted into a fire that swept across the field. One veteran noted that "The almost cheerful "Pop! Pop!" of cartridges gave no hint of the dreadful horror their noise bespoke. Swept by the flames, the trees, bushes, and logs which Confederates had thrown up ... now took fire and dense clouds of smoke rolled across the clearing, choking unfortunates who were exposed to it.... The clearing now became a raging inferno in which many of the wounded perished. The bodies of the dead were blackened and burned beyond all possibility of recognition."[52]

Many of the wounded attempted to crawl to safety, but most could not make it. For an instant, amid the excitement of brutal conflict, human instinct took over. Both sides, Federals and Confederates, stopped fighting and went into Saunders' Field in a humanitarian attempt to save the wounded of both sides. Soldiers in gray attempted to save soldiers in blue, who just a moment before they had tried to kill. The same was true of the members of the 146th as they tried to save anyone they could. It proved to be a noble but mostly useless attempt. Blackened corpses soon lay everywhere. The odor of burnt human flesh wafted on the hot breeze.[53]

The disastrous assault lasted only some twenty minutes. As the survivors gathered in the relative safety of the woods from whence they began the attack, the sullen mood contrasted sharply with the earlier light-hearted banter. Major James G. Grindlay, a native of Scotland who resided in Boonville where he was a bookkeeper, took command of the shattered regiment as its senior surviving officer. Solemnly, the men listened to the roll call. Of 24 officers who left the woods to charge across Saunders' Field, only ten responded to their names. Of 556 enlisted men present that morning, only 254 answered to their names in the aftermath of the sanguine fight. The Fifth Oneida had lost 316 men in twenty minutes, 54.5 percent of those who made the charge. This was the second highest ratio of losses incurred by all the Federal regiments engaged in the Battle of the Wilderness.[54]

In the immediate aftermath of the day's battle, the Orange Turnpike and the surrounding area were clogged with wounded men. Some wandered about in a daze, others sought directions to the nearest field hospital. Ambulances quickly filled with the wounded. Those who could not find space in an ambulance received treatment on the spot. Rough hewn tables made of wooden slats and logs were thrown up beneath trees, and surgeons began to operate, usually hacking off arms and legs, which was the basic treatment for anyone who had been shot in an appendage. Piles of detached limbs grew at an astonishing rate. It soon became apparent that the battle at Saunders' Field had not only been futile, but an incredibly costly affair. Gen. Charles Griffin, who was in overall command of the failed attempt, immediately began to point fingers of blame for the debacle in which much of his command had been needlessly sacrificed. He went into a tirade against Gens. Warren and Wright, going so far as to visit Gen. Grant's headquarters to demand that both be arrested. His request was denied.[55]

Meanwhile, across from the Federal lines the Confederates were busy gathering up their prisoners and sending them to the rear. Most if not all of the prisoners taken from the 146th were sent to the Confederate prison called Camp Sumter in Georgia, which was known by a more familiar name to the captives— Andersonville. In all, 194 men of the regiment were taken prisoner during the war and sent to Andersonville. Of those, 133 were captured at the Battle in the Wilderness on May 5. Thirty of these men would never live to leave the camp.[56]

When some of the prisoners taken by the rebels were being moved off the front lines, Confederate Gen. Richard Ewell asked "What makes you boys fight so? Your regiment fought like hell."[57] Courage is not only recognized by one's own troops, but by the enemy as well. In the next century, the 146th New York's deeds at Saunders' Field would be immortalized on canvas by artist Keith Rocco in his painting, "Into the Wilderness." The 146th New York, still nicknamed Garrard's Tigers, had certainly proven worthy of its name that day in May 1864 at Saunders' Field.[58]

On May 17, the carnage that had occurred at Saunders' Field began to appear in the northern newspapers, including the Upstate and Central New York areas. The *Rome Sentinel* was one of the first to bring the news to its readers. In its report, the paper stated that the regiment, which it identified as the Fifth Oneida rather than its numerical designation of 146, had been nearly annihilated.[59] Though no casualty lists were provided, people who read the account knew to steel themselves for the worst. The war had been going on for three long and bloody years, and high casualty rates in battle were not only common, but accepted almost with an inevitable resignation.

Despite its decimation, the regiment enjoyed no respite from the active campaigning. Immediately after Saunders' Field, what was left of it took part in the Spotsylvania campaign which included battles at Laurel Hill (May 8), Spotsylvania Courthouse (May 12-21), and the assault on the Salient or Mule Shoe (May 12). The 146th was also involved in the Battle of the North Anna River on May 23-26, Totopotomoy on May 28-31, and Cold Harbor, another debacle for the Union, on June 1-3. These engagements cost the regiment another 81 casualties.[60] Eventually, the 146th would receive replacements for the troops it had lost at the Wilderness and ensuing battles. But it would never again be the same.

When Gen. Ulysses S. Grant headed toward Richmond, he laid siege to the city of Petersburg. Grant had intended to take the city easily, which was the major railroad hub and supply line into Richmond. However, the rebels had heavily fortified the city, and it proved a more difficult task than the Federals had anticipat-

Mary G. Brainard
Author of the First History of the
146th New York. *(Donald Wisnoski)*

ed. Eventually, the battle for Petersburg would take ten long months, from June 1864 to April 1865. The 146th New York took an active part in the siege of the embattled city, losing 17 casualties. The remainder of its service in the Federal cause reads like a list of some of the most famous Civil War battles: Weldon Railroad (46 casualties), Poplar Springs Church (3 casualties), Peeble's Farm, Boydton Plank Road, Hatcher's Run, Dabney's Mills, Lewis Farm, White Oak Road, Five Forks (65 casualties), and ultimately, Appomattox Court House, and the surrender of Lee's army in April 1865.[61]

Following the Confederate surrender at Appomattox, survivors of the 146th New York marched back to Washington, D.C., to take part in the Grand Review of the army held in the reunited nation's capital on May 23. By the end of its career, the regiment could count among its ranks three Medal of Honor recipients. The first was Col. James G. Grindlay who distinguished himself for conspicuous gallantry by being the first person to enter the enemy's works during the Battle of Five Forks, the key engagement forcing Lee's Southern army to abandon Petersburg and Richmond. The second was Private David Edwards of Company H, who also earned his honor at the Battle of Five Forks. Born in Wales, Edwards joined the 146th in Sangerfield, New York. On April 1, 1865, he earned the Medal of Honor by capturing an enemy flag. Likewise, in the same battle Irish born Sergt. Thomas J. Murphy of Company G was awarded the Medal of Honor, also for capturing an enemy standard. This was the highest number of Medals of Honor awarded to any single regiment in the Fifth Corps.[62]

The 146th New York ended its illustrious career on July 16, 1865, near Washington, D.C., when the troops mustered out of their country's service. The regiment had taken part in some of the fiercest and most famous battles of the conflict, including Fredericksburg, Chancellorsville, Gettysburg, the Wilderness, Spotsylvania, Cold Harbor, the siege of Petersburg, and the Appomattox Campaign. When all the figures and statistics had been compiled, the 146th New York had lost a total of 654 men during the fratricidal conflict. Among them were three officers and 81 enlisted men killed in battle; four officers and 46 enlisted men who were wounded and later succumbed to their wounds; and eight officers and 332 enlisted men posted as missing. One officer and 100 enlisted men died of disease, and one officer and 87 enlisted men had been prisoners of war. Included in this total are also thirteen officers and 167 enlisted men who were wounded, but later recovered.[63]

The 146th New York Volunteer Infantry, which began its service as the Fifth Oneida County Regiment, was the last infantry regiment to be raised in the county, but by no means was it the least. Its members distinguished themselves in battle with unflagging and unquestioned heroism and dedication to the "cause." When the country was in peril, they answered the call with determination and loyalty. They sacrificed to put the country back together again, many making the ultimate sacrifice. The people living in Oneida County then, as well as today, can be proud of the service the men of the 146th New York Volunteer Infantry rendered to them and to the nation.

---

[1]Frederick Phisterer, *New York in the War of the Rebellion, 1861-1865* (Albany, NY: J. B. Lyon Company, 1912), Vol. V, 3687; Mary Genevie Green Brainard, *Campaigns of the 146th Regiment New York State Volunteers* (Daleville, VA: Schroeder Publications, 2000), 7, 577; Raymond Smith, ed., *Out of the Wilderness: The Civil War Memoirs of Cpl. Norton Shepard, 146th New York Volunteer Infantry* (Hamilton, NY: Edmonston Publishing, Inc., 1968), 24.

[2]Phisterer, *New York in the War of the Rebellion,*Vol. V, 3687; Brainard, *Campaigns of the 146th*, 7-15.

[3]Brainard, *Campaigns of the 146th*, 15-19.

[4]Brainard, *Campaigns of the 146th*, 19-23, 31.

[5]Brainard, *Campaigns of the 146th*, 32-37.

[6]Brainard, *Campaigns of the 146th*, 68-69.

[7]Brainard, *Campaigns of the 146th*, 72-78.

[8]Brainard, *Campaigns of the 146th*, 83-84, 522; *The War of the Rebellion: a Compilation of the Official Records of the Union and Confederate Armies* (Washington, DC: U.S. Government Printing Office, 1880-1901), Series I, Volume XXV, Pt. 1, 181 (hereafter cited as *O.R.*). Casualties included two men killed; one officer and sixteen men wounded; and two officers and 29 men captured.

[9]Christopher Daley, *Uniform Study: 146th New York Zouave Uniform,* C. J. Daley Historical Reproductions Web Site, http://www.cjdaley.com/146th NYSV, May 21, 2008, 1-2; Brainard, *Campaigns of the 146th*, 92.

[10]Brainard, *Campaigns of the 146th*, 110-11.

[11]Brainard, *Campaigns of the 146th*, 111-12, 117-19, 523; *O.R.*, I, XXVII, Pt. 1, 180, 651. Casualties included four men killed and two officers and 22 men wounded.

[12]Brainard, *Campaigns of the 146th*, 343.

[13]Daley, *Uniform Study*, 1.

[14]Smith, *Out of the Wilderness*, 1-2.

[15]Smith, *Out of the Wilderness*, 2.

[16]Smith, *Out of the Wilderness*, x-xi; Brainard, *Campaigns of the 146th*, 173.

[17]Gordon C. Rhea, *The Battle of the Wilderness, May 5-6, 1864* (Baton Rouge, LA: Louisiana State University Press, 1994), 124-125; Smith, *Out of the Wilderness*, xi. Also spelled in some sources as Sanders' Field.

[18]Smith, *Out of the Wilderness*, xi.

[19]Smith, *Out of the Wilderness*, xi; Brainard, *Campaigns of the 146th*, 179.

[20]Brainard, *Campaigns of the 146th*, 181.

[21]A.P. Case and Patrick A. Schroeder, *Then Highest Praise of Gallantry: Memorials of David T. Jenkins of the 146th New York Infantry and Oneida County* (Doleville, VA: Schroeder Publications, 2001), 11; Brainard, *Campaigns of the 146th*, 185.

[22]John Cannan, *The Wilderness Campaign, May 1864* (Conshohocken, PA: Combined Books, 1993), 103.

[23]Cannan, *Wilderness Campaign*, 103.

[24]Edward Steere, *The Wilderness Campaign* (Harrisburg, PA: The Stackpole Company, 1960), 157.

[25]Rhea, *Battle of the Wilderness*, 102.

[26]Brainard, *Campaigns of the 146th*, 189.

[27]Charles Brandegee Livingstone, *Charlie's Civil War: A Private's Trial By Fire in the 5th New York Volunteers – Duryée Zouaves and 146th New York Volunteer Infantry* (Gettysburg, PA: Thomas Publications, 1997), 193.

[28]Brainard, *Campaigns of the 146th*, 187.

[29]Rhea, *Battle of the Wilderness*, 143-44.

[30]Rhea, *Battle of the Wilderness*, 143; Brainard, *Campaigns of the 146th*, 186, 188; Livingstone, *Charlie's Civil War*, 193.

[31]Cannan, *Wilderness Campaign*, 105; Brainard, *Campaigns of the 146th*, 189.

[32]Gregory Jaynes, *The Killing Ground* (Alexandria, VA: Time-Life Books, 1986), 64; Cannan, *Wilderness Campaign*, 105; Brainard, *Campaigns of the 146th*, 189-90.

[33]Steere, *Wilderness Campaign*, 158; Smith, *Out of the Wilderness*, 5; Cannan, *Wilderness Campaign*, 105.

[34]Smith, *Out of the Wilderness*, 5.

[35]Cannan, *Wilderness Campaign*, 107.

[36]Cannan, *Wilderness Campaign*, 107.

[37]Steere, *Wilderness Campaign*, 158; Smith, *Out of the Wilderness*, 5; Cannan, *Wilderness Campaign*, 105.

[38]Steere, *Wilderness Campaign*, 160.

[39]Rhea, *Battle of the Wilderness*, 150.

[40]Cannan, *Wilderness Campaign*, 110.

[41]Rhea, *Battle of the Wilderness*, 150.

[42]Noah Andre Trudeau, *Bloody Roads South: The Wilderness to Cold Harbor, May-June 1864* (Boston: Little, Brown, and Company, 1989), 57.

[43]Smith, *Out of the Wilderness*, 5, 8.

[44]Brainard, *Campaigns of the 146th*, 193-94.

[45]Brainard, *Campaigns of the 146th*, 196-98.

[46]Brainard, *Campaigns of the 146th*, 196-99; Howard Thomas, *Boys in Blue from the Adirondack Foothills* (Prospect, NY: Prospect Books, 1960), 189-90.

[47]Jaynes, *The Killing Ground*, 64.

[48]Brainard, *Campaigns of the 146th*, 194-95.

[49]Steere, *Wilderness Campaign*, 173.

[50]Steere, *Wilderness Campaign*, 174.

[51]Rhea, *Battle of the Wilderness*, 168.

[52]Steere, *Wilderness Campaign*, 174.

[53]Brainard, *Campaigns of the 146th*, 195.

[54]Smith, *Out of the Wilderness*, xii; Brainard, *Campaigns of the 146th*, 196.

[55]Trudeau, *Bloody Roads South*, 63.

[56]National Park Service, Andersonville National Historic Site Web Page, http://www.nps.gov/ande/, May 21, 2008.

[57]Smith, *Out of the Wilderness*, vii.

[58]Steere, *Wilderness Campaign*, 158.

[59]Smith, *Out of the Wilderness*, ix.

[60]Brainard, *Campaigns of the 146th*, 523.

[61]Brainard, *Campaigns of the 146th*, 524-25.

[62]Brainard, *Campaigns of the 146th*, 513; New York Civil War Medal of Honor Recipients Web Site, 16, (h), May 21, 2008; *O.R.*, I, XLVI, Pt. 1, 1258-60.

[63]Phisterer, *New York in the War of the Rebellion*, Vol. V, 3688.

CHAPTER 9

"FRATERNITY, CHARITY AND LOYALTY"
THE BOYS IN BLUE AFTER THE WAR

by

James S. Pula

Within six months of Robert E. Lee's surrender of the Army of Northern Virginia at Appomattox on April 9, 1865, the Union army had been mustered out, its former members free to resume their civilian lives. Few would ever forget what they had experienced. Utican Daniel Butterfield spoke for them all when called upon to give the official address presenting the remains of New York battle flags to the governor. "I am requested to present you these flags on behalf of your soldiers, who have borne them with courage and honor in the changing fortunes of battle," he began. "The brave hearts that yielded life whilst bearing these banners in defense of liberty, the majesty of the law, the safety, honor and welfare of the country, are buried on every field of our recent conflict."[1]

To those who fought, bled, and saw their friends, neighbors, and relatives die under the folds of their regimental colors, these emblems of their units became symbols of their common suffering, an unexplainable experience that bound them together for the rest of their lives. "We all love and revere the old tattered flags that were with us in our marches by day and night, in camp and on battlefield," commented Henry H. Miller of Clinton. "Many a comrade willingly sacrificed his life in defense of those flags and to preserve this beautiful land of ours." J. B. Wicks of Paris recalled the many hard-fought fields on which their colors formed "the rallying centre of the regiment," in the end to be brought "back to the old home, tattered and torn, but new and blessed, in every wide rent and stain—in every faded stripe and star. The colors of the old regiment embody three years of marching, fighting, enduring. They mean life, alive and alert, in holy things." John D. Ernst of Rome, color sergeant of the 117th New York Volunteer Infantry, captured the deep reverence the veterans shared for their regimental colors in the comments he offered on the presentation of the Fourth Oneida's banners to the Oneida County Historical Society for safekeeping.

Five and thirty years ago the patriotic ladies of the city of Utica and the great county of Oneida presented to the Fourth Oneida Regiment a beautiful silken flag, fashioned by their fair hands. You were borne by brave hearts, strong and willing hands through many a field of carnage and bloodshed to be planted in triumph upon the fortress of Fort Fisher. Your course is marked by the bodies of many brave men strewn along your pathway, whose deeds and sacrifices will live in the history of our country long after your tattered silken folds shall have passes into dust and oblivion. Our enfeebled limbs and trembling hands admonish us that we can no longer protect and care for you with our old time strength and vigor, so we consign your sacred folds to the outstretched hands waiting to receive you, with implicit faith and trust in their guardianship. Good bye, old flag, good bye.[2]

To continue their relationship with their old comrades-in-arms, Union veterans held regimental reunions on a regular basis, meeting at different locations around the county each year. In April 1867, a national veterans organization, the Grand Army of the Republic, began in Illinois under the motto "Fraternity, Charity and Loyalty."[3] The movement spread throughout the country, with Oneida County eventually home to 25 G.A.R. posts.

Reunion of the 26th New York Volunteer Infantry held in Utica, May 25, 1885.
(Oneida County Historical Society)

No.	Location	Named For	Chartered
14	Utica	Capt. John F. McQuade, 14th N.Y. Inf.	April 5, 1879
23	Waterville	Sgt. Andrew T. Russell, 117th N.Y. Inf.	May 22, 1868
31	New York Mills	1st Lt. George W. Ross, 117th N.Y. Inf.	May 23, 1868
36	Utica	Maj. William R. Reynolds, 14th N.Y.H.Arty.	May 18, 1878
39	Prospect	Capt. John T. Thomas, 117th N.Y. Inf.	May 3, 1875
47	Rome	Lt. Col. Charles H. Skillen, 14th N.Y. Inf.	Aug. 29, 1873
53	Utica	1st Lt. William K. Bacon, 26th N.Y. Inf.	Oct. 24, 1867
56	Lee Center	1st Sgt. Emory C. Starr, 146th N.Y. Inf.	Feb. 14, 1876
86	Clayville	Sgt. William E. Pettee, 146th N.Y. Inf.	Dec. 14, 1871
88	Camden	Pvt. W. Bradford Willis, 117th N.Y. Inf.	1872
97	Boonville	Gen. Charles Wheelock, 97th N.Y. Inf.	July 11, 1868
146	Utica	Maj. Henry Hastings Curran, 146th N.Y. Inf.	
181	Forestport	Pvt. Henry Walker, 117th N.Y. Inf.	May 26, 1881
227	Clinton	Sgt. Nathaniel B. Hinckley, 117th N.Y. Inf.	Aug. 17, 1881
345	New Hartford	Richard Updyke Sherman, politician	Oct. 27, 1896
413	Sauquoit	George W. Chadwick, Sr., businessman	May 7, 1888
437	Utica	Capt. Frederick "Fritz" Harrer, 14th N.Y. Inf.	Dec. 29, 1883
482	Camden	Capt. J. Parsons Stone, 117th N.Y. Inf.	May 12, 1884
510	Holland Patent	Capt. William J. Hunt, 117th N.Y. Inf.	Aug. 20, 1884
526	Vernon	Capt. James Edgar Jenkins, 146th N.Y. Inf.	Jan. 14, 1889
537	Vienna	Pvt. George Barton Meays, 14th N.Y. Inf.	1886 ?
551	Taberg	Capt. Willard W. Ballard, 81st N.Y. Inf.	April 7, 1885
602	Florence	2nd Lt. Evan R. Jones, 117th N.Y. Inf.	Oct. 6, 1886
615	Verona	1st Lt. Joseph Warren, 97th N.Y. Inf.	July 2, 1887

The Grand Army of the Republic pursued the social, charitable, patriotic, and political interests of its members. Socially, it promoted continuing brotherhood among the veterans by providing them with places and occasions to meet, renew acquaintances, and recall their wartime experiences. Its charitable activities were largely concentrated on providing relief for the widows and orphans of soldiers and for needy veterans. Among its more successful activities was the founding of veterans' homes for aged and infirm comrades-in-arms. To promote patriotism, the organization decorated veterans' graves, distributed patriotic literature and appeared in fraternal uniform at annual patriotic celebrations. In 1867, its commander, former general John A. Logan, issued General Order No. 11 calling on all affiliated departments and posts to set aside May 30 each year as a day for remembering the sacrifices of their comrades, thus inaugurating Memorial Day as a remembrance of those who served in the Civil War. Politically, the G.A.R. was closely associated with the Republican Party because it was associated with the preservation of the Union and the ending of slavery. Over time, the G.A.R. became arguably the most influential groups in America, successfully lobbying Congress to provide pensions to veterans, invalids, and widows of veterans. Five G.A.R. members were eventually elected President of the United States and, between the elections of U. S. Grant and William McKinley, backing by the

G.A.R. was almost a requirement for any Republican interested in running for presidential office. Its last annual national encampment was held in 1949.[4]

Locally, the various G.A.R. posts held annual reunions, turned out for patriotic celebrations and the funerals of their members, and engaged in a variety of social and community projects. Some sponsored lectures, raised funds for local projects, and spoke at educational and community events. As time went on, they increasingly worked with affiliated groups that came into being such as the Women's Relief Corps, Ladies of the G.A.R., Daughters of Veterans, Sons of Veterans, and the Sons of Veterans Auxiliary.[5] Several annual meetings of the New York Department of the G.A.R. were held in Utica, and Oneida County provided three commanders for the Department of New York including James McQuade of Utica, Joseph I. Sayles of Rome, and John S. Koster of Port Leyden. Charles A. Shaw of New York Mills went on to become national president of the organization.[6]

In 1881, as its members began to age and pass away in increasing numbers, the G.A.R. formed the Sons of Veterans of the United States of America to preserve its memory and continue its activities once the original veterans were no more. In 1925, the organization changed its name to the Sons of Union Veterans of the Civil War. It received a federal charter in 1954, only two years before the last known Union soldier died.[7]

On July 1-4, 1938, Henry Fike of Rome, Charles Jennette of Old Forge, James Miller of Forestport, and Philemon Woods of Boonville were among the

Bayne Camp, Sons of Union Veterans, New York Mills.
(Oneida County Historical Society)

eighty New Yorkers and 1,845 veterans who attended the final grand reunion of the blue and gray held in Gettysburg, Pennsylvania. On the third day of the reunion, they witnessed the unveiling of the Eternal Light Peace Memorial. In his remarks on that occasion, President Franklin D. Roosevelt noted that the aged veterans assembled for the last time on the fields of the war's most famous battle had answered their nation's call to duty, "seeking to save for our common country opportunity and security for citizens in a free society."[8] Long before the Civil War began, citizens of Oneida County and the surrounding area emerged as leaders in the anti-slavery crusade. When the speeches subsided to be replaced by the weapons of war, Oneida County continued to play a central role in the battles that preserved the union, ended the reprehensible institution

Charles A. Shaw
(Grand Army of the Republic)

of slavery, and determined the future orientation of the nation's political and economic systems. As General Butterfield remarked in his presentation of New York colors to the governor, men from Oneida County had turned out "in defense of liberty, the majesty of the law, the safety, honor and welfare of the country," and they had done so "with courage and honor."

[1]*Fifth Annual Report of the Chief of the Bureau of Military, with Appendices* (Albany: C. van Benthuysen & Sons, 1865), 29.

[2]*Presentation of the Battle Flags of the Oneida County Regiments to the Oneida Historical Society, Utica, N.Y.* (Madison County Historical Society, No. 414; *Utica Morning Herald*, December 14, 1897).

[3]Stuart McConnell, *Glorious Contentment: The Grand Army of the Republic, 1865-1900* (Chapel Hill: University of North Carolina Press, 1992), 24-27; Wallace Evan Davies, *Patriotism on Parade* (Cambridge: Harvard University Press, 1955), 31.

[4]Davies, *Patriotism on Parade*, 189-92; McConnell, *Glorious Contentment, passim*.

[5]*Sixty-Third Annual Encampment, Grand Army of the Republic and Allied Organizations* (Utica, NY: G.A.R., 1929); *Abstract of General Orders and Proceedings of the Seventy-eighth Annual Encampment, Department of New York, G.A.R., Held at Utica June 12-15, 1944* (Albany: Williams Press, Inc., 1945); *Abstract of General Orders and*

Proceedings of the Seventy-ninth Annual Encampment, Department of New York, G.A.R., Held at Utica June 11-14, 1945 (Albany: William Press, Inc., 1945); *Thirty-Fourth Annual Encampment, Department of New York, Grand Army of the Republic, Held at Utica, New York, May 16th and 17th, 1900* (Utica: G.A.R., 1900); *Thirtieth Annual Encampment, Department of New York, Grand Army of the Republic, Utica, N.Y., May 19th and 20th, 1896* (Utica: L. C. Childs & Sons, Printers, 1896); *Report of the Fourth Regular Meeting of the Committee on Teaching Civics, History and Patriotism in the Public Schools of the State Under the Auspices of the Grand Army of the Republic Department of New York* (Albany: James B. Lyon, State Printers, 1900); Davies, *Patriotism on Parade*, 38.

[6]*Abstract of General Orders and Proceedings of the Fortieth Annual Encampment, Department of New York, G.A.R.* (Albany: Brandow Printing Company, 1906), 6.

[7]Davies, *Patriotism on Parade*, 37.

[8]Paul L. Roy, *The Last Reunion of the Blue and Gray* (Gettysburg, PA: The Bookmart, 1950), 71-72.

BIOGRAPHIES

The following biographies are included here because they highlight prominent Oneida County residents who are not otherwise covered in the major chapters of his book.

Monument of the 146th New York at Gettysburg
(Cheryl A. Pula)

SAMUEL LIVINGSTON BREESE

Samuel L. Breese
(National Archives)

Samuel L. Breese entered the world in Utica, New York, on August 6, 1794, the son of Arthur Breese and Catherine Livingston. Following his early education in Whitesboro and Utica, he entered Union College, but left before graduation to accept appointment as a midshipman in the U.S. Navy on September 10, 1810. During the War of 1812, he fought in the Battle of Lake Champlain under Commodore Thomas McDonough and was awarded a sword and a vote of thanks from Congress for gallant conduct at the Battle of Plattsburgh. Commissioned a lieutenant on April 28, 1816, he was assigned to duty against the North African pirates in the Mediterranean Sea in 1826-27 and in the Levant during the war between Turkey and Greece. Promoted to commander in December 1835, he was assigned to the Philadelphia Navy Yard in the following year before being promoted to captain on September 8, 1841 and assigned to the naval facility at Baltimore. Four years later he was designated commanding officer of the frigate *USS Cumberland* attached to the Mediterranean Squadron.[1]

With the outbreak of the war with Mexico in 1846, Breese participated in the capture of Vera Cruz, Tabasco and Tuspan, after which he was named military governor of Tuspan. Following the war he was assigned to duty on the Great Lakes in 1848 before being named commanding officer at the Norfolk Navy Yard in Virginia in 1853. Three years later he assumed command of the U.S. naval squadron in the Mediterranean as commodore, a position he held until 1859 when he began a stint as commander of the New York Navy Yard in Brooklyn. In the latter position he played a key role in fitting out warships during the early stages of the Civil War when the North was attempting to create the blockade of Southern ports that became a key factor in the Northern victory.[2]

In recognition of his services, he was promoted to commodore in July 1862 and when Congress created the rank of "rear admiral" in the same year, Breese was one of the thirteen commodores originally promoted to the new position. Following 1862 he was assigned as inspector of lighthouses before being reassigned to special duties at the New York Navy Yard in 1865. His last official duty was as port admiral in Philadelphia, a position he assumed in 1869. He died at Mount Airy, near Philadelphia, on December 17, 1870, and was buried in Forest Hill Cemetery in Utica.[3]

by James S. Pula

———

[1] *The National Cyclopædia of American Biography* (New York: James T. White & Company, 1897), Vol. 4, 438; Edward Elbridge Salisbury, *Family Memorials—A Series of Genealogical and Biographical Monographs, on the Families of ..., Breese* (New Haven: Tuttle, Morehouse and Taylor, 1885); *History of Oneida County New York From 1700 to the Present Time* (Chicago: The S. J. Clarke Publishing Company, 1912), Vol. II, 528; obituary, *New York Times*, December 19, 1870.

[2] *National Cyclopædia of American Biography*, Vol. 4, 438; Salisbury, *Family Memorials*; obituary, *New York Times*, December 19, 1870.

[3] *National Cyclopædia of American Biography*, Vol. 4, 438; Salisbury, *Family Memorials*; obituary, *New York Times*, December 19, 1870.

DANIEL ADAMS BUTTERFIELD

Daniel Butterfield
(National Archives)

Born in Utica on October 31, 1831, Daniel Butterfield was the son of John Warren Butterfield, a prominent Oneida County businessman and owner of the Overland Mail Company, a forerunner of the American Express Company. After local schooling at the Utica Academy, Butterfield graduated from Union College in Schenectady in 1849, joined the Utica Citizens' Corps, and began preparing himself for a career in law. He soon abandoned this plan to engage in business activities in New York City, rising to superintendent of the Eastern Division of the American Express Company through obvious family connections. While in New York City he joined the 71st Militia Regiment as a captain and was subsequently promoted to major and lieutenant colonel. In December 1859 he gained election as colonel of the 12th regiment of militia. Although this would appear to provide good experience for the impending conflict, it those days state militia regiments were greatly under-strength and served more social functions than military.[1]

With the outbreak of the Civil War in 1861, Butterfield raced to the nation's capital where he hastily joined the rag-tag Clay Guards that was formed from among local citizens and government officials to guard the capital until loyal troops could arrive. On April 20 he returned to New York where he quickly filled the ranks of the 12th New York State Militia with additional volunteers and left the city on the following day with his regiment aboard the transport *Baltic* headed for federal service. His prompt response during the national emergency earned him appointment as lieutenant colonel in the regular army, despite his lack of serious military training or experience, and brigadier general of volunteers.[2]

Assigned to the Army of the Potomac under General George B. McClellan, Butterfield was soon given command of a brigade in Major General Fitz John

Butterfield photographed on his horse during the Peninsula Campaign in 1862.
(Library of Congress)

Porter's Fifth Corps during McClellan's Peninsula Campaign in the spring of 1862. During the advance down the York Peninsula toward Richmond, Butterfield's brigade was constantly in the advance where it skirmished almost daily. Butterfield's brigade was involved in the first advance on Big Bethel, Harold's Mill, and Yorktown, and was engaged at Hanover where Butterfield left a sick bed to command his troops as soon as the firing broke out and his men captured two artillery pieces. He was again engaged at Mechanicsville and on June 27, 1862, his brigade was in the thick of a major Confederate attack at Gaines' Mill. Though he was wounded in the action, when his troops began to falter under the rebel assault Butterfield grasped a regimental flag, inspiring them to hold firm by his own example. The Prince de Joinville, a French observer who witnessed the act was so taken with Butterfield's heroics that he gave the general the gift of a horse. His country awarded him the Medal of Honor. The citation explained that he had "seized the colors of the 83rd Pennsylvania Volunteers at a critical moment and, under a galling fire of the enemy, encouraged the depleted ranks to renewed exertion."[3]

Following the Peninsula Campaign, while the Union Army recovered from the ordeal at Harrison's Landing in Virginia, Butterfield began think about the bugle call *Lights Out* played each evening in the Union camps to signal the end of the day. He never really liked the music, so he decided to try to experiment with something new to replace it. The new version would thereafter be known as *Taps*. According to a letter written to *Century Magazine* in 1898 by Oliver W. Norton, bugler in the 83rd Pennsylvania, in response to an article on Civil War music by Gustav Kobbe,

> During the early part of the Civil War I was bugler at the Headquarters of Butterfield s Brigade, Morell s Division, Fitz-John Porter s Corp, Army of the Potomac. Up to July, 1862, the Infantry call for Taps was that set down in *Casey's Tactics*, which Mr. Kobbe says was borrowed from the French. One day, soon after the Seven Days battles on the Peninsula, when the Army of the Potomac was lying in camp at Harrison's Landing, General Daniel Butterfield, then commanding our Brigade, sent for me, and showing me some notes on a staff written in pencil on the back of an envelope, asked me to sound them on my bugle. I did this several times, playing the music as written. He changed it somewhat, lengthening some notes and shortening others, but retaining the melody as he first gave it to me. After getting it to his satisfaction, he directed me to sound that call for Taps thereafter in place of the regulation call. The music was beautiful on that still summer night, and was heard far beyond the limits of our Brigade. The next day I was visited by several buglers from neighboring Brigades, asking for copies of the music which I gladly furnished. I think no general order was issued from army headquarters authorizing the substitution of this for the regulation call, but as each brigade commander exercised his own discretion in such minor matters, the call was gradually taken up through the Army of the Potomac. I have been told that it was carried to the Western Armies by the 11th and 12th Corps, when they went to Chattanooga in the fall of 1863, and rapidly made it's way through those armies. I did not presume to question General Butterfield at the time, but from the manner in which the call was given to me, I have no doubt he composed it in his tent at Harrison's Landing.[4]

In response to the letter, the editors of *Century* wrote to Butterfield for his comments. He responded as follows:

> I recall, in my dim memory, the substantial truth of the statement made by Norton, of the 83rd Pa., about bugle calls. His letter gives the impression that I personally wrote the notes for the call. The facts are, that at the time I could sound calls on the bugle as a necessary part of military knowledge and instruc- tion for an officer commanding a regiment or brigade. I had acquired this as a regimental commander. I had composed a call for my brigade, to precede any calls, indicating that such were calls, or orders, for my brigade alone. This was of very great use and effect on the march and in battle. It enabled me to cause my whole command, at times, in march, covering over a mile on the road, all to

halt instantly, and lie down, and all arise and start at the same moment; to forward in line of battle, simultaneously, in action and charge etc. It saves fatigue. The men rather liked their call, and began to sing my name to it. It was three notes and a catch. I can not write a note of music, but have gotten my wife to write it from my whistling it to her, and enclose it. The men would sing , Dan, Dan, Dan, Butterfield, Butterfield to the notes when a call came. Later, in battle, or in some trying circumstances or an advance of difficulties, they sometimes sang, Damn, Damn, Damn, Butterfield, Butterfield.

The call of Taps did not seem to be as smooth, melodious and musical as it should be, and I called in some one who could write music, and practiced a change in the call of Taps until I had it suit my ear, and then, as Norton writes, got it to my taste without being able to write music or knowing the technical name of any note, but, simply by ear, arranged it as Norton describes.[5]

Following the Peninsula Campaign, Butterfield commanded his brigade at Second Bull Run and Antietam before being promoted to division command and then assigned to lead the Fifth Corps at Fredericksburg in December 1862 where his troops were ordered by General Ambrose Burnside to repeatedly launch near-suicidal attacks on Confederate positions along the heights above the city. When Burnside was subsequently replaced by Butterfield's good friend Joseph Hooker as commander of the Army of the Potomac, Hooker named Butterfield his chief of staff in January 1863 and he was promoted to major general in March of the same year. Working together, Hooker and Butterfield managed to increase the low morale of the army through a series of reforms including payment of accumulated back pay, new uniforms and equipment, better and more abundant food, improved medical, and other such changes. One of these, credited to Butterfield, was the development of corps insignia for better identification of troops and a means of instilling unit pride. Butterfield designed most of those used by the Army of the Potomac.[6]

Following the disappointing Chancellorsville Campaign, Hooker was removed from command just prior to the Battle of Gettysburg. Given the imminence of the engagement, Gen. George G. Meade, the new army commander, retained Butterfield as chief of staff during the battle despite his dislike for the Utican. During the bloody three days on the fields about Gettysburg, Butterfield performed well and was again wounded in action when a piece of an artillery shell struck him just below the heart. Following what proved to be a pivotal engagement in the war, Meade wrote to Butterfield on July 14 to tell him: "I shall never cease to remember, and to bear testimony to the efficient assistance you so heartily rendered me, and without which I hardly know how I should have gotten through with the new and arduous duties imposed upon me."[7]

Despite the praise, Meade soon replaced the convalescing Butterfield as chief of staff. Butterfield, who belonged to the Hooker faction of the army along with Daniel Sickles, responded by accusing Meade of wishing to retreat from Gettysburg rather than face Lee's army. Butterfield repeated his charges, which were supported by Sickles, when the two appeared to testify before the Joint Committee on the Conduct of the War, a Congressional committee that appears to have been a thinly disguised political "witch hunt." When Sickles claimed a major credit for the federal victory despite disobeying Meade's orders, a major brouhaha ensued with Sickles and Butterfield attacking Meade's handling of the battle in a long series of articles in the press that brought forth an equally acrimonious response from Meade and his supporters. It was not one of Butterfield's more shining moments.

When he returned to duty after his convalescence, Butterfield was assigned as chief of staff of the Eleventh and Twelfth Corps when they were sent west in the fall of 1863 under Gen. Joseph Hooker to relieve the Confederate siege of Chattanooga. When the two corps were consolidated into the Twentieth Corps in the spring of 1864, Butterfield received command of the 3rd Division which he led in the initial phases of Gen. William Tecumseh Sherman's campaign to Atlanta. Illness forced him to retire from the field following the Battle of Resaca where his men captured four Confederate guns. He spent the balance of the war on special assignments. He mustered out of the volunteer forces on August 24, 1865, but continued in service in the regular army as colonel of the 5th Infantry and superintendant of army recruiting until 1870.[8]

Following his retirement from the army, Butterfield returned to the family business and to veterans affairs, becoming widely known for his philanthropic support of education and veterans. He served as master of ceremonies at the Washington Centennial Celebration in 1889, at General Sherman's funeral in 1891, and at celebration of Admiral George Dewey's return after his victory at the Battle of Manila Bay in the Spanish-American War (the celebration was in 1899). Upon his death at Cold Springs, New York, on July 17, 1901, he was accorded the special honor of burial with full military honors at the U.S. Military Academy at West Point.

by James S. Pula

––––––––––––

[1]*History of Oneida County New York From 1700 to the Present Time* (Chicago: The S. J. Clarke Publishing Company, 1912), Vol. II, 526; Ezra J. Warner, *Generals in Blue* (Baton Rouge: Louisiana State University, 1972), 62; obituary, *New York Times*, July 16, 1904.

[2]*History of Oneida County*, Vol. II, 526; *Harper's Weekly*, February 14, 1863, 109; Warner, *Generals in Blue*, 62.

[3]*History of Oneida County*, Vol. II, 526; Warner, *Generals in Blue*, 62; *Harper's Weekly*, February 14, 1863, 110; obituary, *New York Times*, July 16, 1904; R. J. Proft, *United States of America's Congressional Medal of Honor Recipients and Their Official Citations* (Columbia Heights, MN: Highland House II, 2002); *The Medal of Honor of the*

United States Army (Washington, DC: U.S. Government Printing Office, 1948).

[4]Letter, Oliver W. Norton to *Century Magazine*, August 9, 1898, appearing in an August 1898 issue.

[5]Letter, Daniel Butterfield to *Century Magazine*, August 31, 1898, appearing in a September 1898 issue.

[6]Warner, *Generals in Blue*, 62; *History of Oneida County*, Vol. II, 526; Warner, *Generals in Blue*, 62. The promotion to major general was to rank from November 29, 1862.

[7]*History of Oneida County*, Vol. II, 526; letter, George G. Meade to Daniel Butterfield, July 14, 1863; Warner, *Generals in Blue*, 62.

[8]*History of Oneida County*, Vol. II, 527; Warner, *Generals in Blue*, 62; obituary, *New York Times*, July 16, 1904.

[9]*History of Oneida County*, Vol. II, 527; Warner, *Generals in Blue*, 63.

ROSCOE CONKLING

Roscoe Conkling
(National Archives)

Roscoe Conkling was born to politics. The son of U.S. Representative and judge Alfred Conkling, he was born in Albany on October 30, 1829, attended the Washington Collegiate Institute in New York City, and at the early age of seventeen in 1846 joined the firm of Spencer & Kernan in Utica, through his father's influence, to read law. He was admitted to the bar in 1850, the same year in which Governor Hamilton Fish appointed him Oneida County District Attorney. A Whig, he was an important leader in the formation of the Republican Party in New York in 1854 and a year later cemented his political future through marriage to Julia Catherine Seymour, the younger sister of prominent New York political leader Horatio Seymour. Election as mayor of Utica followed three years later, followed by selection to the U.S. House of Representatives as a Republican in November 1859.[1]

Conkling served two terms in the House before being defeated for re-election by Francis Kernan in 1862. Two years later he redeemed his position at the expense of Kernan, serving from March 1865 to March 1867. A strong supporter of President Abraham Lincoln and the war to preserve the Union, he was in Congress during an especially important time given the political battles that raged at the end of the Civil War regarding the nature and control of the "reconstruction" of the South.[2]

Although re-elected to the House of Representatives in 1867, he resigned to accept a U.S. Senate seat from New York. There, he continued to align himself with the Radical Republican faction and sponsored such controversial proposals as the confiscation of land from former slaveholders and its redistribution to former slaves. As a member of the Committee of Fifteen that drafted Reconstruction legislation, Conkling assisted in writing the Reconstruction Acts that imposed military occupation on the South and required the former Confederate states to meet specific criteria before they could be readmitted to the Union. He was instrumental in adoption of the Civil Rights Act of 1875, strongly supported equal civil and political rights for blacks, and backed disenfranchisement of ex-Confederates. Conkling assisted in drafting both the Fourteenth and Fifteenth Amendments to the Constitution. The former defined citizenship and voting rights, while the latter made it unconstitutional to deprive citizens of their right to vote because of "race, color, or previous condition of servitude."[3]

Conkling was a leader of the pro-Grant "Stalwart" faction of the Republican Party in the Senate, in return President Grant rewarded him with control over patronage appointments in his home state which solidified Conkling's position as leader of the state political machine. When U. S. Grant decided not to seek a third term as president, Conkling received 93 votes for nomination at the Republican National Convention in Cincinnati in 1876, but threw his support behind Rutherford B. Hayes in a successful effort to deny the nomination to James G. Blaine, leader of the "Half-Breed" faction of the party that opposed Conkling. In the disputed election that followed, Democrat Samuel J. Tilden received more popular votes than Hayes, and seemingly more votes in the Electoral College, but twenty of the Electoral votes were contested. With the election in doubt and threats of legal actions, and even civil war if Tilden was not seated, Conkling was a key member of the committee that formed the Electoral Commission to sort out the mess and prevent a national crisis.[4]

Conkling resigned from the Senate in 1881 to protest President James A. Garfield's appointment of Conkling's political rival to the lucrative position of customs collector for the port of New York, a key plum in that era of spoils politics. The following year he declined nomination to the U.S. Supreme Court.[5] After leaving national politics, Conkling returned to New York where he pursued his legal practice and reportedly made a fortune. He died in New York City, on April 18, 1888, and was buried in Forest Hill Cemetery in Utica.[6]

by James S. Pula

---

[1]M. M. Bagg, ed., *Memorial History of Utica, N. Y. From its Settlement to the Present Time* (Syracuse: D. Mason & Company, Publishers, 1892), 560.

[2]Bagg, *Memorial History of Utica*, 560.

[3]Bagg, *Memorial History of Utica*, 561.

[4]David M. Jordan, *Roscoe Conkling of New York: Voice in the Senate* (Ithaca, N.Y.: Cornell University Press, 1971).

[5]Jordan, *Roscoe Conkling of New York*.

[6]Bagg, *Memorial History of Utica*, 562

Henry Wager Halleck

Henry W. Halleck
(Donald Wisnoski)

The third of fourteen children of a farm family, Henry Wager Halleck was born in Westernville, New York on January 16, 1815. His maternal grandfather, Henry Wager, was a friend of Revolutionary War hero Baron Friedrich Wilhelm von Steuben and was among the first settlers of the small village of Westernville, outside of Rome, arriving there in 1788. His mother was Henry's daughter Catherine, a descendant of Barent and Elizabeth Sheffer Wager of Baden-Baden, Germany. His father, Joseph Halleck, had served as a lieutenant in the War of 1812.[1]

When only a boy, Halleck ran away from home because he detested farm work. He was taken in by a relative, David Wager of Utica, who adopted him. Receiving very little in the way of formal education as a child, he did subsequently attend the Hudson Academy and qualified for admittance to Union College in Schenectady where he graduated Phi Beta Kappa, then continued on to the United States Military Academy at West Point in 1835. He did well at "The Point," eventually graduating third out of a class of 31 cadets. Upon graduation in 1839, he received a coveted appointment to the engineers. Halleck did so well in this field that he became assistant professor of engineering at the Academy under Prof. Dennis Hart Mahan, a job he held for a year. Leaving West Point, from 1841 to 1844 he was stationed in New York with the Board of Engineers for Atlantic Coast Defenses where he authored a report on the seacoast fortifications titled *Report on the Means of National Defense*. The War Department sent him abroad in 1845 to study the major military installations of several countries. Completing this assignment, he returned to the United States and delivered a series of lectures on his experiences overseas, mostly at the Lowell Institute of Boston, Massachusetts. His lectures were so well received that he decided to write a book, *The Elements of Military Art and Science*, considered one of the leading texts in the country on military tactics.[2]

Upon being promoted to first lieutenant, Halleck went west to California. When the war with Mexico began in 1846, he saw action under the command of Generals Winfield Scott and Zachary Taylor, earning promotion to the rank of captain for meritorious service at the Battles of Palas Prietas and Urias in November 1847. Halleck distinguished himself further at the Battles of San Antonio and Todos Santos, where, with only a few mounted cavalry, he made a forced march of 120 miles in 28 hours and totally surprised a garrison of several hundred Mexican soldiers, nearly capturing the governor of California himself.[3]

Shortly thereafter, Halleck became a member of the staff of Commodore William Bradford Shubrick on the Pacific coast, was a participant in the capture of the Mexican port city of Mazatlan, and became its lieutenant-governor. This led to his appointment as the Secretary of State for the province of California from 1847 to December of 1849. The same year, he served as a member of the committee that drafted the Constitution for California's application for admission to the Union as a state in 1850. Between 1850 and 1859, he served as Inspector of Lighthouses and Judge Advocate.[4]

Resigning his commission, Halleck quit the military and decided to remain in California to study and practice law in San Francisco. He quickly became a senior partner in one of the largest law firms in the state, but turned down an opportunity to become both a judge on the California Supreme Court and a United States Senator to accumulate a sizeable personal fortune through practicing law and activities as a land developer. He also served as director of the New Almaden Quicksilver Mine in San Jose, the largest mercury mine in the world.[5] Halleck married Elizabeth Hamilton, a granddaughter of the famous Revolutionary War patriot Alexander Hamilton. They had one child, a son named Henry Wager Halleck, Jr., who was born in 1856. Halleck purchased 30,000 acres of land in Marin County that became his family's home, which he named Rancho Nicasio. Noted for his scholarship, Halleck performed what would eventually be recognized as a fine feat of historical preservation while living in California. At the time, he proved to be quite a collector, obtaining literally thousands of official documents pertaining to the state's Spanish missions and the early settlement of California. He had all the papers copied, which proved fortuitous, as the originals were destroyed in the fire which would ultimately burn most of San Francisco to the ground after the great earthquake on April 18, 1906. These copies are now held in the Bancroft Library at the University of California, and have proven invaluable to historical researchers.

By 1861, his administrative skills led him to the presidency of the Atlantic and Pacific Railroad. Although no longer on active duty with the army, he did become the commander of the California militia with the rank of major general, so he had not completely severed all his ties to the military. With the growing tension between North and South, Democrat Halleck was known by acquaintances for having Southern sympathies, but with the outbreak of the Civil War he re-entered the military, gaining an appointment as one of only a few major generals on August 17. At that time, only three other Union officers outranked him: Gen. Winfield Scott, Gen. George Brinton McClellan, and Gen. John C. Frémont.[6] Three months later, he became the commander of the Western Department, succeeding Frémont. Halleck stepped in, brought a new sense of order to the command, and is credited with keeping Missouri in the Union.[7]

Professionally respected by his peers, Halleck quickly earned the nickname "Old Brains" because he had the reputation of being a good military theoretician, administrator and public relations man, always fostering good relationships between the army and the press. Nevertheless, as time went on few associates and subordinates could get along with Halleck. One early conflict developed between Halleck and Gen. Ulysses S. Grant. In January 1862, Grant ventured to St. Louis to confer with Halleck about a plan he had devised to attack Forts Henry and Donelson on the Cumberland and Tennessee Rivers. According to Grant, Halleck cut him off, declaring he had been contemplating the same operation for several weeks. From that point on, the two were continually at odds. Halleck was reluctant to authorize Grant to advance, which frustrated Grant all the more. When Halleck finally issued orders for the advance, Grant quickly captured both forts, becoming a national hero.[8] Grant's sudden popularity drove a further wedge between him and Halleck, especially when Halleck wired Washington to suggest that he, not Grant, be given command of all the troops in the west in return for the taking of Forts Henry and Donelson.[9] Relations between the two men were even further strained by the incident.

On March 11, 1862, the Department of the Missouri was expanded with the addition of armies in Ohio and Kansas, including the Army of the Ohio, commanded by Gen. Don Carlos Buell, and was renamed the Department of the Mississippi. Still under Halleck's overall command, Grant pushed south until by mid-March he reached a small town called Pittsburgh Landing. Halleck, seeking to unite the commands of Grant and Buell into a larger striking force, wired Buell to join Grant while the latter awaited his arrival at Pittsburgh Landing.[10] On the morning of April 6, Confederate forces under Gen. Albert Sidney Johnston launched an attack against Grant's army hoping to drive the Yankees back into the Tennessee River before Buell's army could arrive. The fighting became confused as the rebel and federal lines battled back and forth, with the Union men retreating back toward Pittsburgh Landing where Grant's lines finally held. When Buell's reinforcements arrived early the following morning, Grant counterattacked, driving the Confederates back. The Battle of Shiloh cost the federals over 13,000 casualties, while Confederate losses numbered almost 11,000.

In the wake of Shiloh, Halleck assumed field command himself with a plan to advance on Corinth, Mississippi; but the movement languished as Halleck waited to complete elaborate preparations. When his army finally moved, the Confederates under Gen. Pierre G. T. Beauregard evacuated the town, destroying any useful supplies as they fled. When the Federals finally moved in and occupied Corinth, they took an empty town, devoid of anything of real value.[11] Halleck had proven his worth in the west as an organizer and administrator, but had not proved particularly aggressive as a field commander. With the continuing build-up in federal forces, by the summer of 1862 President Lincoln made the decision that he needed someone with a great deal of experience in administration in Washington, D.C., to assume overall management of various generals with their commands. On July 11 he appointed Halleck to the post with the title of General-in-Chief, and authority to command all land-based forces in the United States. Halleck took office four days later, replacing Gen. George Brinton McClellan.[12]

To his credit, once Halleck assumed his new duties he proved excellent at facilitating the equipping, training and deploying of troops in the field. He proved to be an outstanding administrator and, despite his earlier contention with Grant, took particular attention to see that Grant's army in the west had sufficient supplies to assure its success capturing the crucial port city of Vicksburg, Mississippi.[13] Whereas there had been friction between the two of them before, with Halleck in Washington the two formed a good working relationship.

Halleck took his work seriously, remained close to his office, and was not one to socialize very much. He also did not visit the front, and his lack of diplomacy earned him many enemies in Washington, not the least of whom was the Secretary of the Navy, Gideon Welles, who wrote in his diary that Halleck "originates nothing, anticipates nothing … takes no responsibility, plans nothing, suggests nothing, is good for nothing."[14] Often cited as the reason for his unpopularity was his demeanor of superiority and the fact that he seldom shared his thoughts or plans with anyone.[15]

With Grant's growing success in the west, in the spring of 1864 President Lincoln decided to appoint him to replace Halleck as General-in-Chief. Grant assumed his new responsibilities in March. One of his first decisions was to utilize Halleck's organizational and administrative skills in Washington as "Chief of Staff." Grant would run the armies from the field, accompanying the Army of the Potomac, while Halleck would make sure that supplies, equipment, munitions, and reinforcements arrived where and when needed, and attend to the other myriad administrative functions required to keep the armies in the field. As he had earlier during the siege of Vicksburg, Halleck saw to it that Grant's massive army was well supplied and equipped, and reinforced when necessary. It was this constant supply of men and materiel that eventually won the war of attrition against the Confederates. This was particularly evident during the Overland Campaign and the Siege of Petersburg, and when Halleck gave Gen. William T. Sherman the final authorization to begin what would become his famous March to the Sea from Atlanta to Savannah, Georgia. Halleck also supported Gen. Philip H. Sheridan's campaign in the Shenandoah Valley of Virginia.[16] Halleck's administrative ability contributed much to the eventual Union victory.

After Lee surrendered at Appomattox in April 1865, Halleck was sent to Virginia, where he took over command of the District of Virginia and the Army of the James, with his headquarters in Richmond. Just a few days later, he served as a pall bearer at President Lincoln's funeral. During Reconstruction, Halleck continued performing mostly administrative duties. He commanded the Division of the Pacific (1865-69) and the Division of the South (1869-72).[17] In addition to his career as an Army officer, land speculator, lawyer and government official, Halleck aided in building the pedestal for the Statue of Liberty at old Fort Wood on Bedloe's Island in New York Harbor. He wrote and published several scholarly works, including *Practical Treatise on Bitumen and its Uses; Report on Military Defenses; International Law and the Laws of War* and translations of *Mining Laws of Spain and Mexico* and *De Fooz on the Law of Mines*.[18] He also published a translation of Antoine-Henri Jomini's four volume biography of Napoleon Bonaparte, *Vie Politique et Militaire de Napoleon*.[19] Henry Wager died in Louisville, Kentucky, on January 9, 1872.[20] The city of San Francisco, which had become his home prior to the war, remembered him with a street that bears his name and a statue located in Golden Gate Park.

by Cheryl A. Pula

---

[1] John F. Marszalek, *Commander of All Lincoln's Armies: A Life of General Henry W. Halleck* (Cambridge: Harvard University Press, 2004), 5.

[2] Obituary, *New York Times,* January 10, 1872.

[3] Obituary, *New York Times,* January 10, 1872.

[4] Ezra J. Warner, *Generals in Blue: Lives of the Union Commanders* (Baton Rouge: Louisiana State University Press, 1992), 195; obituary, *New York Times,* January 10, 1872.

[5] Obituary, *New York Times,* January 10, 1872.

[6] John C. Fredriksen, "Henry Wager Halleck," in David S. Heidler, ed., *Encyclopedia of the American Civil War: A Political, Social and Military History* (New York: W. W. Norton and Co., 2000), 909; Warner, *Generals in Blue,* 196.

[7] Obituary, *New York Times,* January 10, 1872.

[8] David Nevin, *The Road to Shiloh: Early Battles in the West,* 60-61; Edwin C. Bearss, "Fort Henry," *Battle Chronicles of the Civil War* (New York: Macmillan Publishing Company, 1989), Vol. 2, 18.

[9] Nevin, *Road to Shiloh,* 96.

[10] Nevin, *Road to Shiloh,* 104.

[11] Nevin, *Road to Shiloh,* 157.

[12] Obituary, *New York Times,* January 10, 1872.

[13]Fredriksen, "Henry Wager Halleck," 910.

[14]Warner, *Generals in Blue*, 196.

[15]"Henry Halleck," Ohio State University, *eHistory Archives,* http://ehistory.osu/edu.

[16]Fredriksen, "Henry Wager Halleck," 910.

[17]Answers.com website, http://www.answers.com, 1.

[18]Obituary, *New York Times,* January 10, 1872.

[19]Answers.com website, http://www.answers.com, 2.

[20]Obituary. *New York Times*, January 10, 1872.

FRANCIS KERNAN

Francis Kernan
(National Archives)

By the decade of the 1830s, Ireland was already the largest source of immigrants to America, and it would continue so until it was surpassed by arrivals from the German states in the late 1840s. Among the first ripples that led to this massive wave was William Kernan who arrived in New York by ship from County Cavan in 1800. After two years in the crowded port city he ventured north to live the life of a farmer in the Town of Tyrone in Steuben County (now in Schuyler County) where he purchased a plot of uncleared woodland. There he met another Irish immigrant, Rose Anna Stubbs, who came from the Emerald Isle in 1808. The two soon married, leading to the birth of their son Francis in Wayne, Steuben County, on January 14, 1816. The son grew to maturity working on the family farm and, when time would allow, being educated in small local schools. At the age of seventeen he enrolled in Georgetown College (now Georgetown University), a Jesuit institution in the District of Columbia, graduating in 1836. Thereafter he took up the study of law in the office of Edward Quinn, Kernan's brother-in-law, in the village of Watkins.[1]

In 1839, Kernan moved to Utica to take a position in the prestigious office of the Hon. Joshua A. Spencer. He was admitted to the bar in 1840, and three years later married Hannah A. Devereux, the daughter of Nicholas Devereux, one of the city's most prominent citizens. Kernan quickly became a partner in Spencer's firm under the new name of Spencer & Kernan, where he earned a solid reputation for legal expertise, the clarity of his arguments, and his ability to find every advantage for his clients. Spencer & Kernan eventually dissolved in 1853, replaced by Kernan & Quinn, and in 1857 when William Kernan joined the firm it was renamed Kernan, Quinn & Kernan. In 1854 Kernan accepted a position as reporter of the Court of Appeals, a position he held until 1857, during which time he edited the eleventh through fourteenth volumes of *New York Reports*. A man of seemingly boundless energy, during this period Kernan also served as Utica school commissioner and manager of the New York State Hospital.[2]

Throughout the 1850s, as sectional antagonisms began to tear the nation apart, Kernan's interest in politics grew apace with the growing crisis. An early leader in the Free Soil movement in central New York, in 1860 he secured the Democratic nomination for New York Assembly. Although Oneida County's First District was by 1860 a Republican stronghold, and had been won by James McQuade by a plurality of some 1,500 votes in the most recent election, Kernan managed to squeeze out a 200 vote majority that launched him on a lengthy career in state and national politics. According to M. M. Bagg's *Memorial History of Utica*, the city "had few more powerful and gifted defenders of the Union and his war speeches were frequent and intensely loyal and eloquent."[3]

In 1862, Kernan ran for Congress against Roscoe Conkling who had won the same seat two years previously by the wide margin of 3,500 votes. In a very hard-fought contest, Kernan eked out a victory by only ninety votes. As a member of the Thirty-Eighth Congress, serving during the crucial months between March 1863 and March 1865, he quickly became a prominent member of the so-called "War Democrats" who wholeheartedly supported administration efforts to preserve the Union. Among the other leaders of the War Democrats were Andrew Johnson, Benjamin Butler, Stephen A. Douglas, Joseph Holt, John A. Logan, and Edwin Stanton. Kernan was among this group to whom Lincoln turned for advice in times of crisis. In the presidential election of 1864, the first ever held during a time of war, the Republicans and War Democrats joined forces in the "Union Party" to re-elect Lincoln, but the success did not filter down to Kernan who lost a bid for re-election to Roscoe Conkling.[4]

Following his defeat, Kernan retired to his law practice in Utica, turning his energy once more to the benefit of his clients, yet his interest in politics remained keen. He was an active member of the state constitutional convention in 1867-68, and in 1870 accepted appointment as a regent of the State University of New York, a position he held until his death. Returning to the rough-and-tumble battles of the electoral canvass, Kernan threw his hat in the ring for governor in 1872, the favorite of both the Democratic and Liberal factions, but lost his bid to Republican John A. Dix.[5]

His ardor for politics not diminished by his electoral defeats, Kernan again entered the arena as the Democratic candidate for the U.S. Senate. At that time, senators were chosen by state legislatures rather than through popular vote. With the Democrats holding a majority in the state legislature, Kernan entered the Senate in March 1876, serving until March 1881, joining his old rival Republican Roscoe Conkling in a unique time when both of the state's U.S. Senators called Utica home. Together with Horatio Seymour, the three were known as the "Utica trio."[6]

At the Democratic Party National Convention in St. Louis in July 1876, Kernan nominated New York's Samuel J. Tilden for the presidency. Tilden's subsequent loss to Rutherford B. Hayes, despite winning the popular vote and seemingly the electoral vote, proved to be the most controversial presidential election in U.S. history.[7] Unsuccessful in a bid for re-election in 1880, he left the Senate in 1881 to once again resume his law practice in Utica. He represented Georgetown College at the Catholic Congress of Laymen held in Baltimore, Maryland, in 1889, and became well-known for his charity and *pro bono* legal advice, activities that were recognized with an honorary Doctor of Laws degree from Georgetown. He died in Utica on September 8, 1892, and was buried in St. Agnes Cemetery.[8]

by James S. Pula

---

[1]M. M. Bagg, ed., *Memorial History of Utica, N. Y. From its Settlement to the Present Time* (Syracuse: D. Mason & Company, Publishers, 1892), 36; *History of Oneida County New York From 1700 to the Present Time* (Chicago: The S. J. Clarke Publishing Company, 1912), Vol. II, 250.

[2]M. M. Bagg, ed., *Memorial History of Utica*, 36; *History of Oneida County*, Vol. II, 250-51.

[3]*History of Oneida County*, Vol. II, 250-51; quote from M. M. Bagg, ed., *Memorial History of Utica*, 36.

[4]*History of Oneida County*, Vol. II, 251; quote from M. M. Bagg, ed., *Memorial History of Utica*, 36-37; "Biographical Dictionary of the unied States Congress 1774-Present," http://bioguide.congress.gov.

[5]*History of Oneida County*, Vol. II, 251; quote from M. M. Bagg, ed., *Memorial History of Utica*, 37.

[6]*History of Oneida County*, Vol. II, 251; quote from M. M. Bagg, ed., *Memorial History of Utica*, 37; "Biographical Dictionary of the unied States Congress 1774-Present," http://bioguide.congress.gov.

[7]*History of Oneida County*, Vol. II, 251; quote from M. M. Bagg, ed., *Memorial History of Utica*, 37; "Biographical Dictionary of the unied States Congress 1774-Present," http://bioguide.congress.gov.

[8]*History of Oneida County*, Vol. II, 252; quote from M. M. Bagg, ed., *Memorial History of Utica*, 37; "Kernan, Francis," *Catholic Encyclopedia* (New York: Robert Appleton Company, 1913).

JAMES HEWETT LEDLIE

One of the saddest chapters in the history of the Civil War took place on July 30, 1864, near the besieged town of Petersburg, Virginia. Prominent among those involved was a native of Utica, General James Hewett Ledlie. Born in Utica on April 14, 1832, Ledlie attended the Scientific Department of Union College in Schenectady, where he studied to become a civil engineer. Upon graduation, he worked primarily in railroad construction, though he did see service as a division engineer on the Erie Canal. He later worked for the Seneca River Improvement Company when it drained the marshes near Geneva, New York.[1]

James H. Ledlie
(Donald Wisnoski)

When the Civil War began, Ledlie went off to do his patriotic duty. Through his influential political connections he obtained a commission even though he lacked military experience or qualifications.[2] He was appointed major of the 19th New York Volunteer Infantry, which mustered into federal service at Elmira on May 22, 1861. Ledlie rose steadily to colonel, with the regiment re-designated the 3rd New York Light Artillery Regiment on December 11, 1862. At the battle of Fredericksburg in the same month, Ledlie commanded a brigade.[3] Shortly thereafter, he was promoted to brigadier general and placed in command of the Artillery Brigade of the Department of North Carolina.[4] The regiment itself was assigned mostly to garrison duty in Virginia and North Carolina.

With the beginning of General Ulysses S. Grant's Overland Campaign in 1864, Ledlie was transferred to General Ambrose Burnside's Ninth Corps where he was given command of an infantry brigade. On June 9, 1864, he assumed command of the 1st Division of the Ninth Corps. Ledlie was aided in his climb up the command ladder by several influential friends including William H. Seward, the Secretary of the Treasury, and General George Brinton McClellan. Seward recommended Ledlie to President Abraham Lincoln, while he was also instrumental in getting the Utican his command and general's stars.[5]

By June 1864, the Ninth Corps was involved in the protracted siege of the city of Petersburg, which was a major supply hub for the Confederate capital at Richmond, Virginia, and General Robert E. Lee's Army of Northern Virginia. With the rebels firmly entrenched behind daunting fortifications, the two sides faced each other across several hundred yards of open territory, the fighting in the area effectively at a stalemate. Grant asked for suggestions as to what to do next. The plan that was adopted required the digging of a tunnel, called a "mine" at the time, over 500 feet long beneath the Confederate lines at a place named Elliott's Salient, after Brig. Gen. Stephen Elliott whose troops manned that part of the rebel fortifications. The digging was to be done by the 48th Pennsylvania Infantry, many members of which had been coal miners in Schuylkill County.[6] Indeed, the idea of digging the mine in the first place had been the brainchild of the 48th's commander, Lt. Col. Henry Pleasants, who had been a mining engineer prior to the war.[7] When completed, the mine would be packed with 8,000 pounds of gunpowder and detonated, blowing a huge hole in the enemy lines while killing untold numbers of rebel troops. The plan was submitted to Burnside and approved. Grant and Gen. George Gordon Meade, commander of the Army of the Potomac, were not overly enthusiastic about the plan and voiced misgivings.[8]

The plan involved not just blasting the enemy with tons of explosives. Once the air cleared, the federals were to send several regiments of well-trained U.S. Colored Troops around the hole to attack the rebel lines while the Confederates were still reeling from the shock. The troops would penetrate Confederate lines, drive a wedge into their fortifications, and create a passage for other troops to follow and head toward Petersburg, the objective to be the attainment and capture of the high ground to the rebel rear. The black troops were members of Gen. Edward Ferraro's 4th Division and had been trained specifically for the operation. But as often happens in wartime, modifications were made to the plan. Many people had serious political concerns and misgivings about using black troops in what might turn out to be a suicide mission. Gen. Grant later explained: "General Burnside wanted to put his colored division in front.... I agreed with General Meade in his objection to that plan. General Meade said that if we put the colored troops in front ... and it should prove a failure, it would then be said ... that we were shoving those people ahead to get killed because we did not care anything about them. But that could not be said if we put white troops in front."[9]

The decision was made to select a replacement division composed of white troops to make the initial attack. It was further determined that the white troops to take part in the assault would be from the divisions of Gen. Orlando Willcox, Gen. Robert Potter or Ledlie. Oddly, when the commanders were called together to discuss the plan and who would ultimately lead it, Ledlie was not summoned to the meeting. Someone, either Potter or Willcox, eventually suggested that since Ledlie's division might be involved, he be included in the planning session and he was called to the meeting.[10] After several hours of discussion, no one was willing to volunteer to lead to attack. Burnside was not happy about the development, so he held a lottery to choose a replacement for the black division. The division that literally drew the "short straw" was Ledlie's. The Utican, who had never commanded troops in battle before, grumbled that he was the "unlucky victim."[11]

Ledlie was the newest commander on scene and did not have much combat experience. His own officers made it clear they had a great deal of contempt for him, and felt he was nothing short of totally incompetent. Regis de Trobriand, a French born brigadier attached to Gen. Winfield Scott Hancock's corps, also knew that the "luck of the draw" was sometimes very unlucky. When he found that Ledlie's division was to lead the attack, he stated: "The lot—which is of course blind, and sometimes is pleased to give us some severe lessons—fell upon the very division which, if it was not worse than the others, was certainly worse commanded."[12]

Burnside, however, thought Ledlie would be a good choice to command the operation based on what he had been told about the Utican's actions at the battle of Cold Harbor. It had been reported that Ledlie had led a successful attack on a Confederate position at Ox Ford on May 26, 1864. In truth, Ledlie had sent the 35th Massachusetts regiment to deal with some rebel sharpshooters. When the regiment attempted to carry out the order, it found not Confederate sharpshooters, but a line of quite formidable rebel fortifications on high ground, supported by rifle pits. No officer would even think of attacking such a position, but Ledlie did. When it became evident the 35th was in trouble, instead of withdrawing it, he sent in the 56th, 57th and 59th Massachusetts to press the attack. It proved to be a disaster. The regiments were decimated by rebel artillery firing canister. Only the advent of a timely thunderstorm saved them from complete annihilation. While all of this was transpiring, Ledlie had been safely ensconced in the rear keeping company, according to witnesses, with a bottle. By July 1864, it was common knowledge among the officers of the 1st Division that Ledlie was a heavy consumer of alcohol, as they were his drinking guests many times.[13] After the ill-fated attack at Ox Ford, Lt. Col. Stephen Weld from the 56th Massachusetts had disgustedly told everyone who would listen that Ledlie "made a botch of it. Had too much booze on board, I think."[14] Yet, instead of being censured for this, Ledlie was recommended for promotion by Gen. Thomas Crittenden and was subsequently given Crittenden's division when that officer stepped down.

When Burnside gathered his senior officers to outline his plan to break the rebel defenses of Petersburg, witnesses stated later that it appeared Ledlie had been drinking and did not comprehend most of what the general was telling him. The plan was to explode the mine, then have Ledlie's men charge around the resulting crater to take and occupy the high ground beyond known as Cemetery Hill. His men would be supported by Gen. Orlando Willcox's 3rd Division, which would follow Ledlie, freeing Ledlie's men to continue their advance. Ledlie would then move forward to take the Jerusalem Plank Road while Willcox would guard against any rebel counterattack, with both divisions being supported by Potter's 2nd Division.[15]

Ledlie did not brief his subordinate officers and men on what they were supposed to do nor what was expected of them. He did not tell them that when the explosion occurred, they were supposed to go *around* the resulting hole to attack the Confederates on the high ground beyond rather than down into the crater. As a result, the troops were totally unprepared for the assault. Further, Ledlie's division was posted farthest from the actual site of the mine, so it had to march the longest distance to get to its staging area. As a result, many of the men were tired by the time they arrived at the jump-off point. It was after midnight before the entire division was in its proper position for the assault, which was scheduled to take place only a little over three hours later.[16]

On the morning of July 30, 1864, volunteers lit the fuse. The resulting explosion blew a 135-foot wide crater in the ground, sending aloft tons of dirt, rocks, and rebel body parts. The rebels were not the only ones surprised. Many federal troops were shocked by the explosion, which some thought was an actual earthquake. When the explosion took place, Ledlie's ill-prepared men stood immobilized by the sight, some even attempted to retreat, and it was only through the efforts of their officers that they finally went forward. Ledlie had personally ordered two very capable subordinates to head the attack. Col. Elisha G. Marshall and the 2nd Brigade were to lead, followed by Brig. Gen. William Francis Bartlett's 1st Brigade. As the men went over the parapet into battle, Ledlie retired, heading away from the action.[17]

When they finally did move, the men marched unopposed across the empty yards separating them from the Confederates, then headed down *into* the crater instead of moving around its flanks. More and more men followed the leading units into the huge hole. The result was unmitigated disaster. Once into the massive hole in the ground, they could not get out and were at the mercy of counterattacking rebels. Gen. Meade wrote: "the troops kept crowding into this crater, which was a large hole some 150 feet in length by 50 feet in width and 25 feet in depth. The troops just crowded into that hole and the adjacent parts of the enemy's lines which had been abandoned for about a hundred yards on each side of the crater. That was immediately filled by our troops. There they remained, and the more men there were ... the worse it was. Their commanders could not keep order...."[18]

Because their leader was not with them, the men of the 1st Division did not push their charge on the enemy as they were supposed to do. Instead, they stopped to gawk at the destruction caused by the mine and to help injured and wounded Confederates who had been buried in the debris of the explosion rather than going for their objective, the high ground to the rear of the Confederate lines.

While his men battled for their lives, Ledlie remained behind the lines in a bombproof bunker far removed from the front lines. Even more damning was the fact that he was drinking liquor. The bombproof had recently served as a regimental headquarters, and during the assault was being utilized as a field aid station. O. B. Chubb, surgeon of the 20th Michigan Volunteers was inside the bombproof treating wounded after the explosion of the mine when Ledlie arrived. Chubb had already heard that Ledlie's men had gone into the fray without proper support. He asked Ledlie if this was true. The general replied that his men were being supported.[19] Chubb later testified,

> ... I took position in a bomb-proof ... located at a point about ten rods in the rear of our line. Shortly after I took up that position General Ledlie ... and Ferraro ... came in and took seats. This was in the morning about half an hour after the explosion of the mine ... during the last moments of his stay there, he sent an aide to ascertain how things were going on, and remarked that he could not go himself as he had been hurt in the side by a spent ball. I cannot state positively when this occurred ... but I recollect him having mentioned that fact quite late in the forenoon, nearly noon, for the first time....[20]

Another witness to Ledlie's actions was surgeon Hamilton E. Smith of the 27th Michigan Volunteers of the Ninth Corps. He said,

> General Ledlie asked me for stimulants, and said he had the malaria and was struck by a spent ball. He inquired for General Bartlett, as he wanted to turn the command over to him and go to the rear. It was one of General Bartlett's aides ... who replied that he was in the crater.... I had rum and whiskey there, and I think I gave them rum.... I think that once was the only time. I was not in the bomb-proof all the time while they were there. It was perfectly safe in there, but it might not have been outside....[21]

At some time during this period, Lt. William Powell arrived with a message telling Ledlie his men where in trouble, but Ledlie replied by saying the troops were to keep pressing the attack and take the high ground beyond the Confederate positions. Ledlie made no attempt to ascertain for himself what was transpiring. Powell later said, "This talk and these orders, coming from a commander sitting in a bomb-proof inside the Union lines were disgusting."[22] Powell told Ledlie that it would be impossible to carry out his orders and returned to the attack, leaving the general in the bomb-proof. Shortly thereafter, an order arrived from Burnside instructing Ledlie to move his troops to the crest of the hill beyond the Confederate works. Ledlie complied with the order by telling an aide to go to the front and tell the commander on scene to carry out the order.[23] By all reports, Ledlie remained in the bomb-proof until after the fateful attack was done. By the time it was over, more than 3,500 Federal troops had been killed. The attack failed.

Ledlie later faced a court of inquiry which reviewed his conduct at what was by then being called The Battle of the Crater. Gen. Meade created the court when he issued Special Orders No. 205 to look into the facts of the fiasco. It convened in August 1864. Testimony was given by Grant, Meade and several other officers who had been involved in the tragic attack. Unfortunately, both Bartlett and Marshall, who had actually led the attack instead of Ledlie, had been captured and were unable to testify. Ledlie had fortuitously taken a leave of absence during the course of the investigation.[24]

Burnside was found to be one of those responsible for the failure of the assault. One of the reasons cited was that when Ledlie's men made the assault, Burnside did nothing to get them out of the Crater and on the move. Because they were blocking the way, troops supporting from behind could not follow up the assault. But the court followed this up by saying it was satisfied that Burnside had done everything he believed to be necessary to insure that the plan would work. In others words, he did not do anything during the assault to rectify the ugly situation, yet could not really be blamed because he thought he had done everything he could to insure success.

Though Ledlie was not present for the court, he was the target of special censure from the officers. He was cited for not sending word to Burnside about the hold up at the Crater caused when his men went into the hole instead of around it, which also caused the following divisions to jam up behind them, unable to move forward. This may have been caused by the fact that Ledlie had given his subordinates specific orders to take the area around the crater then proceed to the high ground beyond, but his subordinates who were present at the meeting where he gave his orders emphatically stated he gave them orders not to proceed beyond the crater.[25] This assertion was backed up by Capt. Thomas W. Clark, an assistant adjutant general for one of the brigades assigned to Ledlie. He said,

> The plan as given by General Ledlie to Bartlett and Marshall, and as given by Marshall to his battalion commanders, was to this effect...The Second Brigade was to be formed in column of battalion front...On the explosion of the mine it was to move forward and occupy the enemy's works on the right of the crater ... but not going into it. The First Brigade was to follow with about the same front and occupy the works on the left of the crater, but not going into it. When the lodgment had been made, it was to be secured and connected to our lines by ... 35th Massachusetts ... the colored division was then to pass through the crater and assault the hill in the rear. Marshall's distinct instructions were that the security of the lodgment was the prime duty of the First Division and the hill was a subordinate object; and General Ledlie's instructions ... conveyed no other meaning to me, or ... to General Bartlett....[26]

Ledlie was also censured for remaining behind in the bombproof while his men tried to press the attack.[27] Two months later, he was mustered out of federal service by the commander of the Army of the Potomac, Gen. Meade, on Grant's orders. Ledlie resigned his commission on January 23, 1865. Some historians rank him as the worst federal general officer of the war.

Now a civilian, Ledlie went back to being an engineer, working on projects in the south and west. He was the first person to demonstrate that it was practical to move rafts of lumber across Lake Michigan to Chicago.[28] As an employee of the famous Union Pacific Railroad, he aided in the construction of the transcontinental railroad, and while doing so was responsible for building many trestles, bridges and snow-sheds that served as avalanche protection in the Rocky Mountains. After the railroad was completed, he was responsible for building the breakwater in the harbor at Chicago.[29] He also took part in building the Nevada Central Railroad from Battle Mountain to Austin, Nevada, in 1879.

He served as first vice-president of the company, as well as chief engineer and general manager of the Santa Rosa and Sonoma Central Railroads in California. He was also chief engineer of the Nevada Southern Railroad, and had interests in the Indian River Railroad in Florida. Ledlie was serving as president of the Baltimore, Cincinnati and Western Railroad Company when he died on August 15, 1882, in St. Mark's Hotel, New Brighton, Staten Island, New York. At the time of his passing, Ledlie was a member of the Military Order Loyal Legion. He is buried in the Forest Hill Cemetery in Utica.[30]

by Cheryl A. Pula

---

[1]*New York Times*, "Obituary of Gen. James H. Ledlie," August 16, 1882.

[2]Alan Axelrod, *The Horrid Pit: The Battle of the Crater: The Civil War's Cruelest Mission* (New York: Carroll & Graf, 2007), 103.

[3]*New York Times*, August 16, 1882.

[4]*New York Times*, August 16, 1882.

[5]John F. Schmutz, *The Battle of the Crater: A Complete History* (Jefferson, NC: McFarland & Company, Inc., Publishers, 2009), 101,

[6]William C. Davis, *Death in the Trenches: Grant at Petersburg* (Alexandria, VA: Time-Life Books, 1962), 65.

[7]Davis, *Death in the Trenches*, 67.

[8]Davis, *Death in the Trenches*, 67.

[9]Axelrod, *The Horrid Pit*, 101.

[10]James Cannan, *The Crater: Burnside's Assault on the Confederate Trenches, July 30, 1864* (Cambridge Center, MA: Da Capo Press, 2002), 48.

[11]Axelrod, *The Horrid Pit*, 102.

[12]Cannan, 48; Schmutz, *Battle of the Crater*, 100, 124.

[13]Axelrod, *The Horrid Pit*, 103-05.

[14]Schmutz, *Battle of the Crater*, 101.

[15]Axelrod, *The Horrid Pit*, 105-06.

[16]Axelrod, *The Horrid Pit*, 110-11.
[17]Axelrod, *The Horrid Pit*, 119, 121, 126.
[18]Axelrod, *The Horrid Pit*, 133.
[19]Cannan, *The Crater*, 108.
[20]Axelrod, *The Horrid Pit*, 126-27.
[21]Axelrod, *The Horrid Pit*, 127.
[22]Cannan, *The Crater*, 110.
[23]Cannan, *The Crater*, 110.
[24]Schmutz, *Battle of the Crater*, 322; Cannan, *The Crater*, 150.
[25]Schmutz, *Battle of the Crater*, 153.
[26]Schmutz, *Battle of The Crater*, 153-54.
[27]Cannan, *The Crater*, 150.
[28]Obituary, *New York Times*, August 16, 1882.

HORATIO SEYMOUR

Horatio Seymour
(National Archives)

The man that author Irving Stone called "one of the most farsighted and creative" people ever to run for the office of president was born in Pompey Hills, Onondaga County, New York, on May 31, 1810. The son of a banker, Horatio Seymour moved with his family to Utica at age ten. After completing his early education, he enrolled in Geneva College (now Hobart College) in 1824, but after two years left for the American Literary, Scientific and Military Academy in Middleton, Connecticut. He returned to Utica in 1827 to read law with Greene C. Bronson and Samuel Beardsley and was admitted to the New York bar in 1832. In the following year he was named private secretary to Governor William M. Marcy, a post he held for six years, gaining an intense interest in politics.[1]

Seymour returned to Utica in 1839 where he assumed management of the family's property and business interests following his father's death. Two years later he ran successfully for the state assembly as a Democrat, and the following year was elected mayor of Utica. He held the two positions simultaneously in 1842-43. In the assembly, he was a member of the more conservative "Hunker" faction of the Democratic Party led by Marcy against the "Barnburner" faction led by Martin van Buren. Seymour was elected Speaker of the Assembly (1845-47) and, as chair of the Committee on Canals, developed a report that influenced state canal policy for decades. By 1850, he had distinguished himself sufficiently to be nominated as the Democratic candidate for governor, but was defeated by a mere 262 votes.[2]

Two years later Seymour was again the gubernatorial candidate, this time winning election. As a delegate to the Democratic National Convention in Baltimore in the same year, 1852, Seymour supported William Marcy's unsuccessful attempt to gain the presidential nomination. When Franklin Pierce received the nomination, Seymour actively campaigned on his behalf. Though his popularity had up to this time continued to increase, he gained many enemies within the state when he alienated a strong temperance movement by vetoing a prohibition bill passed by the legislature. This, along with the unpopularity of Democratic support for the Kansas-Nebraska Act, led to his defeat in the following gubernatorial canvass.[3]

Although no longer governor, Seymour had by this time established himself as a major player in New York Democratic politics and had gained a national reputation. In 1856 he was a delegate to the Democratic National Convention in Cincinnati where he spoke eloquently in favor of restraint of centralized government in favor of local authority at a time when the controversy over the admission of new states into the Union was threatening to tear the nation asunder. In part, he argued "That government is most wise which is in the hands of those best informed about the particular questions on which they legislate, most economical and honest when controlled by those most interested in preserving frugality and virtue, most strong when it only exercises authority which is beneficial to the governed." In keeping with this, he argued in favor of "the right of the people of the territories to settle the slavery question for themselves, assuming that under such a policy there would be a rapid increase of free states."[4] He supported Stephen A. Douglas of Illinois for president in 1856 and again in 1860.

When the election of Abraham Lincoln in 1860 led to the secession crisis, Seymour was a strong supporter of compromise to save the Union. With the outbreak of war, he took a moderate stance that supported restoration of the Union but stridently criticized Lincoln's leadership of the war effort. He was particularly critical of Lincoln's violation of civil liberties, such as the writ of *habeas corpus*, guaranteed under the Constitution, and the president's efforts to concentrate political power in the presidential office.[5]

Yet, although Seymour disagreed emphatically with Lincoln's policies, this did not mean that he was pro-South. At a meeting in Utica in October 1861, Seymour explained: "In common with the majority of the American people, I deplored the election of Mr. Lincoln as a great calamity; yet he was chosen in a constitutional manner, and we wish, as a defeated organization, to show our loyalty by giving him a just and generous support."[6] Seymour took an active part in raising troops in Oneida County, including financial contributions from his own funds for the support of the soldiers, and was named Oneida County recruitment chair by the state adjutant general. In another speech in the summer of 1862, he further explained that "we were bound in honor and patriotism to send immediate relief to our brethren in the field."[7]

In 1862, New York Democrats again nominated Seymour for governor after the incumbent Republican, Edwin D. Morgan, declined to run for another term. No doubt helped by war-weariness, Seymour was one of several Democrats to replace Republicans in governorships and the U.S. Congress as a result of the 1862 elections. In his inaugural address, Seymour explained his feelings on the war and the Lincoln administration:

> The assertion that this war was the unavoidable result of slavery is not only erroneous, but it has led to a disastrous policy in its prosecution. The opinion that slavery must be abolished to restore our Union creates an antagonism between the free and the slave states which ought not to exist. If it is true that slavery must be abolished by the force of the Federal government, that the south must be held in military subjection, that four millions of negroes must for many years be under the direct management of the authorities at Washington at the public expense, then, indeed, we must endure the waste of our armies in the field, further drains upon our population, and still greater burdens of debt. We must convert our government into a military despotism. The mischievous opinion that in this contest the north must subjugate and destroy the south to save our Union has weakened the hopes of our citizens at home and destroyed confidence in our success abroad.[8]

As governor, Seymour quickly gained a reputation for outspoken opposition to Lincoln's policies. He opposed conscription, vetoed a state bill that would have provided absentee balloting for members of the armed forces, and was accused of going easy on rioters in the wake of the New York City draft riots in 1863. Accused of being a Copperhead, a Northerner who was sympathetic to the South, Seymour's popularity steadily declined. In 1863 the Republicans gained control on the state assembly, and in the following year Seymour's bid for re-election failed.[9]

Seymour served as chair of the 1864 Democratic National Convention where he was for a time being considered as a candidate for president until he withdrew his name from consideration. He supported George B. McClellan against Lincoln in 1864, and following the war was a strong supporter of President Andrew Johnson in his battle against the Republicans over Reconstruction policies.[10]

Seymour again served as chair of the Democratic National Convention in 1868. Although he at first refused suggestions that he run for the nomination, as the convention continued on through more than twenty votes without anyone receiving a majority of the votes, Seymour was finally nominated and agreed to run. Running against the popular Republican candidate Ulysses S. Grant, Seymour continued to speak out in favor of limited central government and against Republican Reconstruction policies. Republicans responded by focusing on Seymour's Civil War record as the basis for accusations of treason during the conflict. In the end, Grant won a decisive victory by an Electoral College vote of 214-80.[11]

Following the losing presidential campaign, Seymour continued to be active in state politics, but not as an active candidate. He was named chancellor of Union College in 1873, Commissioner of State Fisheries in 1876, President of the

Board of Commissioners of State Survey in 1878, president of the American Dairyman's Association, and president of the Oneida County Historical Society from its founding until his death. He declined nomination to the U.S. Senate in 1874 in favor of fellow-Utican Francis Kernan. Likewise, he declined inquiries that he run for governor in 1876 and 1879, and also rejected another presidential run in 1880. His last active political effort was campaigning on behalf of Grover Cleveland's presidential campaign in 1884. He died on February 12, 1886, and was buried in Forest Hill Cemetery in Utica.[12]

by James S. Pula

[1]M. M. Bagg, ed., *Memorial History of Utica, N. Y. From its Settlement to the Present Time* (Syracuse: D. Mason & Company, Publishers, 1892), 3-4; *History of Oneida County New York From 1700 to the Present Time* (Chicago: The S. J. Clarke Publishing Company, 1912), Vol. II, 259; Stewart Mitchell, *Horatio Seymour of New York* (Cambridge, MA: Harvard University Press, 1938), 33.

[2]Bagg, *Memorial History of Utica*, 4; *History of Oneida County*, Vol. II, 259.

[3]Bagg, *Memorial History of Utica*, 5; *History of Oneida County*, Vol. II, 259; *Appletons Encyclopedia of American Biography* (New York: D. Appleton and Company, 1900).

[4]Bagg, *Memorial History of Utica*, 5; *Appletons Encyclopedia*.

[5]Bagg, *Memorial History of Utica*, 5; Mitchell, *Horatio Seymour*, 224-25, 249; James G. Randall, *Lincoln the President: Midstream* (New York: Dodd, Mead, 1952), 278; *Appletons Encyclopedia*.

[6]*Appletons Encyclopedia*.

[7]Bagg, *Memorial History of Utica*, 5; *Appletons Encyclopedia*.

[8]*Appletons Encyclopedia*.

[9]Bagg, *Memorial History of Utica*, 5; James G. Randall, *Lincoln the President*, 278; Mitchell, *Horatio Seymour*, 351; *Appletons Encyclopedia*.

[10]George Fort Milton, *Abraham Lincoln and the Fifth Column* (New York: Vanguard Press, 1942), 223; *Appletons Encyclopedia*.

[11]Bagg, *Memorial History of Utica*, 6; *Appletons Encyclopedia*.

[12]Bagg, *Memorial History of Utica*, 6-7.

MONTGOMERY SICARD

Montgomery Sicard
(National Archives)

Born in New York City on September 30, 1836, Montgomery Sicard was the son of Stephen Sicard of New York and Lydia E. Hunt of Utica. When his father died, his mother moved the family to Utica where young Montgomery, named in honor of his mother's father, Montgomery Hunt, grew to maturity. He was appointed as a midshipman at the U.S. Naval Academy in Annapolis, Maryland, in 1851, graduating four years later. Assigned to duty on the frigates *Potomac* and W*abash* in the Mediterranean and the *Dacotah* with the East Indian Squadron, he was promoted to lieutenant on May 31, 1860.[1]

With the outbreak of the Civil War he was ordered home to become executive officer of the *USS Oneida*, on which he served in the West Gulf Blockading Squadron under Admiral David G. Farragut during the campaign that led to the capture of New Orleans in 1862. Following the fall of New Orleans, he took part in two separate bombardments of Vicksburg, the bombardment of Grand Gulf, and an engagement against the Confederate ironclad *Arkansas* at Milliken's Bend. Promoted to lieutenant commander on July 16, 1862, Sicard was reassigned as executive officer of the steam frigate *Susquehanna* for the campaign against Mobile, Alabama.[2]

Following a brief stint at the Portsmouth Naval Yard in New Hampshire, Sicard was assigned as executive officer of the *USS Ticonderoga* engaged in pursuing Confederate commerce raiders. In late 1864 he was promoted to command of the *USS Seneca* and assigned to Admiral David Dixon Porter's forces assembling for an attack on Fort Fisher, the gateway to the Confederate port at Wilmington, North Carolina. He commanded the vessel in both campaigns against the fort in December 1864 and January 1865, and in the latter engagement he commanded the left wing of the naval assault forces in the land attack. After the fall of the fort, he commanded the *Seneca* into the Cape Fear River to bombard Fort Anderson and then in the occupation of Wilmington.[3]

Following the war, Sicard was assigned to the U.S. Naval Academy until 1868 teaching ordnance and gunnery and serving as a department head. In 1868 he was assigned as executive officer of the *USS Pensacola*, flagship of the North Pacific Squadron, and in 1870 was assigned as commanding officer of the *USS Saginaw*. Reassigned briefly to the New York Navy Yard, in the spring of 1872 he was named inspector of ordnance at the Washington Navy Yard where he supervised construction of the first steel, breech-loading rifled guns for use on naval vessels. Sicard designed the special carriages necessary for these guns. In 1878 he published a revised and updated edition of Ordnance Instructions for the Navy. Following some brief appointments to other posts, the president named him chief of the Bureau of Naval Ordnance in 1880 with a promotion to commodore. Promoted again to captain in August 1884, he was responsible for developing the first naval rapid-fire guns, the first armor-piercing shells, and pioneered the development of torpedoes.[4]

In 1894, Sicard assumed command of the New York Navy Yard, the most important facility of its type in the nation at that time. Promoted to rear admiral, he was assigned to command U.S. naval forces in the North Atlantic in 1897, but deteriorating health soon caused his retirement from active service after a career of forty-seven years. He died in Westernville, New York, on September 14, 1900, and was buried in the village Presbyterian cemetery. The destroyer *USS Sicard* (DD-346) was named in his honor, as was Sicard Street at the Washington Navy Yard in the District of Columbia.[5]

by James S. Pula

---

[1]*History of Oneida County New York From 1700 to the Present Time* (Chicago: The S. J. Clarke Publishing Company, 1912), Vol. II, 528-29; *New York Times*, April 8, 1897.

[2]*History of Oneida County*, Vol. II, 529; *New York Times*, April 8, 1897.

[3]*History of Oneida County*, Vol. II, 529.

[4]*History of Oneida County*, Vol. II, 530; *New York Times*, April 8, 1897.

[5]*History of Oneida County*, Vol. II, 531; *Dictionary of American Naval Fighting Ships*; *New York Times*, April 8, 1897.

APPENDIX A

STATISTICS OF ONEIDA COUNTY REGIMENTS

The following information on Oneida County units is compiled from Frederick Phisterer's *New York in the War of the Rebellion, 1861-1865* (Albany: J. B. Lyon Company, 1912) and Samuel Durant's *History of Oneida County New York, 1667-1878* (Philadelphia: Everts & Faress, 1878).

BATTERY A, 1ST NEW YORK LIGHT ARTILLERY
"EMPIRE BATTERY"

MUSTERED IN: September 12, 1861
MUSTERED OUT: June 28, 1865*

RECRUITMENT AREAS: Bridgewater, Burlington, Clinton, Edmeston, Jordan, Little Falls, New Berlin, Phoenix, Sauquoit, Sherburne, South Brookfield, Utica

BATTLE HONORS: Siege of Yorktown, Williamsburg, Bottom's Bridge, Fair Oaks.

CASUALTIES:	OFFICERS	MEN	TOTAL
KILLED	-	2	2
DIED OF WOUNDS	-	2	2
DIED OF DISEASE AND OTHER CAUSES	-	-	-
DIED IN PRISON	-	-	-
WOUNDED	-	1	1
MISSING	=	=	=
AGGREGATE	-	5	5

---

* Note that the muster out date is the date that the reorganized Battery A eventually left the service. The initial Battery A for all practical purposes ceased to exist on June 15, 1862, when its survivors were transferred to other organizations. Only Captain Bates remained to return to Utica to recruit a new group to fill the ranks of the reorganized battery. The casualties listed were those for the original battery.

14TH NEW YORK VOLUNTEER INFANTRY
"FIRST ONEIDA REGIMENT"

MUSTERED IN: Albany, May 17, 1861.
MUSTERED OUT: Utica, May 22-24, 1863

RECRUITMENT AREAS:

Company A – Utica	Company F – Boonville, Forestport,
"Utica Citizens Corps"	Port Leyden
Company B – Utica	Company G – Rome
Company C – Utica	Company H – Syracuse
Company D – Utica	Company I – Lowville
Company E – Utica	Company K – Hudson

BATTLE HONORS: Ball's Cross Roads, Widow Childs' House, Howard's Bridge, Siege of Yorktown, New Bridge, Hanover Court House, Mechanicsville, Gaines Mill, Malvern Hill, Harrison's Landing, Second Bull Run, Shepardstown, Antietam, Kearneyville, Fredericksburg, Richards's Ford, Chancellorsville.

CASUALTIES:	OFFICERS	MEN	TOTAL
KILLED	3	35	38
DIED OF WOUNDS	1	21	22
DIED OF DISEASE AND			
OTHER CAUSES	-	42	42
DIED IN PRISON	1	6	7
WOUNDED	16	178	194
MISSING	1	15	16
AGGREGATE	22	297	319

26TH NEW YORK VOLUNTEER INFANTRY
"SECOND ONEIDA REGIMENT"
"CENTRAL NEW YORK BATTALION"
"UTICA REGIMENT"

MUSTERED IN: Elmira, May 21, 1861.
MUSTERED OUT: Utica, May 24-28, 1863

RECRUITMENT AREAS:

Company A – Utica	Company F – Whitestown
Company B – Utica	Company G – Rochester
Company C – Utica	Company H – Rochester
Company D – Hamilton	Company I – Oriskany
Company E – Utica	Company K – Candor

BATTLE HONORS: Pohick Church, Cedar Mountain, Rappahannock Station, Thoroughfare Gap, Groveton, Second Bull Run, Little River Turnpike, Chantilly, Hall's Hill, Falls Church, South Mountain, Antietam, Fredericksburg, Pollock's Mill Creek, Chancellorsville.

CASUALTIES:	OFFICERS	MEN	TOTAL
KILLED	3	62	65
DIED OF WOUNDS	2	41	43
DIED OF DISEASE AND			
OTHER CAUSES	-	41	41
DIED IN PRISON	-	1	1
WOUNDED	12	231	243
MISSING	-	56	56
AGGREGATE	17	432	449

97TH NEW YORK VOLUNTEER INFANTRY
"THIRD ONEIDA REGIMENT"
"BOONVILLE REGIMENT"
"CONKLING RIFLES"

MUSTERED IN: Boonville, February 18, 1862
MUSTERED OUT: Washington, D.C., July 18, 1865

RECRUITMENT AREAS:

Company A – Boonville	Company F – Salisbury
Company B – Lewis County	Company G – Herkimer County
Company C – Boonville	Company H – Utica and Lowville
Company D – Salisbury	Company I – Little Falls
Company E – Prospect & Vicinity	Company K – Rome

BATTLE HONORS: Cedar Mountain, Rappahannock Station I, Rappahannock Station II, Thoroughfare Gap, Second Bull Run, Chantilly, South Mountain, Antietam, Fredericksburg, Pollock's Mill Creek, Chancellorsville, Gettysburg, Bristoe Station, Mine Run, Raccoon Ford, Wilderness, Laurel Hill, Piney Branch Church, Spotsylvania, North Anna, Totopotomy, Bethesda Church, White Oak Swamp, Cold Harbor, Petersburg, Weldon Railroad, Hicks' Ford, Hatcher's Run, Quaker Road, White Oak Road, Five Forks, Appomattox Court House, and Lee's Surrender.

CASUALTIES:	OFFICERS	MEN	TOTAL
KILLED	7	97	104
DIED OF WOUNDS	5	73	78
DIED OF DISEASE AND			
OTHER CAUSES	1	102	103
DIED IN PRISON	-	54	54
WOUNDED	26	418	444
MISSING	12	253	265
AGGREGATE	51	997	1,048

117TH NEW YORK VOLUNTEER INFANTRY
"FOURTH ONEIDA REGIMENT"

MUSTERED IN: Oneida, N.Y., August 8-16, 1862
MUSTERED OUT: Raleigh, N.C., June 8, 1865

RECRUITMENT AREAS:

        Company A – Rome, Utica and Vernon

        Company B – Utica, Camden, Verona and Vienna

        Company C – Utica, Westmoreland, Rome and Bridgewater

        Company D – Whitestown, Sangerfield, Utica, Vienna and New Hartford

        Company E – Rome

        Company F – Oriskany, Trenton, Utica, Floyd, Rome, Steuben and Deerfield

        Company G – Rome, Clayville, Paris and Utica

        Company H – Utica, Vienna, Rome and Camden

        Company I – Rome, Boonville, Ava, Utica, Western and Clayville

        Company K – Clinton, Remsen, Augusta, Boonville, Deansville, Marshall and Vernon

BATTLE HONORS: Siege of Norfolk, Hill's Point I, Hill's Point II, Siege of Battery Wagner, Bombardment of Fort Sumter, Swift Creek, Drewry's Bluff, Bermuda Hundred, Cold Harbor, Siege of Richmond, Siege of Petersburg, The Crater, Chaffin's Farm, Darbytown Road, Fort Fisher I, Fort Fisher II, Cape Fear, Capture of Wilmington, Carolinas Campaign, Bennett House.

CASUALTIES:	OFFICERS	MEN	TOTAL
KILLED	5	75	80
DIED OF WOUNDS	3	54	57
DIED OF DISEASE AND			
OTHER CAUSES	1	125	126
DIED IN PRISON	-	21	21
WOUNDED	17	274	291
MISSING	2	47	49
AGGREGATE	28	596	624

146TH NEW YORK VOLUNTEER INFANTRY
"FIFTH ONEIDA REGIMENT"
"HALLECK INFANTRY"
"GARRARD'S TIGERS"

MUSTERED IN: Rome, October 10, 1862
MUSTERED OUT: Washington, D.C., July 16, 1865

RECRUITMENT AREAS:

Company A – Utica

Company B – Vernon, Rome and Annsville

Company C – Utica and Rome

Company D – Boonville, Hawkinsville, Rome and Whitestown

Company E – Camden, Augusta, Rome, Utica and Marshall

Company F – Utica, Lee, Rome, Florence, Annsville, Ava, Marcy and Whitestown

Company G – Clinton, Kirkland, Bridgewater and Plainfield

Company H – Utica, Rome and Sangerfield

Company I – Trenton, Remsen, Western, Westmoreland, Steuben, Lowell, Rome, Vernon and Verona

Company K – Paris, Clayville, Utica, Marcy, Clinton, Deansville, Marshall and Whitesboro

BATTLE HONORS: Fredericksburg, Chancellorsville, Gettysburg, Williamsport, Rappahannock Station I, Rappahannock Station II, Bristoe Station, Mine Run, Wapping Heights, Wilderness, Spotsylvania, Piney Branch Creek, Laurel Hill, Gayle's House, North Anna, Totopotomy, Bethesda Church, White Oak Swamp, Petersburg, Weldon Railroad, Poplar Spring Church, Chapel House, Hatcher's Run I, Hatcher's Run II, Hicks' Ford, White Oak Ridge, Five Forks, Appomattox Court House, Lee's Surrender.

CASUALTIES:	OFFICERS	MEN	TOTAL
KILLED	3	81	80
DIED OF WOUNDS	4	46	57
DIED OF DISEASE AND			
OTHER CAUSES	1	100	126
DIED IN PRISON	1	87	21
WOUNDED	13	167	291
MISSING	8	332	49
AGGREGATE	30	813	843

APPENDIX B
COMMUNITY RECRUITMENT

Although regiments, and even smaller units, were comprised of men from several local communities, some contained large numbers of people from a single township. As near as can be determined, the following list identifies the companies of various regiments that were enlisted mainly from individual townships. The list is taken from Frederick Phisterer's *New York in the War of the Rebellion, 1861-1865* (Albany: J. B. Lyon Company,1912), Vol. 1, 72-77.

Township	Infantry	Artillery	Cavalry	Engineers
Annsville	A, F–146th			
	K–189th			
Augusta	I–3rd			
	K–117th			
	E–146th			
Ava	I–117th			
	F–146th			
Boonville	F–14th	H–10th	G–3rd	
	A, C–97th	G, H, K–14th	H–7th	
	I, K–117th			
	D–146th			
	K–189th			
Bridgewater	C–117th	A–1st		
	G–146th			
Camden	B, H–117th	L–2nd		
	E–146th	A, E, M–14th		
	K–189th			
Clayville	G, I–117th		C, D–1st Mtd Rfls	
	K–146th			
Clinton	I–81st	A–1st		
	K–117th			
	K–146th			
Deansville	K–117th		I–8th	
	K–146th			
Deerfield	F–117th	M–14th		
Florence	F–146th			
	K–189th			
Forestport	F–14th			
Floyd	F–117th	M–14th		
Hawkinsville	D–146th			

Township	Infantry	Artillery	Cavalry	Engineers
Holland Patent		M–2nd		
Kirkland	G–146th	M–14th		
Lee	F–146th			
	K–189th			
Lowell	I–146th			
Marcy	F, K–146th			
Marshall	K–117th			
	E, K–146th			
New Hartford	D–117th			
	H–164th			
North Bay		I–8th		
Oriskany	I–26th	M–15th		
	F–117th			
Paris	G–117th	G, H–13th	I–8th	
	K–146th	M–14th		
	K–189th			
Prospect	E–97th			
Remsen	K–117th			
	I–146th			
Rome	G–14th	D–4th		C, E–50th
	K–97th	C–14th		
	A, C, E, F, G, H, I–117th		C, D, E–16th	
	B, C, D, E, F, H, I–146th		F–13th	
	K–189th	G, I, M–20th		
		C–22nd		
		F–24th		
Sangerfield	D–117th			
	H–146th			
Sauquoit		A–1st		
Steuben	F–117th			
	I–146th			
Taberg		M–2nd		
		F–24th		
Trenton	F–117th	M–14th		
	I–146th			
Trenton Falls		M–2nd		
Utica	A, B, C, E–14th	A–1st	G–3rd	I, L–15th
	A, B, C, D, E–26th	G, L, M–2nd	C–11th	
	B–57th	L–4th	F–13th	
	D–78th	G, H–13th	K, M–15th	
	H–97th	C, E, G, M–14th	B, M–22nd	
	E–101st	A, C, D, I–16th	B, F, L, M–24th	
	A, B, C, D, F, I–117th			
	A, C, E, F, H, K–146th			
	H–164th			
	K–189th			

Township	Infantry	Artillery	Cavalry	Engineers
Vernon	I–3rd		M–15th	
	A, K–117th			
	B, I–146th			
	K–189th			
Verona	B–117th		L–1st Mtd Rfls	
	I–146th			
	K–189th			
Vienna	B, D, H–117th		Oneida Cav.	
	K–189th			
Waterville			I–8th	
Western	I–117th			
	I–146th			
Westmoreland	I–3rd		M–15th	
	C–117th			
	I–146th			
	K–189th			
Whitesboro	K–146th			
Whitestown	F–26th		M–15th	
	D–117th			
	D, F–146th			

Appendix C
Oneida County Colors
Returned to the Governor of the State

The following information on the colors returned to the State of New York by Oneida County units is taken from *Second Annual Report of the Chief of the Bureau of Military Statistics of the State of New York* (Albany: C. Wendell, 1865) and *Fifth Annual Report of the Chief of the Bureau of Military, with Appendices* (Albany: C. van Benthuysen & Sons, 1865). One must note that the regiments also turned over colors to the Oneida County Historical Society which still holds them. Except where noted, the national colors were generally returned to the state which had provided them, while the "state" colors, which had been presented by local groups, were placed on deposit for safekeeping in the historical society.

14th New York: turned in a national banner presented to it by Governor Morgan. "It was returned to Gov. Seymour soiled and tattered, but not dishonored."

26th New York: turned in one national flag. Col. R. H. Richardson wrote: "We return them to the State from which we received them, well knowing they will be cherished as momentoes of the living and the dead. They bear the marks of bullets, and of the blood of those who defended them, and, as such, will always be regarded with respect and veneration by those who are left to mourn the loss of their comrades on the field of battle."

97th New York: turned in one national flag inscribed: "Colonel Wheelock, 97th Conklin Rifles, N.Y." that was presented by ladies of Boonville.

117th New York: turned in five flags including two guidons, one blue silk regimental "nearly all gone but fringe" with broken staff, one silk national flag in good shape except for the fringe, and one blue silk regimental new with arms and motto of U.S.

146th New York: turned in a blue silk regimental with arms of U.S. and motto and inscribed "Halleck Infantry" and "146th N. Y. Vol. Regiment Infantry."

INDEX

For military units, see "Artillery Units," "Cavalry Units," and "Infantry Units."